The Ages of The Flash

ALSO EDITED BY JOSEPH J. DAROWSKI

The Ages of the Justice League: Essays on America's Greatest Superheroes in Changing Times (2017)

The Ages of the Incredible Hulk: Essays on the Green Goliath in Changing Times (2016)

The Ages of Iron Man: Essays on the Armored Avenger in Changing Times (2015)

The Ages of Wonder Woman: Essays on the Amazon Princess in Changing Times (2014)

The Ages of the X-Men: Essays on the Children of the Atom in Changing Times (2014)

The Ages of the Avengers: Essays on the Earth's Mightiest Heroes in Changing Times (2014)

The Ages of Superman: Essays on the Man of Steel in Changing Times (2012)

The Ages of The Flash

Essays on the Fastest Man Alive

Edited by JOSEPH J. DAROWSKI

McFarland & Company, Inc., Publishers

Jefferson, North Carolina

LIBRARY OF CONGRESS CATALOGUING-IN-PUBLICATION DATA

Names: Darowski, Joseph J., editor.
Title: The ages of the Flash : essays on the fastest man alive /
    edited by Joseph J. Darowski.
Description: Jefferson, North Carolina : McFarland & Company, Inc.,
    Publishers, 2019 | Includes bibliographical references and index.
Identifiers: LCCN 2019010932 | ISBN 9781476674445
    (paperback : acid free paper) ∞
Subjects: LCSH: Flash (Fictitious character) | Garrick, Jay
    (Fictitious character) | Allen, Barry (Fictitious character) |
    West, Wally (Fictitious character) | Superheroes in literature. |
    Comic books, strips, etc.—United States—History and criticism.
Classification: LCC PN6728.F53 A38 2019 | DDC 741.5/973—dc23
LC record available at https://lccn.loc.gov/2019010932

BRITISH LIBRARY CATALOGUING DATA ARE AVAILABLE

    ISBN 978-1-4766-7444-5 (softcover : acid free paper)
    ISBN 978-1-4766-3566-8 (ebook)

Front cover illustration © 2019 Digital Vision

Printed in the United States of America

McFarland & Company, Inc., Publishers
    Box 611, Jefferson, North Carolina 28640
    www.mcfarlandpub.com

To Kate—you always loved The Flash

Table of Contents

Preface

There is a simple elegance to the very concept of the Flash. For a new reader encountering the Flash, everything is instantly accessible and understandable. The Flash is fast. No further explanation needed. This is not always the case in the popular American superhero genre. Superman has an incredible, constantly expanding number of powers, Batman has an endless array of gadgets, and Wonder Woman has ambiguously multi-faceted powers. But the Flash is a uni-tasker. He is simply fast. As comic book writer Mark Waid notes, the Flash is the genre's first "specialty superhero" (6). He's not super strong, he can't fly, he doesn't teleport, and he can't survive the vacuum of space. He's just very, very fast.

That simplicity serves particularly well when looking at the long-term history of the character. Though the Flash has had different men behind the mask in different eras, the core conceit of the character is consistent. Combine that with an iconic scarlet costume and add some lightning bolts that denote speed, and the character is easily comprehended, even by audiences who are not well-versed in comic book lore and history. Anyone can quickly grasp the nature of the Flash in a way that is not as intuitive with characters such as Martian Manhunter or Captain Marvel (any of the characters who have gone by that name).

The Flash first appeared in *Flash Comics* #1 in a story which was written by Gardner Fox and drawn by Harry Lampert. *Flash Comics* was an anthology title that also featured the adventures of other characters in every issue. It was published by All-American Publications, a company that would eventually merge with other publishers to form DC Comics. This original version of the Flash was Jay Garrick, a college student who studies science and plays for the school football team. The Flash's first appearance had a cover date of January 1940, and the character continued to appear for almost a decade. During the 1940s, the Flash also appeared in *All-Flash Comics*, which was the first comic book dedicated solely to the Flash's crime-fighting adventures. Jay Garrick's Flash also made appearances in anthology titles such as *Comics*

Cavalcade and *All-Star Comics*, and was a member of the first superhero team, The Justice Society of America. While superhero comic books were very popular during World War II, following the war, fan interest waned as consumer interests turned to other genres and avenues of entertainment. *Flash Comics* was canceled near the end of the decade, and its final issue, #104, had a cover date of February 1949.

Less than a decade later, due to many issues affecting the comic book industry, an attempt to revive the popularity of the superhero genre was launched. Launching an era that has come to be called the Silver Age of comics, DC editor Julius Schwartz[1] decided to bring the Flash back. Rather than reintroduce Jay Garrick to new readers, this version of the Flash would be Barry Allen, a police scientist who gains powers when a lightning bolt strikes a shelf of chemicals near his work station. This version of the Flash was created by writer Robert Kanigher and artist Carmine Infantino and first appeared in *Showcase* #4 (Oct. 1956). Barry Allen would gain a pseudo-sidekick, Wally West, who went by the superhero identity of Kid Flash, in 1959's *The Flash* #110. West was created by writer John Broome and artist Carmine Infantino.

In 1986 DC Comics published the massive crossover comic event called *Crisis on Infinite Earths*, and as part of the series, Barry Allen died. Wally West took over the mantle of the Flash at that point. Similar to Wally West acting as a sidekick to Barry Allen, a new young speedster named Bart Allen was introduced in 1994. Bart Allen, co-created by writer Mark Waid and artist Mike Wieringo, goes by the name Impulse initially before adopting West's original codename, Kid Flash. In 2005–2006 DC Comics published a new crossover mini-series, *Infinite Crisis*, which saw Wally West disappear into another dimension. At this point, Bart Allen became the newest man to be the official Flash, though his tenure was the shortest of all. Soon, Wally West would return, and then Barry Allen was resurrected. As seems inevitable with decades-long narrative universes, the Flash's continuity has become a bit convoluted and complex. Undoubtedly more changes will come in the future, perhaps even a fifth man or woman behind the mask of the Flash. Jay Garrick, Barry Allen, Wally West, and Bart Allen have all had differing personalities, impact, and defining storylines in DC Comics. But each was the Fastest Man Alive.

In this essay collection, scholars examine versions of the Flash from across many decades of the character's comic book adventures. While the Flash has had appearances in cartoon series such as *Challenge of the Super-friends* or *Justice League*, two different live action television series adapting his adventures, many appearances in DC's straight-to-DVD animated films, and a live-action film appearance in *Justice League*, these essays are limited in scope to the comic book appearances of the Fastest Man Alive. With almost eight decades of material in the Flash's comic book history, there is more material to analyze than is possible to cover in this single collection. As future fans and scholars explore the Flash's long history, this collection can serve as a stepping stone to even greater understanding of one of the comic book industry's most iconic characters.

The Golden Age of comic books saw the introduction of many iconic characters, as well as some less-famous creations. Cathy Leogrande examines Flash comic book adventures from the Golden Age, but she does not focus her analysis on the titular character. Rather, "Politically Incorrect Humor: Examining the Three Dimwits Through a Disability Studies Lens" considers three side characters who appeared somewhat frequently in the early Flash comics, but much less frequently in subsequent eras. Winky, Noddy, and Blinky were clearly modeled on The Three Stooges, popular comedic characters who first appeared on film in 1934. Winky, Noddy, and Blinky's misadventures drove the plot of many Flash comic books in the 1940s. Leogrande acknowledges the era in which these characters were created and the social norms that found them inoffensive at the time, but also explores the problematic aspects of these characters reflective of modern disability studies.

Moving into the Silver Age of comics and the creation of Barry Allen as the new Flash, Liam T. Webb's essay, "The Birth of the Silver Age Flash: Reasons and Influences," considers the influence of editor Julius Schwartz on embracing the science fiction genre as a defining element of *The Flash*. Webb establishes the cultural factors and also Schwartz's personal tastes that helped to define the tone of the series.

"'I'm covering the story! Wait here for me': The Two-Career Couple in the Pages of *The Flash*" by Charles W. Henebry also looks at the Silver Age adventures of Barry Allen, but focuses on his relationship with Iris West. West was a character more in the mold of Lois Lane than June Cleaver, and represented a challenge to the portrayals of traditional patriarchy that many associate with popular culture from the 1950s and 1960s. Henebry explores how the character was used in the series both before and after her marriage to Allen.

As the Flash transitioned from a new Silver Age character into an established part of the DC Universe, change was inevitable. Peter W.Y. Lee focuses on how *The Flash* addressed some of the social issues of the day in "Barry Allen's Social Awakening in the 1970s." Among the issues addressed are Communism, the Cold War, student protests, youth movements, and juvenile delinquency.

As comics transitioned into what is sometimes called the "grim 'n' gritty" era, new thematic topics took center stage. Fernando Gabriel Pagnoni Berns explores how the economics of the Reagan era were presented in his essay "From Riches to Rags: The Rise and Fall of Wally West."

Tom Shapira also addresses comic books from this era, but "Wrestling with Legacy: How 'The Return of Barry Allen' Shaped DC Superheroes in the 1990s" addresses the manner in which *The Flash* comic books were representative of overall trends in superhero comic books. Whether it was the Flash's role in launching the Silver Age or Barry Allen's death signaling a new era after *Crisis on Infinite Earths*, the Flash has often had an under-recognized role in the larger superhero genre. "The Return of Barry Allen" signaled a renewed interest in the legacies of DC superheroes, an interest that would be explored in several subsequent publications.

Superhero comic books are not published in a vacuum, and particularly with the products from Marvel and DC Comics, the series are embracing or reacting to the larger trends in the company's publishing practices. John Darowski's "Flash Back to the Future: Mark Waid's Counter-Narrative to the Superhero Dark Age" analyzes ways in which *The Flash*, under the guidance of writer Mark Waid, began to resist the darker trends of 1990's superhero stories.

Essays by Daniel J. Bergman and Louie Dean Valencia-García both focus on the early adventures of Bart Allen (Impulse), a new speedster character introduced in the 1990s. Bergman's essay examines the series by exploring the role of education, while Valencia-García focuses on the generational stereotypes of adolescents at the time the series was being produced. Both approaches yield unique and valuable insights.

Since its publication in the 1980s, Alan Moore and Dave Gibbons' *Watchmen* has forced creators working within the superhero genre to address its deconstruction of that very genre. In "Restraining Deconstruction: Geoff Johns' Reframing of *The Flash*," Christian Jimenez examines how Geoff Johns attempts to resist that deconstruction of the superhero during his run on *The Flash*. However, in resisting that deconstruction, Johns is still reacting to it, and thus addressing the new status quo of the superhero post–*Watchmen*.

Matthew J. Smith and Tod W. Burke also examine Geoff Johns' run on *The Flash*. Johns was notable for highlighting the Flash's enemies, believing them to be as varied and interesting as Batman's famous rogues gallery. By making use of Smith's expertise in comic book studies and Burke's experience in criminal justice, "Profiling the Rogues: Seeking Criminal Intent in *The Flash* of Geoff Johns" provides a unique insight into the villains who vex the scarlet speedster.

Sara K. Ellis addresses the newest comic book iteration of the Flash in DC Comics' New 52 era. "Minds in the Gutter: The Persistence of Vision and the New 52" is an examination of yet another iteration of this classic character reborn into the modern world. The unexpected blend of classic character and modern technology within an innovative story told by Francis Manapul and Brian Buccellato provides several avenues for analysis.

The Flash is one of the most important creations of American popular culture and has had a more significant role in guiding the superhero genre than the character has been credited. With the relevance of the superhero genre exploding beyond the comic book pages where it was first created, it is time to give the Flash his due. This essay collection provides insights from several expert comic book scholars, but more work remains to be done on the iconic fastest man alive.

NOTE

1. Julius Schwartz is one of the most significant figures in the history of the American comic book industry. He had an undeniable impact on DC Comics. He was inducted into the Jack Kirby Hall of Fame and the Will Eisner Comic Book Hall of Fame, won numerous awards and even had one award named after him. However, following Schwartz's passing in 2004, a number of allegations of unwanted and inappropriate sexual advances that Schwartz made towards female comic book professionals have been made. As with many traditionally male-dominated industries in recent years, there are issues that were long swept under the rug that are now beginning to be addressed, though much work remains in these areas.

Politically Incorrect Humor

Examining the Three Dimwits
Through a Disability Studies Lens

Cathy Leogrande

The characters of Winky Moylan, Noddy Toylan, and Blinky Boylan were introduced in 1943 during early Flash adventures. They closely resembled the Three Stooges, and were known in the stories by various terms, including "Three Idiots," the "Three Numbskulls," the "Three Dopes," or, most often, the "Three Dimwits." Although peripheral to major story arcs, their storylines mainly involved dragging Jay Garrick into ridiculous misadventures that often occurred due to their lack of intelligence. Hilarity supposedly occurs because of their stupidity, lack of common sense, and ineptness with basic survival abilities. Humor at the expense of others who are different and outside the norm has always been a murky subject in comics. While superheroes can be a positive metaphor for the differently abled, that is not always true for others in the stories. Examining these three characters and their storylines through a disability studies lens provides insights into some of the unchallenged prejudices of the time when these comic books were produced.

Disability Timeline Leading to the Flash

The timeline of social action and acceptance for people with disabilities provides a context within which characters such as Winky, Blinky and Noddy were created. Beginning around 1850, humanitarian efforts on the part of social agencies and private foundations sought to educate people identified as lower functioning and help them become socially competent. In Massachusetts and

New York, leaders such as Samuel Howe and Harvey Wilbur spearheaded efforts to care for those who seemed to be less abled in smaller residential schools with a reasonable level of care (United States "MR 75" 4). They fought against establishment of workhouses and almshouses to deal with these individuals. Howe's beliefs were prescient; his report in 1874 contained words that are still relevant:

> Even idiots have rights which should be carefully considered! At any rate let us try for something which shall not imply segregating the wards in classes, removing them from our sight and knowledge, ridding ourselves of our responsibility as neighbors, and leaving the wards closely packed in establishments where the spirit of pauperism is surely engendered, and the morbid peculiarities of each are intensified by constant and close association of others of his class [qtd. in "MR 75" 5].

Sadly, the voices of such advocates would be silenced with the onset of three developments that lead to the perception of less abled individuals as depraved menaces and threats to society: social Darwinism, eugenics and intelligence testing.

Social Darwinism began in 1901 when Francis Galton applied Darwin's theories to the human race and foresaw dire implications. He believed that, "by eliminating the unfit, man could actively assist nature in promoting the survival of the highest quality of human being" ("MR 75" 9). The first step was to close the small home-like schools and create large state-run institutions as the reasonable and efficient method of care for the less able and less fortunate. At the same time, the eugenics movement grew. Sociologists, doctors and policy makers sought to control and improve society by ensuring that persons deemed less able or deficient would not reproduce by government sanctioned sterilization. Genetics was a tool in these efforts. Studies of families such as the Jukes with several criminal members, and the Kallikaks with a number of lower functioning offspring, gave credence to ideas that "feeblemindedness" was genetic and "the potential undermining of the human race" ("MR 75" 10). In the case of Carrie Bell, the Supreme Court ruled 8–1 to allow eugenic sterilization of undesirable citizens for the greater good of the country (Barry "Giving a Name"). Oliver Wendell Holmes famously wrote in the majority opinion, "Three generations of imbeciles are enough" (Cohen 240). The courts upheld ideas that individuals with lower cognitive skills were problems to be eliminated.

The birth of the field of psychometrics further marginalized individuals. In 1905, Binet helped develop a test to measure ability and difference from the norm. In the United States, Stern and Terman used a formula to determine the ratio of mental age to chronological age that became known as the intelligence quotient or I.Q. ("MR 75" 10). Others, such as Goddard, categorized individuals into ranges titled *idiot* (IQ of 0–25), *imbecile* (IQ of 26–50), and *moron* (IQ of 51–70). This final group was considered the most perilous to others. Doctors from diverse disciplines warned that these persons could pass as normal in appearance, but were potentially dangerous in terms of criminal and degenerate behavior. Some, like Fernald, were zealous in attempts to educate lawmakers and the public on the threat these individuals posed. Physicians were advised to especially try to identify borderline cases, individuals with only a slight intellectual deficit, since these were people most prone to depraved morality and criminal acts ("MR 75" 11). The three characters from Flash stories discussed in this chapter seem to fit the highest functioning of these categories.

By the 1930s, understanding of and recommendations for people previously labeled feebleminded had changed. Classification based on numerical scores was criticized, as was isolation in institutions. Appropriate education was seen as an alternative to institutions, which had become overcrowded partly due to economic depression. Welfare services tied to local communities became desirable as the best way to assist people with disabilities ("MR 75" 29). Communities differed in their resources and willingness to assist individuals with such needs. In some cases, schools and industries welcomed these individuals and worked to help them find a place where they could fit. In other places, adults with lower abilities were left to find their own way, often without family support. World War II brought another step forward. Many men and women who may have been classified as mildly mentally retarded were able to assist in war efforts. The structured routine that is the norm in armed services provided an adaptive and successful environment. The same was true in wartime industries, which led to the demonstration of employability under certain conditions, most notably factories with their standardized and repetitive tasks. While some individuals achieved a level of normalcy with or without support, others drifted from one situation to another (Barry "The 'Boys' in the Bunkhouse"). This instability and need for survival are combined in the stories with the Three Dimwits.

From the Three Stooges to the Three Dimwits

Despite the fact that the Three Stooges began as a vaudeville act in the 1920s, they remain among the most iconic and recognizable entertainers in the world (Thorburn 180). They built their success around their characters' lack of intelligence, along with slapstick physical humor and apparent violence (Braund). In 1933, they transitioned to two-reel short comedies that accompanied longer films. The essence of each was basically the same: Moe was the ringleader, Larry was the middle man who gamely went along with whatever plan Moe devised, and the third stooge (Curly, Shemp, or later Joe) ruined things because of his stupidity. The stooges came to prominence during the Great Depression, when Americans wanted to laugh at those less fortunate than themselves. Reality mirrored art in a way; Columbia studio head Harry Cohen took advantage of the actors by repeatedly providing false information about profits, so he could pay them very little in relation to their popularity (Okuda and Watz 61–64). The shorts remained popular for decades, despite changing social norms. It was always fun to laugh at others with less intelligence, whose deficits in thinking got them into trouble with the law, with businessmen and aristocrats and with each other. In *Stoogeology: Essays on the Three Stooges* edited by Peter Seely and Gail Pieper, authors deconstruct aspects of the act and characters, including the simple mindedness of Curly and the lack of problem-solving ability of Moe and Larry. These realistic (but not real) characters had amazing longevity, lasting into the 1950s and beyond via re-releases and remakes. Like comic books, what was once thought of as low-brow humor has been analyzed and deconstructed to uncover the depth and impact of the characters.

The overlap between the Three Stooges and the Three Dimwits is obvious. At the period that Gardner Fox began working on *The Flash* comics, the stooges were well known and widespread. Fox was the writer behind the debut of the Flash in 1940, collaborating with Sheldon Mayer and E.E. Hibbard. These three sought to provide a lighter tone in the Flash stories. Enter Winky, Blinky and Noddy. They began as minor characters in *All-Flash #5*, where they were part of the background, providing comic relief to the story. They were clearly lifted from the Three Stooges. Noddy Moylan was the leader, often physically attacking the other two just like Moe Howard. Winky Boylan had a round head of curly hair similar to Larry. Blinky Toylan had hair that covered his eyes, more similar to Shemp than Curly. Their clothing was odd; Noddy wore a fedora and tie over what appeared to be just a shirt front with no sleeves; Winky wore a very small hat perched on his head and what appeared to be a rope in place of a belt; and Noddy wore suspenders holding up pants that appeared to be much too big for him. In their first story, they were gofers for a criminal who tried to cheat a woman out of her prized racehorse. Their first story included other humorous details not related to the trio. One character disguised the horse by painting him like a zebra and hiding him at the zoo. Winky, Blinky and Noddy mistakenly let a tiger loose because they were looking for the animal with stripes. The boys get talked into betting on a different horse and lose their money. They are nowhere to be found at the end of the story.

Some may have thought these three would only appear in one issue, but *All-Flash #6* made it clear they were much more than that. The cover featured the three attempting to paint a billboard with a photo of the Flash while spilling glue and paint and almost falling from the scaffold. The cover caption announced them: "Another full length four-chapter novel starring the Flash, the fastest man alive aided and abetted by the Three Dimwits—Masters of Confusion." The introduction for "The Adventure of the Riotous Ray" set the stage:

One machine, invented in a luck-ridden moment by three freaks of fortune! A ray, brilliant in its scope, amazing in its effect on human life and emotions, discovered by luck's looney stepchildren, those mighty mopes of mischance, Winky, Blinky and Noddy! [Fox, "The Ray…"].

The story centers on the results of a personality machine made by chance that allowed two individuals to switch personalities. A flashback reveals that the trio has $8.94 to start a business. Noddy suggested they set up on "Poison Alley." The exchange that follows indicates the extent to which the characters were developed as less able:

WINKY: That's a swell idea! Poisonality that's us! We'll teach people how to be great poisonalities!
NODDY: Poison Alley's a place, you dope! It ain't anything you can teach anybody!
WINKY: Don't talk to a dope like that! He's so dumb I'm surprised he can talk!
BLINKY: Go away, you dope! Pssst … what does dope mean anyway?
NODDY: Aw fellers, I'm sorry if I'm sort of stupid. But put up with me, huh fellers? [Fox, "The Ray…"].

They set up shop and place advertisements. A budding actress named Ada White comes in to have her personality improved. The ensuing conversation has the trio mimicking opera and Shakespeare, two things incongruous with their apparent intellectual abilities. Ada angrily leaves stating that they couldn't teach personality even with a machine. The three decide to build such a machine. They begin with an old sun lamp, then send Blinky to buy "juice" for the battery. He enters a drugstore and requests, "A buck's worth of the cheapest stuff you got! In separate bottles! We'll mix it ourselves." In a thought balloon, the druggist's explains, "I sure unloaded a lot of old stuff I don't even know the name of! Stuff that's been here for twenty years or more." The trio mix the materials in the machine. Noddy says, "We're inventors now fellas … like Edison and Don Ameche!" (Fox, "The Ray…"). Ada returns and the great actress Sara Norheart also enters. Within minutes the machine switches their personalities. An additional caption provides further information:

Shades of Monte Carlo! In the mathematical chance of ten billion to one, the three dopey do-nothings have hit on a secret of the universe! They have discovered something tremendous … the chemical formulae of the human personality itself. Depending as it does upon a proper correlation of certain glands and their chemical stimulants… [Fox, "The Ray…"].

Further explanation is provided in another caption:

Explanation! All human conduct is regulated to a great extent by the chemical secretions of the glands…. If these glands were affected, great changes would result in poise, conduct, even in the brain itself! The "personality machine" extracted from Ada White her glandular chemicals and substituted them for Sarah Norhearts! [Fox, "The Ray…"].

The boys next appear wearing suits as a result of their success. However, the caption indicates that not much has changed: "Moylan, Boylan and Toylan here they are: A little changed by success, but otherwise as dumb as ever!" (Fox, "The Ray…"). More slapstick adventures occur.

The Flash takes the group to meet professors at Columbine University in New York. One of the professors observes, "Three such remarkable geniuses! Hmm, your head structure, definitely brachycephalic, shows remarkable concentrative ability! And the cranium is so well developed! My, my!" Blinky takes this as an insult. The professors examine the machine, and spout information well over the heads of the trio, "The cognate adjustors are intertwined with the variable condensers! The simplicity of the barium coordinators amplifies the regulating oscillations of the biaxial perimeters" (Fox, "The Ray…"). During the rest of the story, individuals use the machine with mixed results. At one point the personalities of all Three Dimwits enter the Flash; the three have his spirit and speed, and The Flash talking in their vernacular.

These examples from *All-Flash #6* illustrate the popularity of these three characters. From a small supporting role in *All-Flash #5*, they quickly grew to be regulars in the supporting cast. John Wells, in his essay on Gardner Fox in *The Flash Companion* (2008) notes that "readers were asked if they wanted to see The Three Dimwits return, and the answer was a resounding yes!" The three characters made over thirty appearances in stories in *All-Flash, All-American Comics, Flash Comics*, and *Comics Cavalcade* until 1947. Most of the stories had similar plots: the trio has a scheme to make easy money, or they accidentally get caught up with criminals, and the Flash gets involved to save them. However, a few of these are worthy of a longer description here.

All-Flash #9 has two stories, both connected to World War II. "The Adventure of the Stolen Telescope" finds the boys attempting to write a story to win prize money. They write random ideas on papers and then throw them up in the air for sequencing. They are mistaken for Nazi geniuses called the Terrible Three. The dialogue is tinged with German-sounding syllables, and there is a swastika and portrait of Hitler. The three boys inadvertently help the Flash catch spies, and recover the anti-gravity telescope Jay created. They write up their adventure as a story and try to sell it to Sheldon Mayer, the editor of All-Flash bi-monthly. Blinky says, "It's just the kind of junk he'd buy!" (31). The second story, "The Adventure of the Magic Mirror," includes a mirror that leads to the fourth dimension. There is a science fiction themed legend of creatures from another planet which turns out to be true. When each person goes through, he is shown only as a symbol of his personality. The Flash is a lightning bolt, and Noddy is a zero. Both stories have complex plots with convoluted twists and lots of references to simple-mindedness of the trio. They are referred to as "Mental Midgets" (4) and "Disciples of Dopedom" (10).

All-Flash #11 contains the story "Troubles Come in Doubles." Joan Williams see a spaceship with what appears to be the trio. The spaceship crashes to Earth with three individuals who look exactly like Winky, Blinky, and Noddy. They are Jakko, Wykin and Donno, former dictators on the planet Karma. They had been ousted from power during a rebellion led by Flingo, a Jay Garrick look-alike. The three escaped in a stolen spaceship, and landed on Earth where they had super speed (much like the Flash). These three were not the simple buffoons; they had achieved power through plotting and planning. They trick the boys into taking their places on Karma, using a genius inventor named Evart Keenan. The interplay of abilities and intelligence across this group of characters seem to show that this idea of skills, ability and common sense were all key components. It is not merely the Flash's speed that is important it is the problem solving and creativity of the surrounding characters that saves the trio.

All-Flash #12 has a number of unusual components. The trio buys a restaurant for an amazingly low price. They discover that the previous owner money to a criminal gang, which they now have to repay. Within the story, they argue about stupidity and call each other names

> NODDY: Now see here Winky—if we go into business you've got to stop calling me dumb!
> WINKY: You ain't dumb Noddy!
> BLINKY: Oh yeah! He was sixteen years old before he could wave goodbye! [Fox, "Tumble…"].

Somehow Blinky develops an incredible balanced meal by just reading about vitamins. The balanced meal is a huge success, and they run out of ingredients. Leaves from a plant that they brought back from Karma find their way into the food. They accidentally discover these leaves make anyone or anything temporarily invisible. This issue also includes the origin story of the Clifford DeVoe who became a villain known as the Thinker. The Thinker is known for his brilliant mind, and later develops a Thinking Cap with special powers. He feels that the Flash is a worthy adversary, and he enjoys challenging him with brilliant criminal plans. The juxtaposition of genius and stupidity, invention and luck make this a more layered story.

In *All-American Comics #74* the cover shows the trio on a scaffold trying to paint a billboard but not paying attention to their task and ready to fall. The caption reads:

Let's have no more accidents, hey folks? You guys and girls out there have to be more careful! An accident can happen to anybody.....We're all careless—you and me and Winky Blinky and Noddy! If ya don't believe me, cast your optics on this mess....
And the next time ya fall down a flight of stairs 'cause you didn't see junior's new fire engine—remember......WE WARNED YOU!!! [Beste 30].

Throughout the story, several accidents occur. A woman is burned on her face with a hot pie. Blinky is also burned when he catches fire trying to use a blowtorch. The fire burns through the scaffold ropes and the three fall to the ground. The Flash saves the rest of the residents from the fire, then completes the billboard the boys were painting. It reads, "Be Careful! It is amazing how little carelessness it takes to cause big accidents! National Safety Council" (Beste 36).

With regard to inclusion of characters that appear to be mentally challenged, there is one final bit of irony. The Editorial Advisory Board of the Superman DC Comic Magazines included Dr. Robert Thorndike, an educational psychologist from Teacher's College at Columbia University. Thorndike was the son of Edward Thorndike, a psychologist and proponent of eugenics, which he called "selective breeding." Robert would go on to be a psychometrician who would collaborate with Elizabeth Hagen in 1954 to develop the standardized Cognitive Abilities Test, widely used in schools to measure intelligence. One wonders whether or not Thorndike noticed, supported or opposed characterizations of intelligence in these issues.

The Three Dimwits remained popular characters in issues of *All-Flash, All-American Comics, Flash Comics*, and *Comics Cavalcade*. They disappeared towards the end of the Golden Age in 1947. It is difficult to say why, possibly due to changes within the industry and a desire to modernize the stories. In 1960, the Flash #117 reads "Meet Winky Blinky and Noddy! They possess an I.Q. of 150 (their three I.Q.'s added together, that is)" (Fox, "The Madcap..." 15). The story, titled "The Madcap Inventors of Central City," is said to be the "zaniest case" of the Flash's career. The story begins with each of the characters being fired from their low-level service jobs for inability to carry out basic tasks. Blinky says that they owe two months' rent and haven't eaten in two days. This reference to their inability to maintain basic survival is in opposition to their clothing and the office they have. The story is similar to the earliest versions, but it is a one-shot appearance with little explanation before or after. At the end, they drive off in their car while the Flash thinks, "Hmmm.... I wonder what madcap adventures those three dimwits will have the next time I see them?" (Fox, "The Madcap..." 27). The caption reads, "* Editor's Note: To the Flash—to his discomfort—will soon find out—in a forthcoming issue" (Fox, "The Madcap..." 27).

Despite that tease, they do not appear until forty years later. In *Flash Vol. 2*, they make a brief appearance. Jay Garrick remains after the wedding of Wally West and Linda Park. The other guests (including Jessie Quick, Max Mercury and Impulse) ask Jay to tell them about his wedding to Joan Williams. In a flashback to 1947, the Flash describes taking Joan to Las Vegas before it was a big city. The humorous story has members of the Justice Society of America interrupting the romance to host a celebration at the Blue Heron Hotel and Casino. The manager, Rocky, is involved with gangsters, and but also skimming money for himself. In minor addition to the story, the Three Dimwits are seen jumping from a train. Despite the passage of time, they are still referred to as "dimwits," still involved with low-level criminals, and still call each other "idjits" (McGreal). Villains Fiddler, Shade and the Thinker are there to rob the place, thinking the Flash is nowhere near them. Instead, the Flash spoils the robbery and rescues the JSA. Rocky loses the satchel full of money; Jay states that he searched the desert but couldn't find a trace. The readers see Winky, Blinky, and Noddy get hit over the head with the satchel full of money. They jump on a train and discuss using the money to retire to an island in the Caribbean. In 2007, an Easter egg of sorts has the three featured on the cover of a children's book that Lois Lane is reading to Christopher Kent (the son of General Zod and Ursa who was adopted by Superman/Clark Kent and Lois Lane). The book is entitled, "The Three Dimwits" and the author is Gardner Fox. Lois reads, "And then Winky said, 'We better take this up with the perfessers at th' collitch!' and Noddy agreed. 'Who'da thunk we'd turn out geniamusses!'" Chris replies, "Ha! Those guys're silly!" (Busiek). These are the only post–Golden Age appearances until their final instance.

In *Justice League: Cry for Justice*, several characters deal with the death of close friends and loved ones. Most of the losses come as a result of a series of robberies of technological items from various cities. Ray Palmer mourns the loss of Professor Watt's assistant Mike Dante who was tortured to death in the theft of the time pool technology. Ray tells Killer Moth, "Mike was a nice guy. Retired. Liked to fish. And now dead. Few knew Mike. And few cared. Unfortunately for you, I knew him and I do care. A whole bunch." This theme continues when Ray stops at the Flash Museum in Central City on his hunt for Prometheus. Jay Garrick is there to investigate the theft of the cosmic treadmill. He and Ray discuss the weight of the losses they have experienced. Jay states, "You say you've been hit hard? So has the Flash Museum. They killed three guards. Retired volunteers—they were harmless, good men.—And my dear friends. And why? The only thing taken was the technology from the cosmic treadmill. And my buddies' lives" (Robinson). The silhouettes of Winky, Blinky and Noddy are seen in the background in their last appearance.

These three characters were a staple of many stories and issues. The rationale appears to have been slapstick humor and plot twists that could be directly related to people with lower intelligence, no skills, and poor decision-making. In the 1940s when the Flash comics originated, individuals such as Winky, Blinky, and Noddy may have been classified as feebleminded. They most likely would not have received any social or educational services. They probably would have dropped out of school prior to graduation without enough skills to find suitable employment. Today, Winky Blinky and Noddy may have been classified as intellectually disabled and received educational support. Transition and vocational services may have helped them find gainful employment. However, it is just as possible that they may not have been labeled. Individuals with milder learning challenges are often misdiagnosed and drop out of school with no ability to move forward in society. In the comics, their lack of skills causes them to seek work by offering to carry out smaller jobs for crime figures. This path is often reality for individuals with similar challenges. Research indicates that 3 out 5 prisoners cannot read or read at a level low enough to impact their ability to function independently (Sainato). Certainly the way these three characters were always on the fringes of criminal activity and schemes designed to help them gain financial reward parallels stories of many inmates. In terms of daily living, they may have been able to fend for themselves, although with difficulty. They do not seem to have any other family and it is not clear where or how they live. Various versions of the Flash seem to watch over them to some extent, but they seem to manage somewhat independently by helping each other. Many homeless people form such groups and reflect real life Winkys, Blinkys and Noddys.

Disabilities as Comic Relief: A Certain Brand of Humor

People who seem "different" in some way have been seen as the focus of entertainment for decades. Bakhtin use the metaphor of carnival to explain how humor can subvert the dominant norms, bring unlikely groups of people together, and encourage eccentric behavior that would otherwise be deemed unacceptable ("Carnivalesque"). Circus sideshows and promoters such as P.T. Barnum claimed to help people with disabilities gain acceptance and even fame, but at the cost of being seen as different to an even greater degree (Fiedler; Mateen and Boes). Robert Bogdan ("Freak Show") and colleagues ("Picturing Disabilities") detail the venues by which individuals with disabilities were able to financially survive. In similar ways, vaudeville and minstrel shows took a "difference" and made it appealing to larger audiences (Strausbaugh). In these cases, individuals involved had self-determination; they chose to become part of a system that some say was exploitative.

In other examples in popular culture, people with disabilities are unknowing targets of unwanted pranks and jokes. Comedy has always included characters whose childlike naiveté often results in disastrous situations. This trope can be described as the *comic misadventurer,* a less abled character who gets into trouble because of his or her impairment (Berger "What's So Funny"). Content analysis and other research methods have helped deconstruct aspects of such entertainment as reflection of times and social codes of behavior (Berger "Disability and Humor"; Riley). Ellis and Goggin explored ways the media helps and hinders understanding. Alicia Rieger explore the ways families with children with disabilities mediate representations. The tension is often between the humor that is seen by the majority group, and the hurt and shame felt by those with similar conditions. Respectful representations can be found (Pennell, et al.; Rieger and McGrail), but these rarely have a light tone or humorous theme. In comics and graphic novels, studies that examined disability and diversity find more that is problematic than positive (Alaniz; Foss, Gray, and Whalen; Ogburn; Kirkpatrick and Scott).

The Three Dimwits appeared in print at a time when other entertainers were using slapstick and satire to make audience members think as well as laugh. Nineteen forty saw Charlie Chaplin's *The Great Dictator* brazenly poke fun at Hitler, Mussolini and Nazism while the country was still on peaceful terms with Germany. The risk was less because he used humor rather than drama. Humor can often be used in traumatic situations to help people cope with their painful reality. An example of this was Mayor Rudolph Giuliani's appearance on *Saturday Night Live* a few weeks after the World Trade Center disaster. Near the end of the opening, Mayor Giuliani states that it is important to have the city's institutions up and running to show that the city is open for business, and that *Saturday Night Live* is one of New York's greatest institutions. Lorne Michaels asks the mayor, "Can we be funny?" Giuliani replies, "Why start now?" ("9/11 Tribute"). Many people have pointed to that humorous exchange as a signal that thing could begin to go back to normal (Guerrasio).

In their book *Seriously Funny: Disability and the Paradoxical Power of Humor,* Shawn Bingham and Sara Green describe two vastly different category of humor: "In disability studies, a distinction has been made between *disabling humor* that (like the taunts of school children) degrades people with disabilities by making them targets of derisive jokes, and *disability humor*" (4). The latter "enlightens others about the disability experience, affirms the humanity of individuals with impairments, counters the widespread view that disability is a tragedy, and challenges stereotypes" (4). These categories demonstrate the tensions inherent in humor connected to disabilities. The simple child-like character and the gruff, aggressive overbearing partner were a staple of vaudeville, radio, television and films. Comedy teams such as

Abbott and Costello, or Dean Martin and Jerry Lewis, were seen as extreme personalities at the edges of the norm. Although they were not seen as individuals to be gawked at or pitied, their success did come from the feeling of superiority by the audience. In addition, there is a difference between people who are playing a part, and people with real disabilities. People knew that the actors playing the dim-witted chump were not like their characters off screen. That is not the case with the trio of characters in the Flash comics. As in *disabling humor*, they were drawn as real people with real challenges, being laughed at, and not in on the joke.

Humor can shape perceptions and be a tool for change. Bingham and Green interviewed a number of comedians with disabilities in order to articulate the value of comedy and laughter to educate, question, and reconstruct existing narratives of disability (7). They described comic Geri Jewell's performance in which she jokingly asks the audience what they think the worst thing is about being a woman with cerebral palsy, then breaks the stunned and embarrassed silence by explaining and miming the act of putting on mascara. She breaks the fear and tension on her own terms. These comedians gave examples of ways "relief humor" served as a positive outlet for emotions (21). They controlled their own actions in order to control the way people saw them. Biklen and Burke would see this as a way to "presume competence." That is very different from others making fun of people with disabilities.

Bingham and Green also identify how individuals can use humor in different ways to frame situations on their own terms. One way a person can gain acceptance from others is by putting others at ease with self-deprecating humor. Others gain a sense of relief and can begin to see the person as more normal than abnormal. Jimmy Kimmel uses humor to defuse the negative power of social media platforms that allow individuals to make comments anonymously that they might never say in person (the opposite of name-calling). He regularly features famous people reading mean tweets about themselves from anonymous Twitter users. The result is laughter instead of the intended pain.

Humor is a social interaction, the opposite of the solitary furtive stare that is all too familiar for many individuals with disabilities (Garland-Thomson). How much better it is to exchange words, especially humorous ones, and find commonalities instead of focusing on differences. If the person with the perceived "problem" is laughing and making jokes, others are put at ease. Comics often use a self-deprecating approach to make a deeper statement. Low-key comedians such as such as Bob Hope and Sid Caesar, as well as in-your-face bold performers like Lenny Bruce, George Carlin and Chris Rock laugh at themselves to help the audience laugh but also think and perhaps question. In this way, humor has the power to change beliefs and attitudes. Varying types of humor, such as satire or parody, can make space for representations that could be viewed negatively in a more serious venue. In the same way, humor can also serve as a lens to examine disability within social context.

Idiots, Dopes and Numbskulls: Why Language Matters

The term *politically correct* began to become part of discussions in American politics in the late 1980s. Within ten years, it had begun to be used in a pejorative way along with other terms such as "thought police" to describe limitations placed on previously acceptable terms in attempts to silence certain points of view. Debates over issues of diversity and multiculturalism generally include accusations that movements that claim to be designed to be more inclusive in fact limit free speech (Chow 2016). Some people defend changes in language as reflective of societal progress and new knowledge. They claim that some labels are not just impolite they are factually inaccurate based on knowledge that was not previously available. In heated political debates, in classrooms, and among families and friends, "the issue of language—what and how to talk about certain issues—has become a dominant lightning rod and definitional frame for public interpretations" (Bingham and Green 124).

Terms and phrases can have power. People with disabilities, particularly invisible ones, are often bullied. In the comics, Winky, Blinky, and Noddy are often bullied by others, and sometimes make ridiculous decisions out of fear. The trio is often afraid of the possibility of physical harm if they do not successfully carry out a task. Like many victims of bullying, they tend to bully each other and attempt to prove their worth. This is not limited to people with intellectual disabilities. Television shows such as *The Big Bang Theory* and *Community* have similar examples of brilliant individuals who are also the target of jokes due to their perceived or actual differences (Williamson and Paul 93). The phrases and slurs used by and for the trio unfortunately can still be heard on most schools. Name-calling can sometimes be the first component of the cycle of bulling that may have severe negative results, for example increased cases of suicides and school violence. What is said and how it is said makes a difference.

Laws, along with social pressure, continue to bring about changes in terms as well as attitudes. "Handicap" is now "disability." Person-first language is used to show the humanity of individuals. A person with a disability may not consider himself or herself a disabled person. Terms like differently-abled and developmental disabilities have replaced more negative ones. People use language to show that the disability is not the defining feature; the focus is on what the person can do, rather than his or her limitations (Biklen and Burke). Major changes have shown the power of language to define—or not—individuals and groups. The Muscular Dystrophy Association annual Labor Day telethon hosted by Jerry Lewis was a staple for almost 50 years. Some families have fond memories of raising money, and watching the tote board flip to show the incredible amount of money that was raised. "Jerry's Kids" referred to children usually in wheelchairs or leg braces and crutches who were brought on stage to evoke pity and increase donations. Mike Ervin, a former poster child for the event, was the subject of a documentary in which he was critical of the charity mentality he believed did more harm than good. MDA severed its relationship with Lewis, something that no one would have predicted when the event began in the 1960s. The changes came from insiders (people with disabilities who began to voice their autonomy and independence) and outsiders (allies who recognized the demeaning nature of the purported assistance). Language and images can perpetuate or erase the stigma associated with categories and groups. Signs of acceptance and change are multiplying. One-year-old Lucas Warren is the first Gerber baby with Down's Syndrome (Begley). Perhaps today, this trio of supporting characters would be written in a different way.

The Last Laugh: When Is It No Longer Funny

The twenty-first century has a different social context than the Golden Age of comics.

Passage of legislation such as the Americans with Disabilities Act (ADA) and the Individuals with Disabilities Education Act (IDEA) mandated modifications in schools and elsewhere to provide inclusion and access for people with disabilities. It would seem logical that there would be a shift in representations of individuals with disabilities would be radically different from the type of persona portrayed in the early Flash comics. A closer look, however, questions whether or not this is the case.

Television and films can change minds and attitudes with powerful visual stories, and emotionally moving presentations. Movies such as *Forrest Gump* and *I Am Sam* present high profile actors playing individuals with intellectual disabilities. While these movies tend to have uplifting stories, some criticize them for the unrealistic presentations. In such films, the characters are flawed but endearing, and often overcome great obstacles to achieve incredible feats. Unfortunately, many other movies use characters with disabilities as the object or source of humor in a different, more mean-spirited way. One specific example is *The Ringer*, in which an able-bodied man poses as a person with a disability to participate in Special Olympics in order to win money via gambling on the result. The main character's uncle says, "Come on, a normal guy against a bunch of feebs? You'll look like Carl freakin' Lewis out there." The Farrelly brothers who made the film reached out to Special Olympics executives. In an interview for the Associated Press, they said they decided the film could humanize their athletes and add a new cachet of cool to their organization.

> "The risk was that it would further the stereotypes of people with intellectual disabilities as the brunt of jokes rather than the teller of jokes," said Special Olympics Chairman Tim Shriver. "But the payoff was even more valuable." "I wanted this movie out there," said Peter Farrelly, who co-produced the film with his brother, Bobby. "It's very funny, but I also saw the potential for changing people's perceptions of people with intellectual disabilities…. It really pushes boundaries," he said. "It shows people who are mentally challenged in a way they've never been shown before…. Farrelly said. "You're not laughing at them. You're really laughing with them. There are a lot of jokes in this movie, and they're in on them all."

While Farrelly may believe in the potential for positive results, others question whether such instances ultimately reinforce the stigma associated with intellectual disabilities.

Characters like Winky, Blinky, and Noddy continue to populate movies and television. Many films may not have a character with a stated disability, but they continue to include characters who are less intelligent for humor or plot devices. Movies like *Home Alone*, *Anchorman*, and *The Hangover* perpetuate laughing at people who are seemingly normal but incredibly stupid. One of the most egregious example is *Tropic Thunder*. Ben Stiller plays an actor who is known for his role as Simple Jack. There are 17 instances of the R-word in the film, but like Peter Farrelly, David Cox points to this and other seemingly offensive aspects of the movie as sharp satire that invites introspection.

> "Retard" isn't the only potentially upsetting term that Tropic Thunder deploys. It also cheerfully trots out "idiot," "moron" and "imbecile." In doing so, it invites us to reconsider the whole issue of the euphemistic re-labeling of disadvantaged groups…. Some films have certainly abused the First Amendment by winning cheap laughs at the expense of the vulnerable to no worthwhile end. *Tropic Thunder* isn't among them. The truths it tells are worth the price that their telling may exact [Cox].

Many disagreed with this perspective. Disability groups protested with rallies and calls for boycott. The dialogue was characterized as "hate speech" which promoted discrimination.

Other examples indicate that the lines between *laughing at* and *laughing with* are as blurry as ever. In 2011, comedian Ricky Gervais used the term "mong" (short for "mongoloid") on Twitter to describe people he thinks are stupid. When disability groups and parent of children with disabilities were angered, he boldly continued to defend his comment. However, a few days later, he personally spoke at length with a parent with children with disabilities and issued an apology (Nathan). Two years later, Gervais wrote, directed and starred in "Derek," a Netflix series in which he portrayed an individual who is very clearly intellectually disabled. Some saw this as just as ignorant and misguided as his previous comments (Lawson). Gervais spoke about the sincerity of the role; his descriptions of the goal to connect with audiences and "applaud people like Derek" make one wonder about the degree and motives for his apparent change of attitude (Siekaly). Characters with disabilities are played for outrageous laughs in animated series such as *South Park* and *Family Guy*. Both shows are known irreverent humor on many subjects, so the issue of people with disabilities as the sources of humor is only one of the potentially offensive components. Media representations of individuals with developmental or intellectual disabilities continue to be scrutinized and deconstructed for positive and negative ramifications (Berger 180; Ellis and Goggin; Stein).

Disabling humor seems to have lingering power. Examples from real events provide additional evidence that making fun of individuals with challenges is almost a reflexive response. President Barak Obama was seen as a champion of civil rights for all marginalized groups, including people with disabilities. In November 2009, he signed Rosa's Law, which replaced the words "mental retardation" with the more accurate term "intellectual disabilities." However, earlier that year Mr. Obama was discussing his bad bowling ability on *The Tonight Show with Jay Leno* and referred to his performance as something that might be seen in Special Olympics (Tapper and Kahn). Although he later called Tim Shriver, the chairperson of the Special Olympics organization, and apologized, many noted that thoughtless humor at the expense of those less abled is still present. Twenty seventeen saw additional examples. Donald Trump publicly ridiculed a reporter, Serge Kovaleski of the *New York Times*. Kovaleski has arthrogryposis, an impairment that visibly affects the flexibility and movement of his arms. Unlike Obama, he did not apologize and attempted to deflect the backlash (Borchers). After a loss, baseball player Aroldis Chapman "liked" a tweet that called his manager an "imbecile" (Grossman). Some found this particularly upsetting because Chapman had been involved in charges of domestic violence. Even with his own issues, he still found it easy to disparage his colleague through social media with a derogatory term. Although he apologized, the incident demonstrated the ease with which old habits can be perpetuated.

Reviews of past practice can help see the progress that has been made in understanding and valuing of individuals with challenges (Cobb; Collins & Ferri; Williamson). Yet despite societal move towards inclusion and acceptance, insensitive terms continue to be used publicly and privately. It does not always seem that changes in rights and access have brought changes in language and attitude. Bingham and Green point to the possible reasons this remains the case: "That these kinds of jokes still get exposure at a time when cultural ideas of disability have progressed to at least some degree ... attest to the lingering temptation to make jokes at the expense of others to bolster feelings of self-worth" (98).

Summary

Winky, Blinky and Noddy were products of the Golden Age of comics combined with the social norms of the 1940s and the level of humor that was popular in American culture. Characters with limited intelligence and a propensity for getting into difficult situations were a staple in television, film and other mediums. Closer analysis of characters like these challenges consumers of entertainment to rethink the impact of such seemingly innocent tropes. Was Moe emotionally disturbed? Was Curly intellectually disabled? Does it matter if they are in on the joke or if it is at their expense? Who decides what is funny and what is appropriate?

There are real Winkys, Blinkys and Noddys in the world. There are also those who continue to see people like this as targets for financial scams, jokes, and more. Society has progressed in many ways, but people with disabilities are often invisible, or still treated as "other." Poking fun, often followed by "just kidding" seemingly remains socially acceptable. Examining these characters in through the lens of disability studies makes painfully obvious that in terms of acceptance and value, people with disabilities are still waiting.

WORKS CITED

Alaniz, José. *Death, Disability, and the Superhero: The Silver Age and Beyond.* University Press of Mississippi, 2014.

Associated Press. "The Special Olympics Approve of 'The Ringer.'" 8 December 2005, www.today.com/popculture/special-olympics-approve-ringer-wbnal0385246. Accessed 12 December 2017.

Barry, Dan. "The 'Boys' in the Bunkhouse." *New York Times,* 9 March 2014. https://www.nytimes.com/interactive/2014/03/09/us/the-boys-in-the-bunkhouse.html Accessed 10 December 2017.

_____. "Giving a Name, and Dignity, to a Disability." *New York Times,* 7 May 2016. www.nytimes.com/2016/05/08/sunday-review/giving-a-name-and-dignity-to-a-disability.html. Accessed 10 December 2017.

Begley, Sarah. "This Boy Named Lucas Is the First Gerber Baby with Down Syndrome." *TIME,* 7 February 2018, time.com/5137165/gerber-baby-lucas-down-syndrome/. Accessed 10 December 2017.

Berger, Ronald J. "Disability and Humor in Film and Television: A Content Analysis." *Disability and Qualitative Inquiry: Methods for Rethinking in an Ableist World.* Ronald J. Berger and Laura S. Lorenz. Routledge, 2015, pp. 177–188.

_____. "What's So Funny About Disability?" *Wise Guys—An Online Magazine,* 9 April 2016,

wiseguys2015www/2016/04/09/whats-so-funny-about-disability/. Accessed 11 December 2017.
Beste, Alfred. "Beware of Accidents." *All American Comics,* vol. 1, no. 74. DC Comics. 1946.
Biklen, Doug, and Jamie Burke. "Presuming Competence." *Equity & Excellence in Education,* 39 (2), 166–175. 2006
Bingham, Shawn Chandler, and Sara E. Green. *Seriously Funny: Disability and the Paradoxical Power of Humor.* Lynne Rienner Publishers, 2016.
Bogdan, Robert. *Freak Show: Presenting Human Oddities for Amusement and Profit.* University of Chicago Press, 2009.
Bogdan, Robert, et al. *Picturing Disability: Beggar, Freak, Citizen, and Other Photographic Rhetoric.* Syracuse University Press, 2012.
Borchers, Calluym. "Meryl Streep Was Right. Donald Trump Did Mock a Disabled Reporter." *The Washington Post,* 9 January 2017. hwww.washingtonpost.com/news/the-fix/wp/2017/01/09/meryl-streep-was-right-donald-trump-did-mock-a-disabled-reporter/?utm_term=.c65784bd69d1. Accessed 16 December 2017.
Braund, Simon. "The Tragic and Twisted Tale of The Three Stooges." *Empire.* August 2012, www.empireonline.com/movies/features/three-stooges/. Accessed 12 December 2017.
Busiek, Kurt. "The Weight of the World." *Superman,* vol. 1, no. 662. DC Comics, 2007.
"Carnivalesque." *Wikipedia,* 5 January 2018, https://en.wikipedia.org/wiki/Carnivalesque. Accessed 10 December 2017.
Chaplin, Charlie, director. *The Great Dictator.* United Artists, 1940.
Chow, Kat. "'Politically Correct': The Phrase Has Gone from Wisdom to Weapon." National Public Radio, 14 December 2016, www.npr.org/sections/codeswitch/2016/12/14/505324427/politically-correct-the-phrase-has-gone-from-wisdom-to-weapon. Accessed 15 December 2017.
Cobb, Marion MacDonald. "Characteristics of Slow Learners." *The Clearing House,* vol. 35, no. 6, February 1961, pp. 345–348. *JSTOR,* doi.org/10.1080/00098655.1961.11477641. Accessed 9 December 2017.
Cohen, Adam. *Imbeciles: The Supreme Court, American Eugenics, and the Sterilization of Carrie Buck.* Penguin Books, 2016.
Collins, Kathleen, and Beth Ferri. "Literacy Education and Disability Studies Re-envisioning Struggling Students." *Journal of Adolescent & Adult Literacy,* vol. 60, no. 1, 18 April 2016, pp. 7–12. *Wiley-Blackwell Full Collection,* doi:10.1002/jaal.552. Accessed 10 December 2017.
Cox, David. "The Imbecilic Truth about the Tropic Thunder Retard Debate." *The Guardian,* 22 September 2008. www.theguardian.com/film/filmblog/2008/sep/22/tropicthunder.benstiller. Accessed 16 December 2017.
Ellis, Kate, and Gerald Goggin. *Disability & the Media.* Palgrave Macmillan, 2015.
Fiedler, Leslie. *Freaks: Myths & Images of the Secret Self.* Simon & Schuster, 1978.
Foss, Chris, Jonathan W. Gray, and Zach Whalen, editors. *Disability in Comic Books and Graphic Narratives.* Palgrave Macmillan, 2016.
Fox, Gardner. "Adventure of the Magic Mirror." *All Flash.* vol. 1, no. 9. DC Comics, 1943.
_____. "Adventure of the Stolen Telescope." *All Flash.* vol. 1, no. 9. DC Comics, 1943.
_____. "Case of the 'Patsy Colt.'" *All Flash.* vol. 1, no. 5. DC Comics, 1942.
_____. "The Madcap Inventors of Central City." *The Flash.* vol. 1, no. 117. DC Comics, 1960.
_____. "The Ray That Changed Mens' Souls." *All Flash.* vol. 1, no. 6. DC Comics, 1942.
_____. "Troubles Come in Doubles." *All Flash.* vol. 1, no. 11. DC Comics, 1943.
_____. "Tumble Inn to Trouble." *All Flash.* vol. 1, no. 12. DC Comics, 1943.
Garland-Thomson, Rosemarie. *Staring: How We Look.* Oxford University Press, 2015.
Grossman, Connor. "Aroldis Chapman Reportedly Apologizes for Liking Instagram Comment Calling Joe Girardi an 'Imbecile.'" *Sports Illustrated,* 8 October 2017, www.si.com/mlb/2017/10/08/aroldis-chapman-instagram-comment-apology-yankees. Accessed 11 December 2017.
Guerrasio, Jason. "New 'Saturday Night Live' Documentary Recounts the Emotional First Show After 9/11." *Business Insider,* April 16, 2015, www.businessinsider.com/saturday-night-live-first-show-after-911-2015-4. Accessed 10 December 2017.

Hinds, Pamela J., Tsedal Neeley, and Catherine Durnell Cramton. "Language as a Lightning Rod: Power Contests, Emotion Regulation, and Subgroup Dynamics in Global Teams." *Journal of International Business* Studies, vol. 45, no. 5 June–July 2014. *JSTOR,* pp. 536–561. Accessed 10 December 2017.

Kirkpatrick, Ellen, and Suzanne Scott. "Representation and Diversity in Comics Studies." *Cinema Journal,* vol. 55, no. 1, Fall 2015, pp. 120–124. *Project MUSE,* doi.org/10.1353/cj.2015.0064. Accessed 15 December 2017.

Lawson, Mark. "Ricky Gervais' Derek: Cruel, or Just Unusual?" *The Guardian.* 31 January 2013, www.theguardian.com/culture/2013/jan/31/ricky-gervais-derek-cruel-unusual. Accessed 10 December 2017.

Mateen, F.J., and C.J. Boes. "'Pinheads': The Exhibition of Neurologic Disorders at 'The Greatest Show on Earth.'" *Neurology,* vol. 75, no. 22, 2010, pp. 2028–2032. *PubMed,* doi:10.1212/wnl.0b013e3181ff9636. Accessed 12 December 2017.

McGreal, Pay (w), and Paul Pelletier (a). "Honeymoon in Vegas." *Flash Vol. 2* #161. DC Comics, 2000.

Nathan, Sara. "'I was naive': Finally Ricky Gervais Apologises for 'Mong' Comments After Mother of Two Disabled Daughters Is Reduced to Tears." *Daily Mail Online,* 24 October 2011, www.dailymail.co.uk/news/article-2051938/Ricky-Gervais-admits-naive-offensive-remarks-Twitter.html. Accessed 12 December 2017.

9/11 Tribute with Mayor Giuliani and Paul Simon. *Saturday Night Live,* season 27, episode 1, NBC, 29 September 2001, www.nbc.com/saturday-night-live/video/911-tribute-with-mayor-giuliani/n11612?snl=1. Accessed 12 December 2017.

Ogburn, Carolyn. "Disability in Comic Books and Graphic Narratives." *Disability & Society,* vol. 32, no. 10, 2017, pp. 1683–1684. *ProQuest Research Library,* doi:10.1080/09687599.2017.1372948. Accessed 10 December 2017.

Okuda, Ted, and Edward Watz. *The Columbia Comedy Shorts.* McFarland, 1986.

Pennell, Ashley E., et al. "Respectful Representations of Disability in Picture Books." *The Reading Teacher,* vol. 71, no. 4, 2017, pp. 411–419. *Academic Search Elite,* doi:10.1002/trtr.1632. Accessed 9 December 2017.

Rieger, Alicja. "'It Was a Joke For Him and a Life for Me': A Discourse on Disability Related Humor Among Families of Children with Disabilities." *Disability Studies Quarterly,* vol. 25, no. 4, 2005. dsq-sds.org/article/view/605/782 doi: 10.18061/dsq.v25i4.605. Accessed 12 December 2017.

Rieger, Alicja, and Ewa McGrail. "Exploring Children's Literature with Authentic Representations of Disability." *Kappa Delta Pi Record,* vol. 51, no. 1, pp. 18–23, doi: 10.1080/00228958.2015.988560. Accessed 12 December 2017.

Riley, Charles A. *Disability and the Media: Prescriptions for Change.* University Press of New England, 2005.

Robinson, James. "Cry for Justice: The Gathering." *Justice League,* vol. 1, no. 2. DC Comics, 2009.

"Rosa's Law." *Special Olympics,* www.specialolympics.org/Regions/north-america/News-and-Stories/Stories/Rosa-s-Law.aspx. Accessed 10 December 2017.

Sainato, Michael. "US Prison System Plagued by High Illiteracy Rates." *Observer,* 18 July 2017. observer.com/2017/07/prison-illiteracy-criminal-justice-reform/. Accessed 12 December 2017.

Seely, Peter, and Gail Pieper, editors. *Stoogeology: Essays on the Three Stooges.* McFarland, 2007.

Seikaly, Andrea. "Ricky Gervais on 'Derek': 'I Think This is the Most Sincere Thing I've Done.'" *Variety,* 28 May 2014. variety.com/2014/scene/news/ricky-gervais-derek-most-sincere-thing-1201194856/. Accessed 14 December 2017.

Smuts, Aaron. "Humor." *Internet Encyclopedia of Philosophy.* www.iep.utm.edu/humor/. Accessed 12 December 2017.

Stein, Joel. "Breaking the Last Laugh Barrier." *Los Angeles Times,* 13 December 2005. articles.latimes.com/2005/dec/13/opinion/oe-stein13. Accessed 10 December 2017.

Strausbaugh, John. *Black Like You: Blackface, Whiteface, Insult and Imitation in American Popular Culture.* Jeremy P. Tarcher/Penguin, 2007.

Tapper, Jake, and Huma Kahn. "Obama Apologizes for Calling His Bad Bowling 'Like the Special Olympics.'" *ABC News*, 20 March 2009, abcnews.go.com/Politics/story?id=7129997. Accessed 13 December 2017.

Thorburn, Russell. "Watching the Three Stooges, After Fifty, in the Hospital." *Prairie Schooner*, vol. 80, no. 1, Spring 2006, p. 180. *Project MUSE*, doi.org/10.1353/psg.2006.0100. Accessed 12 December 2017.

United States. "MR 76: Mental Retardation: Past and Present." January 1977, United States Government Printing Office, www.acf.hhs.gov/sites/default/files/add/gm_1976.pdf. Accessed 10 December 2017.

United States Department of Education. *American with Disabilities Act*. 1990. www2.ed.gov/about/offices/list/ocr/docs/hq9805.html. Accessed 12 December 2017.

_____. *Individuals with Disabilities Education Act website*. sites.ed.gov/idea/. Accessed 12 December 2017.

Walker, Pamela Kay. *Moving Over the Edge: Artists with Disabilities Take the Leap*. MH Media, 2005.

Walters, Shannon. "Cool Aspie Humor: Cognitive Difference and Kenneth Burke's Comic Corrective in *The Big Bang Theory* and Community." *Journal of Literary & Cultural Disability Studies*, vol. 7, no. 3, 2013, pp. 271–288. *Project MUSE*, doi:10.3828/jlcds.2013.24. Accessed 12 December 2017.

Wells, John. "Gardner Fox." *The Flash Companion*, edited by Keith Dallas. TwoMorrows Publishing, 2008, pp. 13–18.

Williamson, John, and Jim Paul. "The 'Slow Learner' as a Mediated Construct." *Canadian Journal of Disability Studies*, vol. 1, no. 3. pp. 91–128. cjds.uwaterloo.ca/index.php/cjds/article/view/59/84. Accessed 12 December 2017.

The Birth of the Silver Age Flash

Reasons and Influences

LIAM T. WEBB

The Silver Age Flash made his debut appearance in *Showcase* #4, dated October 1956. The character was a reinvention of the Golden Age character of the same name, whose series was discontinued just seven years earlier in February 1949. Iconic DC Comics editor Julius Schwartz, employed by the company for over 42 years, from February 21, 1944, until the middle of 1986 (Schwartz 69, 151), was the driving force behind Flash's reinvention. Schwartz's editorial vision was assisted by writer Robert Kanigher and John Broome and artists Carmine Infantino, Joe Kubert, Frank Giacoia, and Joe Giella.[1]

The original Flash was created during the Golden Age of comic books, part of a wave of superhero characters that included Superman, Batman, Wonder Woman, Hawkman and many others. In the latter part of the Golden Age, after the superhero boom of the 1940s waned, most publishers diversified their content, exploring Westerns, Romance, Horror, and Crime comic books. At DC Comics, the series of Superman, Batman, and Wonder Woman had survived the cancelations that befell other superhero titles.

In an event that would change the course of popular culture history, on April 21, April 22 and June 4, 1954, the United States Congress held a hearing on comics, exploring a perceived connection between the reading of comic books and juvenile delinquency in young fans (Coville). While couching their conclusion in language that recognized other possible beliefs on the subject, they said:

> There are many who believe that the boys and girls who are the most avid and extensive consumers of such comics are those who are least able to tolerate this type of reading material. The excessive reading of this material is viewed by some observers

as sometimes being symptomatic of some emotional maladjustment, that is, comic book reading may be a workable "diagnostic indicator" or an underlying pathological condition of a child [qtd. In Coville].

Due in part to the perceived correlation between comic books and juvenile delinquency that arose at this time, the comic book publishing industry was irrevocably altered. One of the most significant changes was the adoption of The Comics Code Authority (CCA), a self-censoring board the industry adopted to tightly monitor and control the content that was produced. The CCA would attempt to ensure morally acceptable stories would be published by providing an extensive list of prohibited content. Following the Senate hearings and the adoption of the CCA, most publishers had to reconsider what was being produced to ensure that it would not be objectionable.

The year after the Senate hearings, DC conceived of the *Showcase* title, which would "...put out a single issue showcasing a new character or concept, then wait to see how it sold before we turned it into a regular monthly title. *Showcase* could function as a sort of one-shot comic trial balloon," (Schwartz, 87) so that the company wouldn't lose more money than absolutely necessary. Julius Schwartz recounted why they decided to try the Flash when they did:

> The first three *Showcases* flopped, and we were at an editorial meeting trying to decide what to do in number four when I suggested that we try to revive the Flash, who had died with the demise of the other superhero titles. [...] Some of my co-workers were incredulous and asked me why I thought Flash would succeed now, having failed so dismally a few years before, thus resulting in his demise. I pointed out that the average comic book reader started reading them at the age of eight and gave them up at the age of twelve. And since more than four years had already passed, there was a whole new audience out there who really didn't know that the Flash had flopped, and maybe they might give it a try [*ibid.*].

The public reacted very well to the character, and now *Showcase* #4 is typically cited as the book that started off the Silver Age of comics. As is the case in many recollections of the earlier days of the comic book industry, the details are not always presented consistently. In a 1992 article Schwartz recalled the meeting differently in that he didn't know who suggested reviving the Flash, but, as Schwartz was the editor of *Flash Comics* in the 1940s, the job landed to him to oversee the work anyway (Silver Age Classics DC Showcase 4, 1992).

Schwartz was very familiar with the Golden Age Flash's initial adventures, which started out with almost exclusively human antagonists and situations (with blackmail, gangsters, etc.). While the Golden Age Flash did develop stories with a more sci-fi style, this more down-to-Earth element never completely faded away; even in the last story of the Golden Age Flash, the villain had a gang of men in suits with guns. In contrast, the Silver Age Flash and his adventures were securely ensconced in science fiction from the first issue and remained that way for years. The main reason for this change was the editorship and leadership of Julius Schwartz.

Schwartz was not a "hands off" editor from any account. He often plotted the stories with the writers, and after researching this era, I feel that Schwartz should get a co-writer's credit on many, if not all, of the early Silver Age Flash stories, as well as the other titles he edited. Schwartz tells of plotting books with a writer like Gardner Fox. "[Fox would] say, Do you have any ideas? And then the two of us would work out the basics of what the next story should be and iron it out there in the office" (Schwartz, 94).

Flash Inker Joe Giella confirmed that Schwartz's direction was the reason for the science fiction focus:

> Both [Schwartz's direction and Broome's preference] but more Julie's because Julie was a sci-fi buff, and I think that was very instrumental going with that route. Julie was instrumental in that, I do remember that. … In my personal opinion, it was from the beginning it was that way, due to Julie's history and he told me that. Just like the circle on Batman's chest. I don't know what it was originally, but Julie was responsible for that oval and the Bat enclosed in the oval [Joe Giella, phone interview, October 31, 2017].

Frank Giella, son of Flash inker Joe Giella and companion to Julius Schwartz, by Giella's estimation, on 50 to 70 convention trips, confirmed that Schwartz was the driving force behind the tone of the stories:

> That was pure Julie Schwartz, in my opinion. I spoke with him on the plane and asked him. He used to have people come up to Julie at the shows who wanted to meet someone who knew L. Ron Hubbard. Forrest Ackerman knew Julie, Julie just had a love of science fiction; it was on cutting edge at the time, space and time travel and made that stuff great. It wasn't mobsters, it was villains, he had a lot of fun creating them. That was his obsession, science fiction. I wasn't there but that is my opinion. A lot of that sci-fi stuff was Julie's decision, he got involved in working up stories, working up a cover [Frank Giella, phone interview, November 27, 2017].

When I asked about the extent of Schwartz's influence on the books, Frank Giella reported:

> I'm sure you're on the right track; we have to reevaluate it for group credit. I think everybody would contribute; they would sit around and discuss things like that. [Joe Giella] did have lunch with Julie here and there. Definitely the writers and Julie got together and layout guys and maybe my father had less of impact because [Joe Giella] picked it up after the story written and designed already. My father liked to work at home. But I'm sure the other guys got together, you could see the stories had Julie's influence, which he didn't get credit for. More influence than anyone I would say. Julie would get credit sometimes but not the respect. All of the team should be recognized in some way. Carmine's art was sketchy like that, the inker picked one line of the 20; look at Elongated Man versus Batman and Flash, the finished product looks different. Probably the best inker for Carmine [Infantino] is Carmine [*ibid.*].

Carmine Infantino recalls the creative process somewhat differently, though he does acknowledge some of Schwartz's input on the characters and first concepts. Infantino relates his experiences of when he got the first script for the Silver Age Flash:

> Bob Kanigher handed me the script, and had even laid out a stick-figure idea of the first cover. ... And we went over it a little. That's how I know it was Bob's script. No matter what anybody else says, Bob Kanigher introduced the ring that contained the uniform. Julie may have helped Bob comic up with the combination of lightning and chemicals giving The Flash his abilities and I believe Julie came up with the character's name, Barry Allen (after talk show hosts Barry Gray and Steve Allen). But if you look at the very first script, you can tell it was Kanigher's type of story.
>
> Then Kanigher said to me, "Go create a costume for this guy; forget the old character. You go create something new." So I went home and designed the red outfit that you see today. ... I also designed Flash's "Rogues Gallery" of villains. So the creation of the new character, was a group effort between Julie, Bob, and myself [Infantino, 51].

However, Paul Levitz, former publisher of DC Comics said "Julie was very much involved in the plotting of his titles in the Silver Age, and might devote a half day to working with a writer. He was much less focused on the art, beyond the idea of the cover and working with artists he respected and trusted." Levitz added "Notwithstanding Carmine's claims after Julie's death, artists almost never participated in that part of the process in those years except by creation of covers before stories, which doesn't seem to have been part of the Flash process" (Levitz interview, November 30, 2017).

While I do not doubt what Mr. Infantino related above was his honest recollection, Kanigher and Schwartz shared an office for many years and so I find that it is plausible that, despite a reported mutual dislike between Schwartz and Kanigher (Paul Levitz interview, November 30, 2017), Schwartz may have had some influence on Kanigher's scripting, even if Kanigher wrote in his own style and tone. While this is conjecture, I find it to be more likely than not that they may have discussed ideas for the script, if not essentially co-plotted, together as Schwartz did so many times before and since that time.

In an article in 1992 Schwartz wrote "I had strived to make the new Flash as different as possible. The only thing he had in common with his predecessors was his speed. I wanted originality.... I gave Barry (The Flash) Allen a new origin and an interesting cast of characters," (DC Silver Age Classics Showcase 4, 1992). Note that Schwartz wrote "I had strived" and "I gave," not "Kanigher strived" and "Kanigher gave." Indeed, in the same book, Robert Loren Fleming recalled that "the first appearance of the Silver Age Flash ... to Kanigher [was] just a long-forgotten afternoon. He was busy that year, 1956, editing full time and doing a little writing on the side. ... That particular script [for Showcase #4] exited Kanigher's typewriter doing Mach One, and he didn't even take the time to look up and watch it go" (DC Silver Age Classics Showcase 4, 1992). Schwartz's word choice here, coupled with Fleming's recollections and the general tendency for Schwartz to have given himself less credit than was likely deserved for many things in his career, provide enough evidence that it was at absolute minimum a collaborative effort between Schwartz and Kanigher on the first Flash story, if not lopsided heavily in favor of Schwartz with Kanigher doing the write up. Note, this is not to make a value judgement of any kind on Kanigher or on Infantino's recollections, it is simply a preponderance of research evidence.

Infantino goes on to tell us that Schwartz took Kanigher off the Flash and put John Broome on as writer (Infantino, 54) which coincides with the start of the titular *The Flash* comic book series (*DC Archive Editions: The Flash* Vol 1, table of contents). Schwartz was an editor, an author's agent, a co-plotter of comics but above all, was a lover of science fiction. As a young boy Schwartz enjoyed the fantasy series *Blue Fairy* (Schwartz, 3), and as he got older he recalls that "I devoured dime novels…. I especially liked Dick and Frank Merriwell and Nick Carter detective mysteries—I preferred those featuring the villain Dr. Quartz because his name sounded so much like my name," (Schwartz, 7). Then, in 1926, at age 11, Schwartz received in trade from a friend a copy of the June issue of *Amazing Stories*. Schwartz says that "I devoured that issue, cover to cover…." and "And from that day on, I was hooked [on science fiction]!" (Schwartz, 8). Schwartz also said: "I loved science fiction! It was the real reason I wanted to be an editor, and I even worked with the writers who I had read and agented to the science fiction magazines," (114) which included Flash writer John Broome.

Schwartz drew on his knowledge and background to help shape the Flash and other Silver Age characters. It is nearly certain that John Broome did the same since he too was a science fiction fan (Decker, *The Flash Companion*, 61).

While Schwartz personally wanted to highlight science fiction adventures for the Flash as a science fiction character, this was not contrary to anything the company wanted or needed at the time. In fact, Schwartz was, in this sense, the right person at the right time in American history, riding the then-current crest of optimism and advancement in American culture. Many authors and researchers have posited that the 1950s was a time of forgetting about the horrors of World War II and enjoying the spoils of victory, both financially and as a notion of cultural pride. Frank Giella corroborates this:

> It was on the crest of the 50s and 60s with the space program, and what reflects on society but comics and things at the time. The whole space race was going on, computers started coming around, being worked on; medicine was making big advances. The 60s, 70s, 80s, and 90s were about advancement and Julie tapped into that. I was

born in 1964, and we were fascinated with that stuff [meaning science and space]. He tapped into space race, Kennedy saying we're going to the moon. In 1968–69 Batman and Robin went to the moon because Joker was on the moon. It was in *Detective* 388, it came out right – it came out in June 1969 and we landed on moon in July 1969, so I guess he was tapping into buzzwords of the time. Now, if it came out in June, it was drawn in February to March, with everyone talking about that, going to the moon; so like with sci-fi earlier, he tapped into what was going on in society [Frank Giella, phone interview, November 27, 2017].

While Schwartz clearly tapped into the 1950s trends of optimism, science, space travel, etc., this did not bar him from also drawing on his long history in science fiction fandom and publications. And if anything, as Paul Levitz remarked, Schwartz was a bit ahead of his time: "I think Julie was just a bit ahead of his time in the forensics role [of Barry Allen's identity]. The lack of comedy [in the Silver Age Flash stories] is probably the distance from Shelly Mayer's editorial influence." But for a better look at Schwartz's science fiction influence, we should turn to the early Silver Age Flash stories to see where science fiction really shines through.

In *Showcase* #4, the first Flash story is titled "Mystery of the Human Thunderbolt" and is the Silver Age Flash's origin story and his confrontation with his first adversary, a villain known as The Turtle Man (Kanigher). The Turtle Man was a revived Golden Age character, redefined for the Silver Age with a new personal identity and even different villain name which was just "The Turtle" in the previous incarnation. The Turtle Man did things slowly and planned to use Flash's speed against him, but had no specific powers of his own. This is distinct from the Golden Age Turtle, who had the ability to drain Flash's speed from the hero. The second story in *Showcase* #4 is titled "The Man Who Broke the Time Barrier." It was written by John Broome and concerned a thief from an unspecified future named Mazdan who was sentenced to live in a desolate 50th century Earth, but accidentally went to the 20th century. Mazdan fought Flash with futuristic gadgets like a magnetic rod that shoots circles of heat and a special contact lens that essentially makes lasers from simple electric light. Flash brings the criminal back to his own time and the issue is settled, as the future people say they will make sure Mazdan goes to the right century this second time. The first story presents the reader with a non-powered villain, and the second story has future criminals, gadgets, and faulty time machines. What a stark contrast between the two writers.

In Flash's next appearance in *Showcase* #8, the first story, by Robert Kanigher, was titled "The Secret of the Empty Box" and featured a set of identical triplets who dress as a villainous stage magician and show up separately in succession (as if they are one person) to commit crimes with simple magic tricks which are really athletic and mild technical tricks like a wired suit or hidden parachute. The second story in #8, written by John Broome (and likely co-plotted by Schwartz) features the debut of Captain Cold, a thief that uses a super-science "cold gun" powered by "cyclotron radiation" enabling it to freeze people, objects, and make mirages using absolute zero cold. Again, we see a stark contrast in the tone of the two stories. And again, the Kanigher story has a non-powered villain while the Broome story has a villain rooted in science fiction.

In the Flash's third appearance in *Showcase* #13, the story by Kanigher was "Around the World in 80 Minutes." The title was clearly a nod to Jules Verne, but past that, science fiction was not a concern in the story where Flash had to stop natural disasters or terrorism all within a certain time period. The second story, "Master of the Elements" by John Broome, featured the debut of Mr. Element, another villain with a super-scientific gimmick of using different elements and even wearing the symbol for carbon on his chest. Later in the story, Mr. Element uses the fictional "elemento" which he says is "magnetic light," to shoot Flash into space (Broome, "Master"). Flash escapes by mimicking the trajectory of a comet and banking around the moon to come back to Earth. Both the hero and villain of this story use science and scientific rationale to battle. The title itself, "Master of the Elements," could have been a nod to the classic Verne story "Master of the World" featuring Robur the Conqueror, who used flight to "prove his superiority" the way Mr. Element used elements to "prove" his. At this point, just three issues into this new character, by nature of the dual stories, one could almost wonder if there were two people calling themselves not only Flash, but Barry Allen as well. This problem is resolved in the next issue, which was Flash's fourth and final appearance in Showcase before starting his own title.

Both stories in *Showcase* #14 have a science fiction antagonist. The first story, written by Kanigher, was "Giants of the Time World" which featured UFOs, time travel, and a Lilliputian race who grow into the aforementioned giants. Here we see influences of H.G. Wells as well as Jonathan Swift and many aspects found in many pulp stories. In fact, the Flash is put into a large hourglass in the story, and this predicament is featured on the cover, and this seems to be a definite nod to the multiple pulp covers with women (usually *au naturale* or very close to it) in glass tubes about to be experimented upon— for example the August 1939 issue of *Uncanny Tales*, and the June 1940 issue of *Thrilling Mystery* (Haining, 149 & 143, respectively)—which Schwartz, if not Kanigher as well, would likely have been familiar with.

The second story in *Showcase* #14 was "The Man Who Changed the Earth," which introduced a new villain named Dr. Alchemy, who was actually just Mr. Element in a new identity. This is a first for the Silver Age, if not comics themselves that I could find, where a character changes villain identity on purpose (thus excluding any previous changes-by-mistake such as Lex

Luthor losing his hair due to an artist's mistake). The character changes from Mr. Element to Dr. Alchemy because of the character's stumbling upon the fabled philosopher's stone. He then uses it to commit robberies (however, since earlier in the issue the stone turned a lead pipe into gold why robbing a bank was necessary, no one but Broome and Schwartz know).

After Showcase #14, the Silver Age Flash received his own title, and DC resumed the numbering from the canceled Golden Age title, for business and economic reasons. It was assumed that readers would buy an issue #105 quicker than they would buy a #1, because at the time a higher issue number would indicate staying power and thus quality to a reader more than a #1 issue (Schwartz, 88). Both of the stories in this issue, as well as both stories in *The Flash* #105 were written by John Broome (and presumably co-plotted with Schwartz). The first story was titled "Conqueror from 8 Million B.C." about the telepathic last survivor of an iron-based humanoid society on Earth from eight million years ago. After waking from his suspended animation, this iron-based person tries to crush Flash by making him 1,000 times heavier than normal. Similar to the "Master of Elements" story from *Showcase* #13, Flash escapes this trap using a scientific principle, this time air pressure to turn his tube prison into a makeshift rocket in order to crash and break free upon impact with the ground and deliver the coup de grace to the alien.

The next story from this issue is "The Master of Mirrors" and introduces the recurring villain Mirror Master, who was yet another thief with a scientific process, this time involving mirrors to create illusions and trick Flash's perceptions in a mirror maze. The first story in *The Flash* #106 introduces us to Gorilla Grodd, from a hidden race of intelligent, talking gorillas in Africa, who have their own modern city and rocketry. Grodd's plan was to pose as a traveling human actor in a gorilla suit in order to search for the missing "greatest mind in the world" of Solovar. Grodd learns how to mentally control other gorillas from Solovar (against Solovar's will) and Solovar then enlists the aid of the Flash in overthrowing Grodd who has just taken over Gorilla City with his new powers. This story is high science fiction and nothing else. At this point in the character's history, the generic cross-pollination of science fiction and superhero is solidified with gusto.

The creation and use of Gorilla Grodd as a Flash villain was in fact a holdover from earlier science fiction comics. In the DC series' *Strange Adventures*, a science fiction comic, when they featured a gorilla on the cover, it sold better than other issues (Schwartz, 80). When the editorial staff understood this, they began using gorillas in all of their titles, so much so that eventually DC had to make a rule of no more than one book featuring a gorilla on the cover per month (Schwartz, 171)!

The next story in *The Flash* #106 was "The Pied Piper of Peril" featured an adversary who had a "super sonic flute" to make sound do implausible things. Notably, unlike other villains of this era, the first thing that the Pied Piper does is gather a gang of thugs to him, in an echo of the Golden Age villains who, despite their inhuman powers, rarely let themselves be without a gang to back them up. Also, Piper's motivation is simply to beat the Flash, not pull off a successful heist or conquer a gorilla city. This story serves to change up the formula of the series and introduce a new gadget-based villain more than anything else.

The first story in *The Flash* #107 features the return of Gorilla Grodd and also the appearance of a race of inner-Earth blue bird men who, though also scientifically advanced, were enslaved by Grodd's mental powers. This hollow Earth premise was well established in science fiction by the 1950s, first appearing in Edgar Rice Burroughs' *Pellucidar* series. And while it may be coincidence, the bird people in this story bear a general resemblance to the underground bird people in the 1943 "Underground World" episode from the Fleischer Superman cartoon series.

The second story in *The Flash* #107 was titled "The Amazing Race Against Time" and featured an amnesiac super speedster who was really a robot built on an alien world. This robot crashed on Earth before he could complete his mission, which was to fix a weak spot in a planetoid that kept an alternate dimension from leaking into ours. The treatment that gave the alien robot his memory back also took his super speed, so of course the Flash had to help out in fixing the planetoid's weakness. The next issue, *The Flash* #108, featured other-dimensional alien thieves and the third appearance of Gorilla Grodd who could now turn himself into a human.

All of these stories are high science fiction/science fantasy. As John Broome with Julius Schwartz as editor and perhaps co-plotter took over *The Flash*, they dictated the script, tone, genre, and style of the series and stories. In one of their most iconic stories, the Silver Age Flash meets the Golden Age Flash in the "Flash of Two Worlds!" in *The Flash* #123. Schwartz writes:

> Now, one of the innovations I brought to comic-book editing involved a motif that I had picked up from my early years as a fan of the pulps. When I was growing up I loved the old dime novels that were published by Street & Smith, particularly those that featured my favorite heroic duo, Frank and Dick Merriwell. There were a whole mess of Merriwell stories that featured Frank or Dick, but it wasn't until they were actually teamed up in a single story that I was completely bowled over.
>
> Individually they were great; together they were *super!*
>
> What a team up!
>
> [...] I also remember other team-ups, like the time Tarzan went to Pellucidar to help out David Innes, and crossovers between stories, like when it was revealed that Britt Reed (aka the Green Hornet) was descended from Dan Reed (the nephew of the Lone Ranger).

Team-ups and crossovers were a great hook, and I frequently used them on the titles I worked on, playing around with different pairings and crossovers. One of the best story ideas that I came up with using this motif was "Flash of Two Worlds" [Schwartz, 89–91].

"Flash of Two Worlds" introduced the concept of multiple versions of Earth's heroes that would become a staple of DC Comics. These decisions, which changed the course of comics history for the Flash, for two companies, and now the greater American culture through films and television, were a direct result of Schwartz's love of science fiction and the traditions of the pulps.

The Silver Age Flash was conceived out of a number of factors, including the desire to sell more comics, shifting publishing focuses after the government hearings, and the understanding that the then-current crop of readers didn't know the Golden Age Flash. The tone, nature, and genre of the stories was a group effort; however, it is apparent that they were guided by Julius Schwartz to a greater degree than is often acknowledged. It is Schwartz's influence, and his love of science fiction, that directed the Silver Age Flash's course in the early years, and by doing so, directed the course of the entire comics industry to feature superheroes based on scientific concepts and principles, rather than the more mystic origins of many Golden Age characters.

NOTE

1. In researching the origin and influences on the Flash's reinvention, I had the great fortune to be able to interview Joe Giella, his son Frank Giella, as well as Paul Levitz, former president of DC Comics. While some information that follows is well-known in comics circles, I hope and feel I have helped advance scholarship of the events by these interviews.

WORKS CITED

Brinkley, Allen. *The Fifties.* 2017, The Gilder Lehrmann Institute for American History. https://www.gilderlehrman.org/history-by-era/fifties/essays/fifties. Accessed November 15, 2017.

Broome, John (w), Robert Kanigher (w), Carmine Infantino (p), Joe Kubert (i), Frank Giacoia (i), and Joe Giella (i). *The DC Archive Editions: The Flash Vol. 1.* Mike Carlin, Executive Editor. New York: DC Comics, 1996. Print.

Coville, Jamie. *Comic Books and Juvenile Delinquency Interim Report of the Committee on the judiciary pursuant to S. Res. 89 and S. Res. 190.* 2016, Jamie Coville. http://www.thecomicbooks.com/1955senateinterim.html. Accessed November 1, 2017.

_____. *The 1954 Senate Subcommittee Hearings into Juvenile Delinquency, with the special focus on Comic Books.* 2016, Jamie Coville. http://www.thecomicbooks.com/1954senatetranscripts.html. Accessed November 1, 2017.

The DC Comics Database. http://dc.wikia.com/wiki/Strange_Adventures_Vol_1_9. Accessed November 25, 2017.

Decker, Michael. "John Broome: Words to Run By." *The Flash Companion.* Keith Dallas, editor. Raleigh, NC: TwoMorrows Publishing. 2008.

Estrada, Jackie. *John Broome, Frank Jacobs to Receive 2009 Bill Finger Award.* 2009, San Diego Comic Con. https://www.webcitation.org/5zXoEeISc?url=http://www.comic-con.org/cci/cci_finger_2009.shtml. Accessed November 20, 2017.

Giella, Frank. Personal interview by telephone. November 27, 2017.

Giella, Joe. Personal Interview by telephone. October 31, 2017.

The Grand Comics Database: John Broome. https://www.comics.org/writer/name/John%20 Broome/sort/chrono/. Accessed November 30, 2017.

Infantino, Carmine, and J. David Spurlock, editor. *The Amazing World of Carmine Infantino: An Autobiography.* Lebanon, New Jersey: Vanguard Productions. 2001.

Kahan, Bob, editor. DC Silver Age Classics Showcase 4. DC Comics: New York. 1992. Print.

Levitz, Paul. Personal interview by email correspondence. November 28, 2017, sent, November 29, 2017 returned.

The 1950s: Fact and Summary. http://www.history.com/topics/1950s. Accessed November 15, 2017.

Schwartz, Julius, with Brian M. Thomsen. *Man of Two Worlds: My Life in Science Fiction and Comics.* New York: HarperCollins Publishers. 2000.

"I'm covering the story! Wait here for me"

The Two-Career Couple in the Pages of The Flash

CHARLES W. HENEBRY

The 2014 premiere of *The Flash* on the CW network reinvented Barry Allen and Iris West as a youthful will-they-won't-they pair. The television series' first episode establishes Barry as a charmingly nerdy police scientist who becomes super-speedy after exposure to radiation from an exploding particle accelerator. Iris is his childhood crush and adoptive sister, a young reporter still finding her voice, who writes as an unpaid blogger. Both of them are obviously talented, but both display the shy under-confidence typical of millennials recently graduated from college. The question hanging over their incipient romance is whether Barry can escape the stickiest tar pit of a "friend zone" ever imagined by a television writing team.

By contrast, the Barry Allen and Iris West that first appeared in the pages of DC's *Showcase* (issues #4, #8, #13 and #14, published 1956–58) dressed and acted like people in their early thirties. They had been dating for some time, and were both well-established in their respective professions. The question that hung over this couple was whether her career would doom their love. He was a police scientist of no particular prominence, whereas she was a leading reporter for Picture News.[1] Bad enough that her job put her on a first-name basis with Barry's boss, the police captain (*Showcase* #8A, May–June 1957), but Iris seemingly couldn't help but express her superior status by constantly running Barry down. He may be super-speedy, but according to her he's always running late.

The writers' evident interest in the dynamics of a two-career couple conflicts with prevailing notions of mid-fifties America. Iris will strike today's reader as sharing more in common with Katherine Hepburn's world-renowned lady journalist from the 1940 movie *Woman of the Year* than with iconic '50s figures like June Cleaver or Marilyn Monroe.[?] But while the feminist movement may have been at a low ebb in 1956–58, half a decade before Betty Friedan published *The Feminine Mystique,* there was in fact a lot of concern in mid-fifties America about the social impact of career women, on the logic that women with "masculine" ambitions made men correspondingly less ambitious and more effeminate. As we will see, the Silver Age Flash gave expression to this *zeitgeist* with a twist: while Barry, in his meek acceptance of Iris's dominion, embodied the effeminized midcentury male, in his other identity as the Flash he propounded a paradoxical solution to that problem: the secret hero.

Prior scholarship has focused on the Barry Allen Flash as a resonator for the nuclear jitters of the Cold War. In particular, Richard Wright examines the series through the lens of Alan Nadel's *Containment Culture,* noting how the Flash's speed grants him a near-total freedom from constraint—even as he constrains the illegal activities of others, he does so by working outside the law (57). In this sense, Wright argues, Flash embodies the Cold-War ideology of American exceptionalism, as exemplified by the title page of "Around the World in 80 Minutes!" (*Showcase* #13A, March-April 1958): the costumed figure of the Flash zooms around the globe in response to SOS calls from Eastern Europe, the Middle East, Russia, and elsewhere. But Wright's analysis ignores what makes the Flash different from other superheroes of his era: his almost comical preoccupation with satisfying his girlfriend. Racing around the world on that title page, the hero's thoughts bend toward home: "How can I answer all these calls for help from all parts of the world—and still keep my date with Iris in Center City?" Barry's phrasing implies that his greatest challenge will not be in saving others, but in placating Iris—as if the worldwide threat of Communism were nothing in comparison to the man-crushing scorn of a woman kept waiting.

Of course, keying the hero's sensibility so closely to the gender politics of the mid-fifties had the unintended consequence of giving the character an expiration date. As this essay will explore in its later pages, from 1966–71 writers on *The Flash* struggled to bring Barry's relationship with Iris into line with new gender norms without thereby destroying the couple's dynamism. During this period Iris's personality changed rapidly, sometimes from issue to issue, as different writers tried new approaches to making their marriage an impetus, rather than an impediment, to story and drama. But if the results were uneven, they provide insight into the mores of a period of rapid social change.

A Woman's Scorn

Writer Robert Kanigher invented Iris,[3] debuting her in *Showcase* #4A (September-October 1956) as a critical foil for Barry's superpower: "*Barry—You're always late! Why are you so slow?*" (emphasis, here and in all other quotations, preserved from the original lettering). He may be fast, but he's never fast enough for her. In the next issue, Iris greets Barry even more sharply: "Late *again!* What is it this time? You stop to tie your shoelace?" (*Showcase* #8A, May-June 1957). But with this story Kanigher added a vital complication: Iris isn't just an acid-tongued woman perennially disappointed in her tardy boyfriend; she's an acid-tongued woman with a job. Her job makes her a busy person, justifiably angry when Barry keeps her waiting. More vital, her job makes her a woman of importance: the story opens with Iris in the midst of interviewing the Police Captain about a colossal box first sighted in the middle of Central City Square after two days of thick fog. The whole city is buzzing, and she's in the midst of it, trying to solve the mystery. Barry, meanwhile, has been sidelined: his training as a police chemist is (evidently) irrelevant to plumbing the mysteries of giant boxes, so while uniformed officers and workers clamber around and atop the structure, he was left behind in the lab. He only shows up at the worksite because Iris called him to change the venue for their date, and that change of venue means he's also sidelined romantically, reduced from a paramour to a bystander: after upbraiding him for being late, Iris declares imperiously, "I'm covering the story! Wait here for me while I see how much nearer they are to opening it!" A bit later, she comes back with further news and a request, demoting him to mere go-fer: "There's another box inside the big one! I'll have to wait until it's opened! Please get me a container of coffee and a sandwich—and Barry, honey, try to get back *this* year?"

Of course, being sidelined gives Barry the freedom to pursue the mystery in his own way, as the Flash. And, while Central City's attention remains centered on Iris, Kanigher's narrative follows the crimson streak of Barry's uniform as he criss-crosses the city searching for the criminal operation that he suspects is behind it all: "The story isn't here," Barry thinks to himself when Iris strides off to check on workers' progress in opening the box, "The 'brain' that planted that box wanted the whole city's attention here—while he was elsewhere! I'm going to look for him!" Thus, Iris and the Police Chief stand about on center stage, shaking their heads at the mystery while doggedly pursuing a failing strategy: "*Another* box—*Inside* the big one! This is a Chinese box puzzle, Captain!" to which the Captain replies, "The only way we can solve the puzzle is to open the second box!" Meanwhile, working as the Flash, Barry zips about invisibly "backstage" and manages to find the actual culprits, three criminals dressed (appropriately) as stage magicians. Declining any credit for his heroism, the Flash deposits the first two criminals in jail and leaves the last one to be found by the police once they open the third and final box. In the story's closing panels, Iris walks up to Barry to tell him what's been going on, teases him for failing to ever get her that sandwich and coffee, and suggests that he make it up to her by taking her out for dinner.

While atypical in rendering the Flash's heroics invisible, this story set the pattern for Barry's interactions with his careerist girlfriend: Iris criticizes him for being lazy or late, often on dates that double as reporting assignments, her job giving her the upper hand in their relationship. In his third Flash story, Kanigher opened with the couple walking out of a movie theater; after a brief exchange, Iris abruptly ends the date, right there in the middle of a busy city sidewalk: "Meanwhile, Mister Barry Allen, even if you are an absent-minded scientist, try to move faster than a turtle—and meet me on time tomorrow," a lunch date that turns out to be a photo shoot for a feature she's writing (*Showcase* #13A, March-April 1958). In Kanigher's story from the following issue (May-June 1958), Iris cuts their lunch short because she has an exciting photo assignment that (improbably) requires her to fly what looks like a fighter jet. The secondary writer on the series, John Broome, left Iris out of his first two efforts, but his stories for *Showcase* #13 and #14 both give prominence to Iris and her work. In the first, Iris interrupts a date with Barry when she hears about a nearby bank robbery: "I've got to get over there and cover it for my paper! Come on, Barry! For once in your life—hurry up!" (*Showcase* #13B). In the second story, Iris strikes an unusually conciliatory note when she calls Barry up with the news of Mr. Element's jailbreak: "Sorry, Barry! But this is one time *I'm* going to be late" (*Showcase* #14B). They work in parallel for several days, the Flash chasing down his arch-enemy, now renamed Dr. Alchemy, while Iris reports the results. But when they finally get together the following evening, she's as critical as ever: "Barry, I thought you turned over a new leaf—but you're late again!" Barry makes excuses, insisting that "*Dr. Alchemy* kept us hopping over at headquarters," but she'll have none of it: her job is important, she seems to be saying, his is not: "Well, thanks to a *real* man like *Flash,* you won't have to worry about *Dr. Alchemy* any more! You ought to thank *Flash*—!" (*Showcase* #14B). Barry can only reply, meekly, "I will, Iris…! Now let's eat—I had a hard day!" (ellipsis in original, here and elsewhere, except where noted).

As this exchange suggests, Iris's scorn for Barry is matched only by her admiration of his alter-ego. She repeatedly holds Flash up as a model for Barry to emulate, ironically dismissing Barry himself as a hopeless case: "If you were *half* the man that Flash is" (Broome, *The Flash* #105A) or even "I wonder why I put up with your slowness, Barry—when the man I admire most is *The Flash—the fastest man alive!*" (Kanigher, *Showcase* #14A). In a relationship that strikes us today as nothing short of toxic, Barry takes consolation that Iris's scorn expresses adoration of his other, heroic self. We often catch Barry's pride in this thought, smiling as if this unacknowledged victory redeemed his constant losses in their long running interpersonal war. At the close of the first Flash story in *Showcase* #4, Iris sighs wistfully at the mention of Flash in a news headline: "How exciting it would be to meet a man like that! But I guess it's just an idle dream!" to which Barry wryly responds, "Sometimes dreams come true, Iris!" (Kanigher). Following the 1959 launch of *The Flash* as an independent series, Flash sometimes sits down with Iris to be interviewed about his exploits. On such occasions, hiding behind his crimson mask, Barry basks in Iris's gushing admiration. Nothing better expresses their peculiar relationship dynamic. As Barry Allen he may be a relative nobody to her hard-charging reporter, but as Flash he's the famous one: "Flash, this is a break for me—getting this exclusive interview with you!" (Broome, *The Flash* #118A, February 1961).

Today one might consider Barry's wry submission to Iris's demands a form of passive aggression, but it draws more specifically on a comic trope prevalent in midcentury film and television, the henpecked husband. Barry works hard to please Iris and always says "yes" to her requests, but he does what he likes once she turns her back. For instance, when Iris commands Barry to follow her as she runs off to cover the bank robbery in Broome's story for *Showcase* #13, shouting "For once in your life—hurry up!," Barry responds with "Uh, all right, Iris," then lags behind her for a beat before racing invisibly past her to deal with the crime on his own terms. Having supplanted Kanigher as lead writer, Broome reworked this scenario repeatedly in the years following. In the second issue of the new series, Barry makes a point of arriving on time for dinner at Iris's apartment, but while she's busy in the kitchen he ducks out to respond to a challenge from the Pied Piper. When he returns on the story's final page, Iris opens the door with an air of exasperation: "Barry!? What happened to you?" But he's only flustered for a moment: "Oh, I—just stepped out—to get this paper—!" and hands her a newspaper bearing a headline celebrating Flash's capture of the villain (*The Flash* #106B, April-May 1959). In a story from two years later, Barry agrees to wait in the green room while Iris is being interviewed on television, but he zips off after spotting the Mirror Master running past the studio. This time, he manages to get back before Iris realizes his absence, leaving her with the pleasant impression that "Barry may be *slow and lazy,* but he's certainly *loyal,* staying here the whole hour to be near me during my *TV* appearance!" (*The Flash* #126A, February 1962).

Of course, there's a crucial difference between Barry, who secretly slips out to perform acts of magnanimous heroism, and a typical henpecked husband of the era, someone like Ralph Kramden, whose truant hours in *The Honeymooners* were spent on crackpot schemes his wife deplored. Even as

Barry uses his secret identity to deceive and disobey Iris, he can comfort himself with the thought that he's acting in accord with her underlying wishes. After all, she's always urging Barry to be more like his speedy alter-ego. Barry often feels compelled to justify his little acts of deception, even when he's acting in a way that helps Iris out. For instance, in the opening pages of Gardner Fox's famous "Flash of Two Worlds!" Barry suggests to Iris that Flash could appear in place of a missing stage magician at a charity event she's organizing: "I can't stay, Iris, but to make amends—suppose I phone *Flash* and ask him to come over and fill in? I just left him at police headquarters" (*The Flash* #123, September 1961). Iris is delighted, and Barry steps outside to put on his costume; but as he does so he runs through the preceding conversation in his head, anxious to explain away his lies: "I told Iris *Flash* had been at police headquarters, which was true enough since *I* am *The Flash* ... and that he'd be right over which is—also true!"

Yet Barry's equivocations also run in the other direction: even as he acts in accord with Iris's wishes, he comforts himself with the thought that he's secretly disobeying and deceiving her. Broome dramatized this complication in the opening pages of "The Big Freeze!" While driving Iris to the state prison for a press event, Barry finds out that she's attending a parole hearing for one of Flash's old nemeses, Captain Cold. Iris laments that she wasn't able to contact Flash about testifying before the board, to which Barry replies slyly, "Er—maybe he won't miss it, Iris!" (*The Flash* #114A, August 1960). When they arrive, Iris gets out of the car and Barry watches her walk across the lot toward the prison entrance, thinking: "There goes Iris toward the parole board meeting! She expects me to wait here for her—but I have other ideas!" Even though he's doing what she hoped Flash might do, he insists to himself that he's acting on his own initiative. Barry may be her pliant boyfriend, but Flash isn't her creature.

Working Women, Passive Men

This portrait of the two-career couple is remarkably similar to one presented by Robert Coughlan in a special issue of *Life* magazine dedicated to "The American Woman: Her Achievements and Troubles." A frequent contributor to *Life* who went on to write a number of Time Life Books in the 60s and 70s, Coughlan gave a pointedly negative assessment of working women: when women enter the masculine world, they create a natural imbalance, with consequences not only for themselves, but for their husbands, children, and ultimately society. Citing interviews with contemporary psychoanalysts, Coughlan concluded that "the emerging American woman tends to be assertive and exploitive. The emerging American man tends to be passive and irresponsible…. They are suffering from what the psychiatrists call sexual ambiguity" (109, ellipsis mine).

Coughlan's sense of cultural crisis appears to have been widely shared among *Life*'s editorial staff. On its cover the magazine offered a superficially positive take, with a photogenic "Working Mother" posed in loving embrace of her young daughter. But the editors chose Catherine Marshall, a conservative writer of inspirational books and the widow of a nationally prominent minister, to write the issue's Introduction. Credited in the headline as "Mrs. Peter Marshall," she insisted that although women might pretend otherwise, they were made for love, not worldly ambition: "Ask any thoughtful, honest woman what the most satisfying moments of her life have been, and she will never mention the day she got her first job or the day she outwitted her boss on his ground." Pointing readers to Coughlan's essay, Marshall warned that women who deprive themselves of the satisfactions natural to their sex (romance, marriage, and children) tend to fall prey to psychological maladies. Later in the issue, Jennie Magill, the working mother from the cover, was featured in a photo spread, along with her husband, other children, housekeeper, and coworkers—a spread graced with the provocative title, "My Wife Works—And I Like It" (140–141). But by contrast to the tranquil cover photograph of Magill and her daughter, these black-and-white images presented her as an outspoken woman, easily overmatching her bow-tie-wearing nice-guy husband. Thus, even as the short article's title presented it as a refutation of Coughlan's thesis, the photo editor ran a collection of images that reinforced the notion that women who work create a climate of "sexual ambiguity."

Hitting newsstands in December 1956, a few months after Barry Allen's debut in *Showcase* #4 but five months *before* his second appearance in *Showcase* #8, this special issue of *Life* may have contributed to Kanigher's decision, starting with that second issue, to make Iris a leading reporter. Even if it didn't exert a direct influence on Kanigher, Coughlan's essay sharpens our sense of what's at stake in Barry's relationship with Iris. As we've seen, her worldly success eclipses his rather pedestrian job, an emasculation his manhood can only survive by recourse to a secret identity. We find Barry driving Iris to press events and faithfully offering to wait backstage while she steps in front of an admiring public, both episodes that echo scenes from *Woman of the Year*. But whereas in that movie Spencer Tracy's gruff but personable sports reporter finally rebelled, forcing Katherine Hepburn's culturally refined political columnist to reassess her priorities, Barry merely hunkers down, unable or unwilling to question Iris's dominion. In short, a problem comically raised and no less comically resolved in 1940 had by the late fifties come to seem a widespread, intractable social malady.

Indeed—for in early 1958, less than a year after Kanigher first focused attention on Iris's job in *Showcase* #8, *Life's* rival magazine *Look* ran a three-article series of cultural critique, republished within months by Random House as an illustrated hardback, *The Decline of the American Male.*[4] In the leading essay, J. Robert Moskin argued that America was being systematically feminized—not just by women working in traditionally male fields, but by teachers, wives and mothers whose love and attention trained men for submission to the conformist demands of mass society (4). Moskin's analysis is so hyperbolic in its alarmism as to seem almost tongue-in-cheek: "Scientists who study human behavior fear that the American male is now dominated by the American female" (3). This impression is reinforced by the slender volume's satirical cartoons, executed by Robert Osborn in a style reminiscent of James Thurber. The cover featured a straitjacketed man dangling from marionette strings operated by a pretty young woman; inside, a man is being crushed by industrial apparatus to fit a mold (27); another runs fruitlessly on a treadmill, urged to ever greater efforts by his fire-breathing spouse (60). Despite the manic style of its illustrations, however, the book evidently warranted extensive coverage in the pages of the *New York Times:* a meditation by Charles Poole, a review by A.C. Spectorsky, and a couple of off-hand references by the anonymous author of the paper's "Topics" column. These writers did not all agree with the book's conclusions (Poole in particular mocked the authors roundly), but they did give serious attention to its arguments. Further confirmation of the little book's significance: Arthur Schlesinger's thoughtful response essay, published in the November 1958 issue of *Esquire,* "The Crisis of American Masculinity." One senses that the *Look* artist's satirical hyperbole didn't undercut the book's standing as cultural criticism; to the contrary, the illustrations rendered its anxiety-inducing thesis in a form that could be faced down and laughed about—a catharsis achieved, unfortunately, by scapegoating women.

Here, again, we find a strong parallel to the Flash comics of the period. From 1956 to 1965, Iris functioned as a comic predicament from which Barry could not escape. Her frequent enumeration of his failings reinforced the demarcation between his two identities, one superhuman and the other all too human. Ironically, she criticizes Barry only in the hope of improving him and thereby making him worthy of her love. When he does well she rewards him with praise: "See—isn't it easy to keep an appointment, if you give yourself plenty of time?" (Kanigher, *Showcase* #13A, March-April 1958). But her efforts are self-defeating: you can't scold someone into self-reliance. At one point, in a subplot reminiscent of one of Osborn's cartoons, Iris signs Barry up for a self-improvement course: "Start on the Road to Greatness! Professor Dobill will analyze you—tell you what is holding you back in life!" reads the poster (Broome, *The Flash* #136A, May 1963). Dobill's clinic is far from impressive, located on the second floor of a back-street office building, but

Iris is quite confident that it's just what Barry needs. As she leads him up the stairs, she silences his momentary protest with an attempt at encouragement: "There's nothing wrong with you except that you're slow—and lazy—and ambitionless!" A year later, Barry finally completes Dobill's course, and the couple goes out to celebrate: "Barry, you did it! I—I can hardly believe it," Iris gushes. "You see, Iris, you've been under-estimating me!," Barry responds, "You don't realize what I'm capable of!" But Iris can't resist a final put-down to restore the familiar hierarchy of their relationship: "My goodness! Listen to the 'successful' man talk!" (Broome, *The Flash* #146A, August 1964).

Transcending the Flannel Suit

If Iris embodies the foibles of the career woman, in his civilian identity Barry displays the plight of "Organization Man," William Whyte's term for the malaise gripping midcentury males. Capitalizing on the popularity of Sloan Wilson's bestselling novel *The Man in the Grey Flannel Suit,* Whyte decried the turn from the frontier ethic to the "groupthink" of corporate culture. Conformism was sapping initiative and independent thinking, qualities that had made America great. Now, Flash is no conformist—he stretches a red elastic suit over his grey business outfit and runs around fighting crime. But Barry lives an unassuming, unambitious life, working a job so boring that it never once features as a plot point in the 150 Flash stories published from 1956 to 1972. When Iris drags Barry up the stairs to enroll him in Professor Dobill's course, he muses on his apparent lack of worldly ambition: "Iris doesn't realize it, but as my alter-ego The Flash I've won my measure of fame and success! As Barry Allen I'm perfectly satisfied to remain a 'nobody'" (*The Flash* #136A, May 1963). Intriguingly, Whyte's treatise, published in 1956, singled chemistry out as the scientific field where industry had most thoroughly suppressed individual genius and open-ended research in favor of incremental improvements made by large teams of technicians (208, 214). That same year, challenged to reinvent Flash for the 1950s, Kanigher imagined a chemist, working in a police laboratory, who gains superhuman powers when he's struck by lightning in a freak accident. A bolt from the blue: what more evocative metaphor for genius, for talent that cannot be put to use in a bureaucratized institution like a crime lab? At first the young scientist doesn't know what to use his powers for: he outpaces a cab he's running to catch, he prevents a waitress from spilling food all over him, and he reacts instinctively to save his girlfriend from a stray bullet. Only then, inspired by a comic book from his childhood, does he decide to put on a costume and fight crime (*Showcase* #4A, September-October 1956). In so doing, this mild-mannered working stiff transcended the limits of the role to which society assigned him, working outside the law to achieve well-deserved fame.

In 1965, almost a decade later, John Broome and Gardner Fox were still working out the implications of Barry/Flash's split personality. In the "A" and "B" stories of *The Flash* #154 (August 1965), they offered contrasting meditations on Barry's dead-end career and Flash's celebrity. The second of those two stories, scripted by Broome, introduces the Flash Museum, an impressively futuristic building constructed, as Barry muses to himself, by "The people of *Central City* ... as a tribute to their 'famous fellow-citizen'—*The Flash!*" (ellipsis mine). Fleshing out his claim from #136A that he was satisfied to remain a nobody so long as he could be famous as the Flash, Barry admits that he has visited the Flash Museum weekly since its opening a few months earlier: "Naturally, I get a kick out of coming here!" Who wouldn't enjoy basking in the adulation of one's fellow citizens? Broome highlights Barry's secret pleasure in his alter-ego's fame by introducing a dramatic foil: Dexter Myles, a washed-up, homeless Shakespearean actor whom Barry befriends and manages to install as guide at the Flash Museum. An attention-seeking buffoon reminiscent of Falstaff, Myles shows the folly of stagey self-promotion.

In the "A" story of the same issue, Gardner Fox offered a humorous commentary on Barry's civilian career. The episode opens with Iris using an instant-film camera to snap a photo of Barry smiling, holding up a plaque. Iris is excited, "Her eyes dancing with pride," and she takes the photograph with the plan of publishing "a big spread" in her paper. But what exactly is this chemistry award for? The reader never learns. What's more, once a glitch in Barry's speed power has been fixed and Iris gets a non-blurry photo halfway through the story, we never hear again about her proposed article on his accomplishment. To sum up, in the only episode from 15 years of issues in which he receives public recognition as Barry Allen, we don't even witness the award ceremony—assuming there was one. Fox thus introduces the possibility of Barry standing out in his job, but this episode is the half-hearted exception that proves the rule: in the postwar America of *The Flash,* extraordinary talent must be expressed in secret, outside the bounds of both work *and* home life.

In this issue's dual meditations on fame and anonymity, one can detect a commentary on the predicament of comic book writers and artists. Under work-for-hire rules, Gardner Fox and John Broome enjoyed no rights to the stories and characters they created. They knew this all too well: Fox invented the original Flash in the 1940s, and on the strength of that connection he was given the opportunity to script the 1961 "Flash of Two Worlds" story connecting the Barry Allen Flash to the world of his predecessor. In so doing, Fox invented something even bigger, the DC Multiverse. Yet he had no legal stake in either the character or the fictional universe that he created; not only were creators deprived of royalties, they worked at the whim of editors. At any time, for any reason, they could lose creative control of a character they had invented—as demonstrated when Robert Kanigher was pulled from writing the Barry Allen Flash just prior to the launch of *The Flash* as an independent series. In this sense, comic book writers and artists offer a particularly vivid instance of the travails of Organization Man: paid by the page, forced to labor collectively, producing work which was judged for its conformity to social norms and valued only for its profit to the corporate entity. Indeed, while Marvel had long made a practice of crediting comic book creators on the title page of each story, DC only began doing so about a year after this issue ran, starting with *The Flash* #163 (August 1966). Up to that time, DC's writers and artists labored anonymously—though their names were generally known to fans thanks to the letters page. This helps to explain why artist Carmine Infantino placed profile headshots of himself and editor Julius Schwartz on the restaurant wall where Barry and Iris dined in #154B (August 1965).[5] Jokingly assuming the role of an actor or comedian immortalized on the wall of a tony New York steakhouse, Infantino poses the question, if Flash gets a museum, what of his artist?

This analysis suggests that there was something at stake in Barry Allen's secret identity besides the superhero cliché of creating an "*aura of mystery* surrounding The *Flash* that impresses criminals," as Barry phrases it in the first issue of the new series (Broome, *The Flash* #105A, February-March 1959). Batman's aura of mystery strikes fear in the hearts of criminals, but fear and mystery simply aren't what Flash is about. Indeed, it's difficult to think of a story in which Flash's identity matters to anyone other than Iris—except, of course, a certain kind of reader. By performing acts of heroism only while disguised, by maintaining the lifestyle of an ordinary middle-class man, Barry could channel midcentury male anxiety, even as his extraordinary adventures offered a fantasy of escape from the constraints of a boring job and a nagging wife. The Barry Allen Flash can thus be read as an update on James Thurber's famous 1939 short story "The Secret Life of Walter Mitty." Introduced on an afternoon driving his wife to the hairdresser and performing a series of errands, Mitty is a nebbish of a man who takes refuge from the indignity of serving as chauffeur and go-fer by imagining himself as the male lead in a series of genre adventures—several war stories, a surgical melodrama, and a courtroom scene. With the crucial difference that Barry really *is* the Flash, Barry's secret life is remarkably like Mitty's, an ego-soothing fantasy world in which anything is possible, a refuge from the insults of quotidian existence.

Mitty's unnamed wife is the villain of the piece. While strangers sometimes interrupt Mitty's daydreams with shouted directions or commands, his wife is the reality-principle that brings him down to earth, again and again, just as his imagination is taking flight: "You're driving too fast," "Remember to get those overshoes," "You're not a young man any longer." We've seen Iris play a similar role in Barry's life, acid criticism puncturing his heroic pretensions. Both women demand that their man be at their beck and call: "Wait here for me. I forgot something. I won't be a minute," says Mitty's wife, to which Thurber adds, dryly, "She was more than a minute." The wife in Thurber's story exerts an even greater tyranny, however, insisting that Mitty subjugate not only his daily life to her whims, but his dream world to her pragmatism. By the story's end, Mitty's left with no space to call his own; to his wife's query, "Why do you have to hide in this old chair? How did you expect me to find you?" he gives only the cryptic reply "Things close in."

Thanks to his super-speed or, perhaps, to his unmarried state, things never "close in" for Barry. But at key moments we sense that the "aura of mystery surrounding The Flash" is really about keeping Iris in the dark: for when his secret is threatened, she wavers in her admiration of the hero, and this almost unmans him. At the end of *The Flash* #110A (December 1959–January 1960), for example, Barry is in such a hurry to arrive on time for a date that he runs up to Iris still dressed in his Flash uniform, triumphantly announcing "Made it! I'm here Iris—on time!" (Broome). Iris is at first confused, "Eh? What are you talking about, *Flash?* I have a date here at this time with *Barry Allen!*," but in the next panel she's got a suspicious, knowing look on her face, and Barry/Flash turns to the reader, undone by her gaze, his mask peels up from his cheek. Iris has witnessed his mistake, and suddenly he's just a guy in a costume.

The Fraternity of Superheroes

Notably, while Barry's heroism must remain secret from Iris, it can be shared with other men—and boys. Broome emphasized this point by pairing #110A with the origin of Kid Flash in #110B. Just pages after Barry's embarrassing near-reveal of his heroic identity to Iris, Flash is in the middle of telling her nephew Wally how he gained his powers when an identical freak accident makes the lad super-speedy. The story is more than a little silly, literally asking the reader to believe that lightning can strike the same way twice. But it's more interesting when read as metaphor: whereas Iris's critical frame of mind endangers Barry's heroic powers in #110A, her nephew's credulous admiration *engenders* them in #110B. At the story's start, Barry is tickled to learn Wally is the "President of the Flash Fan Club in his home town." Inspired by the boy's enthusiasm, he changes costume into Flash before welcoming him into the lab to tell him his story. Just as he gets to the part where lightning crashed through the window, lightning literally crashes through the window, drawn from the blue sky as though by the fervency of Wally's imagination. The boy returns home with a new mission in life, as Kid Flash, fighting crime in his home town and occasionally returning to Central City for team-ups with his aunt's boyfriend. Later, Barry becomes close friends with Hal Jordan, the Green Lantern, and the two men pal around in civilian life in between donning their costumes to fend off alien invaders. In Broome's story from *The Flash* #131 (September 1962), Hal and Barry are vacationing together with their girlfriends in southern California when they get caught up in a shared adventure. Hours later, they sheepishly return to the house where Carol and Iris are waiting, worried what the girls will make of their prolonged absence. Both episodes seem a bit fishy from a present-day perspective: two men or, worse, a man and a boy who share a secret life away from the prying eyes of women. But I don't think that's a fair reading. Their mannerisms are clubby rather than sexual, like men who go bowling after work or boys who post "no girls" on their clubhouse door.

Gardner Fox expanded on this trope years later, in a story that ran in *Green Lantern* #43 (March 1966). Carol and Iris both find out about their boyfriends' heroic identities, and insist that the men take them out for dinner dressed as Green Lantern and Flash. Published just seven months before Barry and Iris's wedding in *The Flash* #165 (November 1966), the story presents the women as girlishly excited at their newfound knowledge, not least by the power it gives them over their men. There's a particularly striking moment early in the story when Iris picks up Barry's special ring, puts it on his finger, and presses its secret clasp, causing his Flash costume to spurt out. The symbolism of her actions—referencing both the wedding ceremony and events thereafter—inverts the traditional hierarchy of man and wife by putting her in control. A page later, when Carol and Iris meet up with their dates in tow, the two men stand uncomfortably in their costumes at either end of a long panel by artist Gil Kane, looking away from one another as well as from the cause of their mutual embarrassment, the pair of giggling girls hugging each another in excitement. The secret fraternity of superheroes has plainly been violated. So it seems symbolically appropriate when Flash and Green Lantern both lose their powers just a few pages later, in the wake of an attack by newly minted villain Major Disaster. Though the women nobly pledge to stay true to their now powerless men, Flash wonders whether the Justice League will feel the same way: "They may ask for our resignations!" At the story's end, after recovering their powers in the course of dealing with Major Disaster, the heroes turn to the knottier issue of their girlfriends. Flash muses, "We cleared up that case—all except Iris and Carol! I'd just as soon they didn't know our secret identities—not for the present," to which Green Lantern replies, "Right! I hate to use that corny routine of *power-ringing* them to forget our secret identities! Even I'm getting tired of that!" For a Silver Age comic, their conversation is unusually dark, Barry failing to offer a noble justification for wiping the women's minds even as Hal implies that the procedure has become almost routine.

This uncomfortable moment throws into sharp relief something that was only implicit earlier: keeping super-heroics a men's club wasn't a tenet of these comics' heroic ideology but emerged instead from their psychic underbelly. Invented by John Broome in 1959 for *Showcase* #22 (September–October 1959), Hal Jordan channels some of the same midcentury anxieties as Barry Allen. True, Hal works as a test pilot for the Ferris Aircraft Company, outwardly the opposite of Barry's boring career. But from the first issue his job seems more political than heroic. When a saboteur's treachery threatens the life of a fellow pilot, Hal has to transcend the limits of his identity within Ferris Aircraft by flying to the rescue—not by piloting an airplane but in costume. And, like Barry, Hal is hemmed in by his romantic attachment to a career woman. *Showcase* #22A introduces Carol Ferris as the company president's daughter. Hal presses her for a date and she agrees, "As long as it's not on company time." But, later the same day her father announces he's stepping down, making her Hal's boss. "From now on the relations between us will be *strictly business!,*" she declares. In subsequent stories Carol goes on dates with both Hal and Green Lantern, sometimes playing one off against the other, never realizing they are the same person. Hal can't solve this romantic quandary by revealing his secret identity because secret heroism is itself a solution to a deeper cultural quandary, how to be manly in a world where not even test pilots can be mavericks.

Gender and the Generation Gap

Even though these stories presented heroism as a men's club, their readership was not exclusively male, as witnessed in the comic's letters page. From the launch of "Flashgrams" in 1960 through Barry and Iris's wedding in 1966, to the end of Broome, Fox, and Kanigher's run in August 1971, women contributed roughly 6 percent of letters overall. Their participation started just above that level, around 7 percent for 1960–61, rising to 10 percent for the period of Barry and Iris's engagement (1964–66), then dropping precipitously after their marriage to around 3 percent for April 1967 to August 1971. Women were particularly well represented in the lengthy letters section of issue #168 (March 1967), the first page comprising letters in response to the wedding issue (1 in 4 female) and a second page with letters answering whether Barry should tell his new wife about his secret life as Flash (2 in 10).[6] By contrast, women were wholly absent from the double-sized letters page in issue #179

(May 1968), some 24 letters total, the first page debating whether Flash or Superman won the "Race to the End of the Universe" four issues earlier, and the second weighing the merits of artists Ross Andru and Mike Esposito after Infantino's departure from the title. These percentages offer only a rough sense of the comic's readership: letters chosen for publication don't necessarily reflect letters received, nor should we assume that letter-writers formed a representative sample of the far larger population of readers. Nonetheless, the presence of women on the letters page meant that the comic book wasn't a men's club, even if its stories imagined Flash's heroism that way.

The conversations that took place in "Flashgrams"—between individual fans as well as between fans and the comic's editor—sometimes reinforced the stories' gender dynamics, as for example the reaction when Jennie Smith called for a female Flash in issue #115 (September 1960): "I've read *The Flash* for quite a while and like it very much. I'm not going to gripe or complain, but in *Superman, Batman,* and even *The Blackhawks,* there is a female counterpart of these heroes—Supergirl, Batwoman, and Zenda. Can you please have a Lady Flash, in addition to the very interesting Kid Flash?" Editor Julius Schwartz gave a telling response: "Isn't *Flash*—in his Barry Allen identity—hard pressed enough wooing his girlfriend Iris West without ringing in competition in the form of a *Lady Flash?*" A few months later in issue #118 (February 1961), reader Skip Oakes echoed Schwartz's clannish defense of the superhero men's club by mocking Smith's proposal with a *reductio ad absurdum:* "I think that the introduction of such a character would cripple your magazine a great deal. It wouldn't stop with just a *Lady Flash*, for the next thing you know there'll be a *Dog Flash*, a *Cat Flash*, a *Fish Flash*, and other extremes. You already have a *Kid Flash* and an *Elongated Man*—both of which are terrific—to help *Flash* out of tight spots. Please don't wreck a good thing." Criminals, aliens and super-villains may physically threaten Flash, but to Oakes as also to Schwartz, a female hero represented an absolute, existential peril.

But while Schwartz could successfully invoke the boys against girls rivalry of the playground to rally support for all-male super-heroics, readers of both sexes were left nonplussed by subtler elements of the comic's gender politics. In issue #139 (September 1963) reader Larry Brown demanded that the lead characters tie the knot: "When are you going to allow Barry Allen to marry Iris West? Now don't get me wrong! I'm not some kind of screwy sentimentalist who wants to see every superhero burdened by a wife. It's just that I think you should stop fiddling around and let Barry and Iris get serious." Even as he acknowledged that their marriage would violate longstanding comic-book tradition, Brown seemed not to grasp the core issue that kept them dancing with one another at arms-length, exchanging intimacies but never fully intimate. Schwartz's response cut straight to that point: "Supposing—just supposing, mind you—that Barry and Iris do get married? Should Barry then reveal his secret *Flash* identity to his wife?" Fans' responses to this query, published five months later, in issue #142 (February 1964), offered a variety of views on the viability of Barry and Iris's relationship: Shari Shepard thought Iris lacked the sense of adventure needed for a hero's wife, while Patricia Yanchus pointed to the favorable augury of Jay Garrick's happy marriage to Joan, and Paul Feola insisted that it would be wrong to have secrets in a marriage. Even as these readers disagreed on whether Iris was right for Barry, they all agreed in their essentially idealized conception of marriage, entailing complete candor between soulmates—a vision sharply at odds with that of the comic's creators.

Two years later, Broome and Schwartz polled the comic's readership a second time on this crucial question. On this occasion, they ensured a much more voluminous reader response by having Barry himself pose the question as he drove off with Iris on their honeymoon in the final panels of issue #165 (November 1966). As she lay back in the car's passenger seat, her eyes half-closed after the big day, he hunched forward over the wheel, consumed with worry over whether to confess his secret: "I guess what I could use is some *good advice!* Yes, I sure could! Tell me reader … what you would *you* do if you were in my place?" The response came in strongly in favor of honesty: in issue #168 (March 1967) Schwartz published eleven letters on the question, eight of them calling for an immediate confession.

As with the letters from issue #142, the salient pattern in #168 was the readers' faith in the mutuality of marriage. As Don Akers put it in the letter that ran at the top of the page, "TELL HER! … After all, they (Barry and Iris) spoke the vow that 'makes two people into one.' Has *Flash* any secrets he would keep from his own self?" Even those who argued against such a revelation justified their stance by an appeal to drama, not to principle, as for example Robert Goldman: "Let's not have Barry tell Iris his secret for a few issues. It'll make the stories more interesting to see how he explains his absences."

Thus, though Flash's female fans were, on the whole, more interested in hairstyles and relationships than male fans were, the real divide was not a gender but a generation gap, between the comic's largely Baby Boomer readership and its far older creative staff. Robert Kanigher, John Broome, Gardner Fox, and Julius Schwartz were all born between 1911 and 1915, and artist Carmine Infantino in 1925. Not coincidentally, every one of the cultural critics cited earlier was born between 1913 and 1924: Robert Coughlan, William Whyte, Sloan Wilson, Arthur Schlesinger, and J. Robert Moskin—not to mention Moskin's writing partners George B. Leonard and William Attwood. That generation returned from World War II to marriage and a booming economy; yet its leading lights came to doubt the fruits of peacetime, challenging the ideology of postwar prosperity not just in novels and social treatises but in comic books. In so doing, they created a new ideology, one that explained their discontent by scapegoating women and corporatism. But by 1966, the year of Barry and Iris's wedding, that cultural critique was well past its prime; a new generation had arisen, one that advocated for peace and love as well as personal fulfillment, and that feared something far more sinister than a woman's apron strings.

Transformations

In sum, while the comic's creative staff enjoyed dramatizing the malaise of the midcentury male, the significance of Barry's secret heroism was lost on readers. And reader opinions mattered a lot; when you're working for a corporation, the customer is always right. To Larry Brown's demand for a wedding, Schwartz gave a coy response ("Supposing—just supposing") but he inserted an editor's note in the "A" story of the same issue that for the first time made offhand reference to Iris as Barry's fiancée. It was a soft rollout rather than a big announcement: testing the waters without committing to a specific timetable. Editor's notes, quite rare in comparison to narrator's boxes in the pages of *The Flash,* signaled editorial intervention, generally an effort to explain abstruse details. In this case, Schwartz likely decided to make Iris a fiancée late in the process of assembling issue #139, either without consulting Broome or over his objection. Notably, while Broome wrote close to 90 percent of Flash stories up to this point, after Barry and Iris's engagement his participation slipped to around 50 percent. So it's tempting to conclude that Broome disliked the new direction that Schwartz imposed on the series.[7]

Marriage represented a major change for the title. It necessitated alterations in Iris's character, with a greater focus on gender-normative interests and activities, from antiques (Fox, *The Flash* #161B, May 1966) to finding the perfect wedding ring (Fox, *The Flash* #151, March 1965) to cooing over small children (Fox, *The Flash* #152A, May 1965). Marriage also required a change in the core dynamic of the series. Iris's scorn for Barry's failings had to be softened into fond teasing of his foibles: "Barry—you're early! Such a phenomenon deserves a reward!" Iris declares in Fox's *The Flash* #140B (November 1963), after which she runs up to kiss him. In place of scorn as a source of interpersonal drama, Broome experimented with jealousy (*The Flash* #140A, November 1963), a lead that Fox followed up enthusiastically in #144A, #145B and #150A, with both writers being careful to present a situation where her jealousy seemed a natural response rather than the work of a shrewish temperament. Fox brought Iris's transformation to a completion of sorts in #158A (February 1966), when he had her spring into action at Barry's direction, getting kids to safety during an emergency. It was the first occasion where she treated Barry, not Flash, as a hero.

Fundamentally, marriage required the series' writers to embrace the possibility of change and growth within a comic-book series. Prior to this point, while new characters were introduced from time to time—Wally West, Ralph Dibny, Professor West, Hal Jordan—Iris and Barry themselves hardly changed at all. She worked at Picture News, he worked in a police crime lab; in his spare time he ran around as Flash, a hero whose timeliness she admired no less than she despised her boyfriend's tardiness. This resistance to change was typical of the medium. By 1963, Clark Kent had been trapped in a love-triangle with Lois Lane for over twenty years. Very much like radio and television serials, comic books were structured episodically, with each story's plot resolved in a way that restored the status quo. This allowed writers to work in parallel without interference; it allowed readers to miss an issue without major mishap; perhaps most important, it allowed the corporation to capitalize for years on a winning formula. Intriguingly, Fox introduced the possibility of a comic book hero undergoing major life changes in 1961's "The Flash of Two Worlds" (#123), when he portrayed Jay Garrick, long retired from his labors, now settled down and married to his former girlfriend Joan. But while Jay and Joan spurred readers on in demanding a wedding for Barry and Iris, their example offered only the possibility of such a change, with no guidance as to how to ensure that altering the series' dramatic formula wouldn't destroy its appeal.

If Fox undertook much of the work of reinventing Iris's character during her three-year engagement, Broome's stories in this period drove Barry inward, away from conflict with Iris to conflict with his own conscience. In *The Flash* #152B (May 1965), Barry rescues Iris's father from a team of foreign spies, but interacts with his fiancée only at the end when he gives her a false account to cover up his secret identity: "I hate telling Iris these fibs—but she'll understand some day, when she finds out her *husband* is *The Flash!*" Perhaps most telling were a pair of stories in issues #147 and #153, reintroducing one of Broome's first Flash villains, Mr. Element/Dr. Alchemy, as the reformed criminal Al Desmond. A middle-class chemist engaged to a woman named Rita, Infantino's art presented the dark-haired Desmond as Barry's symbolic twin. As noted earlier, Barry's heroism had a double valence, breaking social norms even as it worked to enforce them; by contrast, the urges that pull Desmond away from his pretty girlfriend are unambiguously criminal. Thus the story presented an opportunity for Barry to wholeheartedly endorse marriage and middle-class existence, in sharp contrast with the homosocial loyalty he showed toward Hal on dates with Iris and Carol. When Desmond abruptly cuts out in the middle of a double date, Barry stays behind with Iris, listening intently as Rita confides that she's worried about her boyfriend's mental state (*The Flash* #147, September 1964). In this two-episode struggle for Desmond's very soul, Barry must contend with the malign influence exerted over Desmond by Professor Zoom, a 26th century speedster who wears a costume that is the color-inverse of the Flash's own. The complex psychomachia of these issues thus pits Flash and his symbolic twin Zoom in a struggle to permanently reform or irremediably corrupt Barry's twin, Desmond.

Echoing this melodrama a year and a half later, Broome's plot treatment for the wedding issue scapegoated Professor Zoom as stand-in for the comic's prior diffidence about marriage (*The Flash* #165, November 1966). After realizing that he'd squandered his chances of happiness in the 26th century, Zoom switched places in the time-stream with Barry, leaving our hero in future-world prison while he assumed both of Barry's identities: superhero and bridegroom. This convoluted scenario enabled (or perhaps arose from)[8] one of the most compelling issue covers of the era: Flash running into church to interrupt the wedding of Barry Allen and Iris West. But the scenario also worked to efface the double-valence of Barry's dual identity. Years earlier, Broome introduced Zoom in the same issue, *The Flash* #139, where Schwartz soft-launched Barry's engagement. Zoom was once a 26th-century loser named Eobard Thawne, but he got a "bolt from the blue" in the form of a time-satellite containing a costume once worn by Flash. Remembering historical accounts of the 20th-century hero, Thawne was inspired to reject his all-too-ordinary life to become Professor Zoom.

As with Al Desmond in issue #147, Zoom's backstory suggested a kinship between the superhero and the supervillain, both of whom use their powers to escape the strictures of modern society. In the wedding issue, though, even as Thawne reshapes his face to look like Barry, his behavior reveals just how different he really is. Determined to play the role of Flash, Zoom goes in pursuit of a criminal gang, but while he enjoys the adulation of bystanders, he finds it impossible to return the recovered goods to the bank safe: "I guess I've thought and acted like a criminal *too long!*" (*The Flash* #165). What's more, as Zoom dresses for the wedding the next morning, he can only conceptualize marriage as "the *great game of impersonation!*"—a sentiment whose folly is suggested in the next panel as he glumly fidgets in the limousine, sandwiched between Barry's parents on their way to church. A proper scapegoat, Zoom experiences pre-wedding jitters that Barry might otherwise have sullied himself by expressing. What's more, Zoom's conception of marriage as impersonation echoes the alienation felt by the "grey flannel suit" generation, while his presumptuous attempt to appropriate marital bliss without doing any work expresses an even more primitive mindset. At one point during his battle with Flash, Zoom uses a futuristic "matter-distributor" to tangle Flash in a ball-and-chain, a sexist joke about the bond of marriage that Barry so desperately wants to enter. In short, by embodying the misogynist, anti-matrimonial venom of the past decade, Zoom allowed Flash to repudiate those sentiments, now recognized as unhealthy and antisocial because they were associated with a criminal rather than with the series' hero.

In focusing attention on Barry's personal struggle, however, Broome reduced Iris to a trophy, fought over by the hero and the villain. She's hardly present in that issue, except as a formulaic bride, blissed out on her wedding day. In the years prior to the wedding, Fox had softened Iris by sanding away her distinctive qualities as an ambitious career woman. After the wedding, while she continued to work as a reporter, writers began presenting Iris doing work around the house, cooking for Barry (Fox #171, Broome #172A, #182A & #188, Bates #179, and Kanigher #199A) and (more amusingly) mending or ironing Barry's Flash costume (Broome #190A, Kanigher #202). A quarter-century earlier, *Woman of the Year* ended with Katherine Hepburn's globe-trotting reporter trying desperately to cook breakfast for her husband—and failing. But Iris experienced no difficulty stepping into the role of a housewife. These glimpses of domesticity reinforced the "happy ending" wedding narrative, but they also reduced Iris's significance within the story from Barry's transcendent goal/obstacle to mere scenery: the pretty apron-clad woman without which no suburban home would be complete. This may explain the decline in female readership implied by the sudden drop-off in women's letters in "Flashgrams." If so, it would seem that Schwartz, in trying to please a key element of the comic's readership, wound up destroying the very thing those readers found appealing. This conclusion, however, is wholly speculative. Alterations to the comic's dramatic formula may simply have coincided with a broad decline in female readership across the industry. Or, indeed, the decline I have noted may be an illusion created by a change in Schwartz's approach to choosing letters for publication.

Flash Forward into the 70s

In any event, a number of stories stand out from the four-year period stretching from the wedding issue up to *The Flash* #209 (September 1971), when Cary Bates took over as principal writer on the series. Immediately after their marriage, in the December 1966 issue, Broome staged a compelling debate between Barry and Iris on the question of whether her career should take precedence: "But Iris—this is important!" he pleads, to which she responds: "So's my article important! It's a front-pager with a by-line! Remember, darling, we agreed it was vital in our marriage for both of us to keep our careers!" (#166A, December 1966) The exchange frames their disagreement not as a conflict between careers, but between her career and his needs: can she be a working woman and also a loving wife? Yet while this question echoes the midcentury literature of male resentment, Broome gives Iris by far the better lines. Unfortunately, this engrossing episode proved to be the exception, rather than the rule for Broome's output in this period.

In two other important issues, both from 1969, Broome reflected on the boys' club model of heroism that he had first outlined a decade earlier. In issue #189, Barry and Iris go on vacation with Wally West. When their rental cabin needs to be restocked with firewood, the men jump at the opportunity to trigger their rings and do the work at super-speed. Iris looks on, bemused: "You two—!" Thus, her presence proves not to be much of a damper on their heroism. But Broome found means to reaffirm the boy's club ideology two issues later, in *The Flash* #191 (September 1969). That story opens with Hal Jordan accusing Iris of trying to marry him off, after finding out that they've invited him over for dinner along with a young lady, Olivia Reynolds. It seems like the first step toward opening Hal's superhero life up to a woman, just as Barry had done with Iris. But Olivia turns out to be a "U–Mind," a being whose extraordinary mental powers can sustain an ancient alien race—but only so long as she remains ignorant and leads a normal life. Soon thereafter, she's captured by evil robots, and while her mental powers play a role in her rescue, the story presents her as little more than a damsel in distress. Given that dynamic, it's far from surprising when Hal agrees with the (male) alien leader that Olivia must be restored to her former state of ignorance, and uses his power-ring to make her forget everything.

In five issues from 1969, Frank Robbins experimented with making Iris into a true partner in adventure, a formula familiar from the Elongated Man and the Golden Age Flash, and dating back to the Thin Man movies of the 1930s and 40s. Robbins' first issues (#180 and #181, June and August 1968) embraced this approach enthusiastically, sending the couple on a samurai-movie-style adventure in Japan. The response from readers (published in issue #183, November 1968) was decidedly mixed, but while Robbins reduced Iris's involvement in his subsequent stories, an element of partnership could still be detected, as in *The Flash* #184 (December 1968) where Iris plays a prominent role in prompting Flash to save Central City from annihilation. Artist Ross Andru took pains to dramatize their collaborative heroism in the panels down the right side of page four: the topmost shows Iris running to her carphone(!) to contact Barry. In the panel just below, Barry rushes out of the police station to become Flash. In the bottommost panel, Flash begins a frantic circuit around Central City. In this celebration of teamwork, as we move vertically down the page her energy translates into his action. After Robbins left the title, none of the other writers chose to follow his example—with one possible exception. In *The Flash* #207 (June 1971), Mike Friedrich pictured Barry and Iris attending a Washington Starship concert, where they witness the collaborative music-making of Grace and Paul (i.e., Grace Slick and Paul Kantner of Jefferson Airplane).[9] When the concert gives way to chaos due to the malign interference of Sargon the Sorcerer, Barry and Iris each spring into action, he as a hero and she as a reporter eager for a story. Apparently, Friedrich saw in Slick and Kantner's sexual and professional partnership a model for Barry and Iris to emulate.

This survey of compelling stories from 1967 to 1971 would not be complete without mention of the work of Robert Kanigher, who in late 1969 returned as a regular contributor more than a decade after being sidelined by Broome. In *The Flash* #192 (November 1969), Kanigher turned the tables on Iris's old complaint that Barry was always arriving late for their dates, having Flash arrive late for an appointment with the U.S. Navy after lingering too long with his wife in bed. The consequences prove dire: a submarine goes missing, all hands presumed lost. The public turns on its erstwhile hero, and Iris is invited by her editor to write a feature on the role Flash played in the disaster. While the latter half of the story is baroque in its complexity, there's a wonderful moment of clarity about a third of the way in, when Iris offers to sacrifice her job to save the Flash's reputation. Barry proves equally magnanimous: "You're a reporter, Iris! You've got to tell it like it is! And—and—don't spare me." Both characters display a quiet heroism in this scene that's distinct from the superheroic norm, not the heroism of the gallant knight-errant or that of the gritty loner, but that of a man and a woman who love and admire one another.

His finger evidently on the pulse of public interest, in February 1971 Kanigher ran a story in *The Flash* #203 that raised the specter of divorce. The cover, by Neal Adams over a photograph by Jack Adler,[10] featured a despairing Flash trying to pull Iris back across a strange inter-dimensional boundary. Flash's side shows a cityscape rendered in realistic detail; on the far side we glimpse a fantastical future-world. Iris straddles the boundary, momentarily held back by Flash's grip on her arm, but as she crosses over her clothes and hairstyle are changing into something radically futuristic. Her mindset appears to have changed as well: "Let me go, Flash! You can't hold me here! I must go back to where I belong!" Bearing the provocative title, "The Flash's Wife is a Two-Timer!," the story tells how Flash arrived home to find the house deserted, the table set as if for dinner but no trace of Iris—except a note on the refrigerator that sends him scrambling for his cosmic treadmill. When catches up to her, one thousand years in the future, she's still dressed her 1970s turtleneck and pants, and she screams at her husband like a woman determined to make a fresh start: "*Get away from here! Go back to where you belong!*" Of course it turns out that Iris was pulled into this strange unsettling future against her will; after that initial protest she melts into Barry's arms and lets him rescue her. But even as this revelation denies divorce was ever a possibility in Barry and Iris's relationship, the narrative reads as a fantasy of remarriage: after falling prey to some kind of a consciousness-raising seminar, a wife leaves home only to be pulled back from the radical future of divorced life by her husband's timely intervention.

In short, Barry and Iris's wedding broke the dramatic formula on which the series was based, forcing writers in the years following their marriage to experiment with new approaches to the characters' relationship. From the results, we may surmise that Schwartz insisted that their marriage be a happy one, a dictate that severely limited dramatic possibilities. The sheer variety of approaches that writers took from 1967 to 1971 suggests that none of them was ever sufficiently compelling to become canonical. So, in spite of the editorial dictate of a happy marriage, their characters' relationship felt unsettled, ever-changing. In that sense Iris remained true to her roots: in spite of everything a challenge to male dominion.

NOTES

1. Likely a reference to the *New York Daily News,* with its distinctive camera logo.

2. The notion that Iris was based on a character from an old movie isn't as far-fetched as it may sound. Writer Robert Kanigher was 25 years old when *Woman of the Year* premiered, and artist Carmine Infantino would have been 15. Intriguingly, the final panel in *The Flash* #115B from September 1960 depicts Iris sitting at her desk with a 1920s era telephone and a typewriter of similar vintage. In a manner reminiscent of Hepburn's haughty world-news correspondent, she's too busy with a teletype report to look up when Barry walks in the room. He's dressed in a fedora and a rumpled trench coat, looking like a beat reporter or a gumshoe from a noir movie. Reader Carl Yaffe commented on the anachronistic telephone in a letter published in issue #120 (May 1961); the editor's response confirms the influence of old movies on the comic: "Blame it on watching too many Hollywood films! Because the movies depict stereotyped newspaper reporters using the outmoded upright phone—so did we!"

3. In a 1996 interview with Paul Kupperberg, editor Julius Schwartz claimed that the idea of reviving Flash in the pages of *Showcase* came out of an editorial meeting (Kupperberg 5). Abetted by Kupperberg, Schwartz's recounting glosses over Kanigher's role in creating the Barry Allen Flash, focusing instead on John Broome's decade-long run as writer for the character. Broome scripted the "B" stories in the Flash issues of *Showcase* and supplanted Kanigher entirely once *The Flash* launched as a series in 1959 (6–7). But artist Carmine Infantino credits Kanigher as principally responsible for inventing the Barry Allen Flash. According to him, Kanigher resented losing a series he considered his creation (Amash, 58 and 60). To return to the question of who created Iris West, given that Broome didn't use her at all in his first two *Showcase* stories, I feel confident in crediting Kanigher, though Schwartz may have contributed in his role as editor.

4. This book, together with the larger debate in late-50s America over the perceived crisis of masculinity, has been extensively discussed by historians, among them Barbara Ehrenreich, K.A. Cuordileone and James Gilbert.

5. The identities of Infantino's portraitures were confirmed by Julius Schwartz on the letters page of issue #157 (December 1965), writing in response to an inquiry from reader Dick Flinch.

6. These statistics are provisional. I was unable to examine the letters column for about 10 percent of the hundred-odd issues published from 1960 to 1971. And I could not determine the gender of about 6 percent of letter writers: those who signed anonymously or

with initials, as well as those with ambiguous names, were left out of my calculations. Finally, I chose to count the total number of letters published regardless of how frequently a particular fan's name appeared. Some fans appeared quite regularly—in one case sometimes more than once an issue.

7. Broome half-humorously broadcast his feelings about women and marriage in issue #155, with a story in which Gorilla Grodd defeats Flash but then is himself defeated by a female gorilla he'd taken up with, leaving Grodd to bewail his losses in the final panel: "humans know what they're talking about when they say … the *female* of the species is more deadly than the *male!*"

8. Infantino describes how, as he rose in Schwartz's esteem, the editor began accepting interesting cover ideas from him, based on which writers were invited to craft a storyline (Amash, 64). A famous instance from this era is the cover where Barry walks away from a tree where he has hung up his Flash uniform. Fox used it as the basis for "The Flash's Final Fling!" in #159A, following which Kanigher managed to talk Schwartz into running his own story in response to that cover in #161A, "The Case of the Curious Costume."

9. Weirdly, the comic's use of "starship" in the band's name came 3 years before the formation of Jefferson Starship as a touring group—though the name did appear on an album released in 1970 by Kanter, "Blows Against the Empire."

10. Credited by Schwartz in response to a letter published in *The Flash* #207.

WORKS CITED

Amash, Jim. *Carmine Infantino: Penciler, Publisher, Provocateur.* Raleigh, NC: TwoMorrows Publishing, 2010.

Austin, Charles. "Obituary; Catherine Marshall, 68, Author." *New York Times,* March 19, 1983.

Bates, Cary. "The Flash—Fact or Fiction?" *The Flash* #179 (May 1968).

Broome, John. "The Big Freeze!" Story A in *The Flash* #114 (August 1960).

_____. "Captives of the Cosmic Ray!" *The Flash* #131 (September 1962).

_____. "Case of the Explosive Vegetables!" Story B in *The Flash* #152 (May 1965).

_____. "Challenge of the Weather Wizard!" Story A in *The Flash* #110 (December-January 1959).

_____. "Conqueror from 8 Million B.C.!" Story A in *The Flash* #105 (February-March 1959).

_____. "The Death-Touch of the Blue Ghost" *The Flash* #189 (June 1969).

_____. "The Doom of the Mirror Flash!" Story A in *The Flash* #126 (February 1962).

_____. "The Doomed Scarecrow!" Story A in *The Flash* #118 (February 1961).

_____. "Gangster Masquerade" Story B in *The Flash* #154 (August 1965).

_____. "Grodd Puts the Squeeze on the Flash" Story A in *The Flash* #172 (August 1967).

_____. "The Heat Is On … for Captain Cold" Story A in *The Flash* #140 (November 1963).

_____. "How to Invade Earth—Without Really Trying" *The Flash* #191 (September 1969).

_____. "Last Stand of the Three-Time Losers" Story A in *The Flash* #166 (December 1966).

_____. "The Man Who Changed the Earth!" Story B in *Showcase* #14 (May-June 1958).

_____. "Master of the Elements!" Story B in *Showcase* #13 (March-April, 1958).

_____. "Meet Kid Flash!" Story B in *The Flash* #110 (December-January 1959).

_____. "Menace of the Reverse-Flash!" *The Flash* #139 (September 1963).

_____. "Menace of the Runaway Missile!" Story A in *Showcase* #22 (September-October 1959).

_____. "The Mightiest Punch of All Time" *The Flash* #153 (June 1965).

_____. "The Mirror Master's Invincible Bodyguards!" Story A in *The Flash* #136 (May 1963).

_____. "The Mirror Master's Master Stroke" Story A in *The Flash* #146 (August 1964).

_____. "The Most Colorful Villain of All!" *The Flash* #188 (May 1969).

_____. "One Bridegroom Too Many!" *The Flash* #165 (November 1966).

_____. "Our Enemy, The Flash" *The Flash* #147 (September 1964).

_____. "The Pied Piper of Peril!" Story B in *The Flash* #106 (April-May 1959).

_____. "Super-Speed Agent of the Flash" Story A in *The Flash* #190 (August 1969).

_____. "The Thief Who Stole All the Money in Central City" Story A in *The Flash* #182 (September 1968).

Coughlan, Robert. "Changing Roles in Modern Marriage." *Life*, December 24, 1956. 108–118.

Cuordileone, K.A. *Manhood and American Political Culture in the Cold War.* New York: Routledge. 2005.

Ehrenreich, Barbara. *The Hearts of Men: American Dreams and the Flight from Commitment.* New York: Anchor, 1987.

Fox, Gardner. "Battle Against the Break-Away Bandit" Story A in *The Flash* #158 (February 1966).

_____. "Captain Cold's Polar Perils" Story A in *The Flash* #150 (February 1965).

_____. "The Catastrophic Crimes of Major Disaster!" *Green Lantern* #43 (March 1966).

_____. "The Day Flash Ran Away with Himself" Story A in *The Flash* #154 (August 1965).

_____. "Flash of Two Worlds!" *The Flash* #123 (September 1961).

_____. "The Girl from the Super-Fast Dimension!" Story B in *The Flash* #145 (June 1964).

_____. "Here Lies The Flash—Dead and Unburied" *The Flash* #171 (June 1967).

_____. "Invader from the Dark Dimension" *The Flash* #151 (March 1965).

_____. "Menace of the Man Missile" Story A in *The Flash* #144 (May 1964).

_____. "Metal Eater From the Stars" Story B in *The Flash* #140 (November 1963).

_____. "Mirror with the 20–20 Vision" Story B in *The Flash* #161 (May 1966).

_____. "The Trickster's Toy Thefts" Story A in *The Flash* #152 (May 1965).

Friedrich, Mike. "The Evil Sound of Music!" *The Flash* #207 (June 1971).

Kanigher, Robert. "Around the World in 80 Minutes!" Story A in *Showcase* #13 (March-April 1958).

_____. "Case of the Curious Costume" Story A in *The Flash* #161 (May 1966).

_____. "The Day The Flash Failed!" Story A in *The Flash* #192 (November 1969).

_____. "Flash?—Death Calling" Story A in *The Flash* #199 (August 1970).

_____. "The Flash's Wife Is a Two-Timer!" Story A in *The Flash* #203 (November 1969).

_____. "Giants of the Time-World!" Story A in *Showcase* #14 (May-June 1958).

_____. "Mystery of the Human Thunderbolt!" Story A in *Showcase* #4 (September-October 1956).

_____. "The Satan Circle" Story A in *The Flash* #202 (December 1970).

_____. "The Secret of the Empty Box!" Story A in *Showcase* #8 (May-June 1957).

Kupperberg, Paul. "Foreword." In *The Flash Archives,* vol. 1. New York: DC Comics, 1996.

Life editorial staff. "My Wife Works and I Like It." *Life* December 24, 1956. 140–141.

Marshall, Catherine. "An Introduction by Mrs. Peter Marshall." *Life* December 24, 1956. 2–3.

Moskin, J. Robert, George B. Leonard, Jr., and William Attwood. *The Decline of the American Male.* New York: Random House, 1958.

Poole, Charles. "Books of the Times." *New York Times* June 3, 1958, 29.

Robbins, Frank. "The Attack of the Samuroids" *The Flash* #181 (August 1968).

_____. "Executioner of Central City!" *The Flash* #184 (December 1968).

_____. "The Flying Samurai" *The Flash* #180 (June 1968).

Schlesinger, Arthur. "The Crisis of American Masculinity." *Esquire* November 1958, 63–65.

Spectorsky, A.C. "Of Man and Mouse." *New York Times* June 15, 1958, BR7.

Thurber, James. "The Secret Life of Walter Mitty." *The New Yorker* March 18, 1939, 19–20.

"Topics." *New York Times* June 15, 1958, E8.

"Topics." *New York Times* July 16, 1958, 28.

Whyte, William H. *The Organization Man.* Simon & Schuster, 1956; reprint U of Pennsylvania P, 2013.

Woman of the Year. Directed by George Stevens, performances by Spencer Tracy and Katharine Hepburn, Metro-Goldwyn-Mayer, 1942.

Wright, Richard A. "'I Can Pass Right Through Solid Matter!': How the Flash Upheld American Values While Breaking the Speed Limit." *Comic Books and the Cold War, 1946–1962: Essays on Graphic Treatment of Communism, the Code and Social Concerns,* edited by Chris York and Rafiel York, McFarland, 2012, pp. 55–67.

Barry Allen's Social
Awakening in the 1970s

PETER W.Y. LEE

For the fastest man alive, Barry Allen was stuck running in place during the early 1970s. The Scarlet Speedster inaugurated the silver age of comics in 1956, which came to symbolize the sixties as the industry exploited public social and political angst. Spider-Man swung through various crises on college campuses, while Green Lantern hung his head in shame for not helping black-skinned people at home. But the Flash couldn't keep up with the times. As a straight-arrow police detective, the Flash's origins showcased a DC Universe based on science, rationality, and a moral affirmation of law and order upholding the status quo. Appropriately, Barry Allen's stomping grounds, Central City, referred to the heartland of traditional American values.

Not so to many of the Flash's younger readers. The baby boomers were restless. In the early 1960s, a surging youth movement countered mainstream American culture, dismissing middle class mores as an aged obsolete "Establishment" needing redress. While youth rebellion was nothing new—the "lost generation" of the 1920s and the "beatniks" and "delinquents" in the 1950s gave social guardians headaches—the disenchanted kids of the sixties weren't thugs or criminals, despite child experts' and parenting guides' attempts to label them as such. Rather, peaceniks, hippies, yippies, and radicals saw themselves as reformers and activists. Earnestly organizing marches to implore the Establishment's "fuzz" to give peace a chance, the youth movement was clearly not a fad. In 1962, the most significant of these New Left groups, the Students for a Democratic Society, issued the *Port Huron Statement*, a utopian declaration for domestic and international progressivism: "In a time of supposed prosperity, moral complacency, and political manipulation, a new left cannot rely on only aching stomachs to be the engine force of social reform"

(Miller 14). With revolution in the air and in the streets, Barry Allen's kiddie book needed a reboot, lest it lose relevancy.

The Flash was still socially hip—if only in name. Back in the Depression, words like "flash" and "streamline" connoted a fast-paced, modern lifestyle as an ideal for cash-strapped Americans to fantasize over (Cogdell 91–92). Streamlined design signified technology and luxury, and early comics such as *Silver Streak Comics* and *Flash Comics*, with their diagonal fonts and streaked pen lines, visualized the theme. Speedster Jay Garrick, with his Mercury-inspired helmet and winged feet, and the futuristic marvel Flash Gordon in comic strips and the movies, were tributes to fast-paced living. This endearing association extended through the 1960s; in the Marvel Universe, "Flash" Thompson was the big man on campus among the Midtown High School in-crowd, especially when compared to puny wall-crawling wall-flowers. In 1962, the name "Flash" even sounded cool to a wishy-washy Charlie Brown in *Peanuts*, who longed for the cool nickname of "Flash" Brown (Schulz). Even if Barry Allen threatened to fall on the outs, his superhero moniker reflected a hopeful, bright future.

However, student-led activism shifted by the decade's end. The early optimism of the sixties, with an emphasis on political reform and individual and social betterment, fractured into factions as civil rights activism grew violent and the Vietnam War escalated. Burnout, in the form of drug culture and a conservative backlash, further divided youths and widened the generation gap. Novelist Hunter Thompson's scathing *Fear and Loathing in Las Vegas* presented a laundry list of disappointments and disillusionment of the time; the "brutish realties of this foul year of Our Lord 1971" included the deaths of John F. and Robert Kennedy, LSD guru Timothy Leary in jail, Muhammad Ali dethroned, and "Bob Dylan clipping coupons in Greenwich Village" (22–23). With the times a-changin' and facing a segmented public, the Flash ran ragged to appease multiple audiences.

A Static-Charged "Fuzz"

As a police officer and a superhero, Barry Allen was first and foremost a protector of the status quo. Long-time, traditional fans wanted him to stay that way. As a lawman and a product of the Cold War, Barry Allen dashed headfirst into anti-communist ballyhoo. In issue #199 (August 1970), for instance, a mysterious "Colonel K" of the U.S. In-T Agency identifies Allen's alter ego and sends him on a secret mission to halt the "Y-Missile." The letter stands for "yellow peril"—unidentified in the comic, but Gil Kane's artwork depicting the Great Wall and a portrait of China's Mao Zedong presents clear evidence of the communist menace. Flash hurdles to the Far East to prevent the missile's launch from hitting the "heart of America," but not before Kane depicts him frozen in horror, as a red mushroom cloud bursts from his imagination at the prospects of his failure (Kanigher, "The Explosive..."). He succeeds, of course, with Colonel K. writing him a thank you note in advance, as if Uncle Sam had no doubt of the inevitable American victory.

In the midst of this top-secret spy stuff, the American hero has inside help: kids. Youth had long served as political agents of cold war culture on both sides, and Flash finds an ally behind the Bamboo Curtain. Even as he recoils in horror at the Yellow Peril enveloping the U.S. in red, he takes heart knowing that China's children are Americans at heart. He encounters a peasant, who says the "*Red Guard*" teaches him to hate the "capitalist enemy" (Kanigher, "The Explosive..."). But the boy knows his superhero mythology, identifying this red guardian as the "honorable Flash" and vows he will not turn the American in to the authorities. This communist fanboy isn't alone: "How my friends' eyes will *pop* when I tell them I have seen the fastest man on earth!" (Kanigher, "The Explosive..."). An underground youth culture, apparently, supports the American Way. For his part, Flash tells the young traitor he's doing the right thing: "With kids like you—some day we will all live in peace!" (Kanigher, "The Explosive"). The child connects with Flash and, by extension, capitalism and American Dream that Flash represents.

While Flash applauds the Asian child who defies his communist masters as a true contributor to peace, he has no doubts about the indoctrination of American children as citizen soldiers. In issue #200 (September 1970), Flash becomes a Manchurian candidate for an assassination plot of the U.S. President. This stripped-down potboiler, a rip-off of Richard Condon's 1959 novel and John Frankenheimer's 1962 film adaptation, re-affirmed Flash's dedication to American norms; the comic omitted the source novel's criticism of McCarthyism. Instead, readers see a shapely "Dr. Lu" heading the Crime-Network, made up of diehard Commies, leftover Nazis, and assorted underworld ne'er-do-wells. Lu kidnaps Iris Allen and forces Flash to undergo brainwashing to do her bidding—just as she had done with 199 previous freedom fighters. Passing herself off as Iris, she cozies up to a hypnotized Flash and kisses him to further her nefarious brainwashing. Her orders: go to "Funland" during a civic Boy's Week in Washington, D.C., and deliver a hairdryer to her. Translation: break into the Oval Office and shoot the President with a laser gun. Flash promptly dashes off.

In his brainwashed state, Flash believes his is on an errand of charity. He sees the boys playing soldier, trying to peg him with fake machine guns and tanks, shouting "bam-bam" and "tut-a-tut." Grinning, Flash envisions that the first two hundred boys who tag him will earn an encyclopedia set, linking educational brain power with military prowess, both of which trump being a superhero: "It's more important for some of the kids to walk away with the encyclopedia—than for me to prove in the fastest man on earth!" (Kanigher, "Count 200..."). Ideally, Funland isn't just fun and games; these boys can partake in the glory of the ideal citizen soldier—both scholar and warrior. Basking in the Cold War zeitgeist for his two hundredth anniversary issue, Flash sees no reason to question the young American kids desperately trying to shoot him down.

Funland, however, is all in Flash's mind. Due to the terrible Dr. Lu, the brainwashed Flash fails to realize the amusement park is actually the nation's capital and the "boys" are G.I.s trying to stop Flash from trespassing on the White House lawn. Flash whizzes by the grown-up versions of his imagined boys, and the real soldiers are helpless to prevent Flash from presenting a "hairdryer" to give to "Iris"—trigger words to gun down the President of the United States. As Flash bursts into the Oval Office and takes aim, the Free World seems doomed. Thankfully, he snaps out of it in time and moves faster than a speeding laser beam to save the Commander in Chief, who doesn't even realize what's going on. Flash comes to his senses only because he recalls that Dr. Lu's hypnotic, oriental "spice" lipstick was not the honey flavor his sweet Iris uses. Flash chastises the brainy Dr. Lu for overreaching her gender role ("You're a scientist who forgot she's also a woman!") after he saves the President. "I feel as if an Iron Curtain's been lifted from my mind!," Flash declares as he promptly wipes out the Crime-Network (Kanigher, "Count 200...").

Even in his brainwashed state, Flash couldn't run too far from rigid American social norms. The realization of flawed, foreign "women scientists" forgetting to use the right flavor of lipstick as a sign of their lack of femininity triggered his wake-up call; everything else around him, including prepping boys for draft-age marksmanship, was simply part of his civic duty. The boys play soldier and Flash accepts their taking potshots at him in the name of American child rearing. Indeed, the Flash and DC at large had little sympathy for uppity youth activism. While Marvel's Stan "the Man" Lee toured college campuses and leaned towards the left in questioning social mores, DC conservatively shied away from radicalism. The company's notorious short-lived series *Brother Power, The Geek* lasted a mere two issues. According to editor director Carmine Infantino, Superman's legendary editor, Mort Weisinger, disdained long-haired hippies and expressed his displeasure to publisher Jack Liebowitz about the swingin' counterculture (Markstein). Even though the first issue wasn't friendly to hippies—one of them eats out of a garbage can—DC had enough of geeks, freaks, and hippies and killed the series. Brother power lost out to the Man.

The Flash never said it outright, but he, too, didn't really care for student protestors. The cover of issue #185 (February 1969) featured the Scarlet Speedster bogged down by uncouth hippies, as they bash him with their peace signs. In issue #189 (June 1969), fan Scott Gibson commented in the letter pages, "What I enjoyed most about the cover was the girl hippy [sic] with her choppers sunk in poor Flash's leg!" Reader Kristy Kindgreen found the image offensive, pointing out one protestor holding a sign reading, "Give a Damn!" She found the sign "one of the worst things you could possibly do. Most kids think that if they see a word like that in a comic it is all right because most comics are smart enough not to use such a word." Lindgreen thought impressionable kids would simply and blindly follow the comic's word usage.

DC's editors replied by pleading innocence. They pointed out the comic merely reproduced the slogan of New York City's youth program that was "officially sponsored and endorsed by the Mayor of New York City," John Lindsay, to help underprivileged youth. DC acknowledged that for readers outside of the Big Apple, the tagline might seem offensive out of context. However, the company had no qualms about distorting the image of hippies who apparently cannot follow through on their messages of tolerance and peace. That the youths violently attack the Flash while mixing authentic slogans (the Civil Rights Movement's "We Shall Overcome" and "Flower Power") with comic book silliness ("Ban the Flash!") trivialized real-world activism. Frankly, these hippies didn't give a damn.

The story itself didn't help the hippies. In #185 (February 1969), Barry and Iris Allen head to Paris to celebrate a second honeymoon where they witness the Eiffel Tower sucked into space by some aliens from Titan.[1] A band of hippies under the magnetic spell of "Le Loup," a loopy conman who wants to steal the alien's ray gun to rob banks, declare their solidarity with "immigrants" with placards declaring, "No Soul-Brother Is Alien to Us" (Robbins). Flash harbors deep suspicions about anyone who is "not an *official* government delegation" and the anti-establishment hippies prove the superhero right. Le Loup nears the trusting Titans and orders his intolerant followers to attack the extraterrestrials via archery (Robbins). Thankfully for interstellar harmony, Flash easily disarms the bowmen and knocks Le Loup for a loop. The aliens learn that not all humans are violent or hostile, no thanks to the uncouth hippies who profess love but make war.

Flash's relationship with nonconformist youths remained tense. In issue #202 (December 1970), the Flash goes to Hollywood to investigate the Satan Circle, a rock band that haunts discotheques with names such as "Hell on Earth"—this particular club confines women in cages. In Tinsel Town—the "capital of merriment and mayhem," the caption notes—Flash learns the Satan Circle is part of a demonic cult that prays on partygoers and young people (Kanigher, "The Satan..."). Fending off misguided roughnecks, like the motorcycle gang Hell's Imps, Flash manages to save his wife from the sacrificial altar of these blood-lusting deviants.

While Flash upheld the Establishment view, not every reader supported such unabashed adherence. In issue #202 (December 1970) some fans commented on the silliness of "The Explosive Heart of America"; reader Jim Vecchio declared, "Good title, baaad story," explaining, "The entire concept of a mysterious Mr. K. employed with a secret-ultra-tiptop-secret American Agency who comes out of nowhere and just *happens* to know The Flash's secret identity is terribly infantile." While some fans enjoyed the traditional, patriotic tale, enough such letters reflected the creators' new direction to update the fastest man alive. The first order of business was a trip to the barber.

Flashing Forward

To join the times, Barry Allen dashed forward without reserve. In issue #194 (February 1970), artists Ross Andru and Mike Esposito hinted at the coming change, depicting Allen sporting his traditional crew cut, but, thanks to a macabre time-traveling ghost story from the 1890s, several panels featured Allen sporting mutton chops. But in the next issue, #195 (March 1970) artist Gil Kane accelerated Allen's hair growth. He began parting his lengthening hair to the left and his sideburns slowly etched down his face. After skipping an all-reprint issue—to let Allen's locks grow out further—the cover of #197 (May 1970) showed him sporting a full, flowing mane, parted and tucked behind his ears. Barry Allen himself remained silent on his new 'do, but Iris compares his new coiffure with his clean-shaven looks: "Your hair comb is even worse than your shave," she quips, "only *one star* for that!" (Kanigher, "Four Star..."). Iris, serving as a fill-in for her newspaper's film critic, mostly kept quiet, but her poor review foreshadowed readers' attitudes toward the Flash's transformation.

Barry Allen's hair length represented a reaction to the counterculture. His signature bowtie, three-button suits in sober, conservative colors were hallmarks of 1950s conformity and normality (Young and Yong 83). The crew cut's popularity originally grew out from ex-servicemen and refugees from World War II as an efficient and cheap way to thwart lice. During the booming military industrial complex of the 1950s, the paramilitaristic hairstyle fit neatly with the public vigilance against communism. In contrast, long-haired beatniks symbolized chaos, a lack of order and respect for social norms, and, for men, signs of unmanliness. By the 1960s, nonconformists rejected the crew cut for its association with the Cold War citizen soldier. For youths acting out, like rockstar Mick Jagger, long hair was not feminizing. Jagger rejected the idea that "being masculine means looking clean, cropped, and ugly"—a rebuke of the 1950s-styled organization man (Luciano 85). For Barry

Allen, the short-short-haired, long-distance superhero not only discarded his hair style, DC ret-conned it out of existence. In issue #203 (February 1971), a flashback recreates the Allens' wedding from issue #165 (November 1966), with Allen sporting his new '70s 'do. Though the wedding was only four years ago in real time, 1971 was culturally light years away from 1966. The "magic year" of 1968, with the assassinations of Martin Luther King, Jr., and Robert Kennedy, the Tet Offensive in Vietnam, a riot at the Democratic National Convention in Chicago, the birth of "black power" movements like the Black Panthers, and various youth "springs" in Czechoslovakia, Poland, and Yugoslavia widened the generation gap. Not wanting to be left behind, Allen mis-remembered his nuptials to fit the times.

Fans picked up on Barry Allen's makeover. In issue #203 (February 1971), reader Dan Jordan complimented the comic's new direction. Citing a non-existent letter from #199 (August 1970), Jordan erringly recalled "one reader [who] states that his hair is getting longer. He states this as a *complaint*, but I state it as a *compliment*. This is 1970, not 1948; I think Barry's hair *should* be longer. Crew cuts are out for a man of his age. Besides, his head looks weird in a crew cut. *Keep Barry's hair long!*" In this reader's recollection, the postwar crew cut was neither efficient nor a sign of mental stamina, but looked outdated and odd. This revisionism extended to Barry Allen's own memories and other fans hoped for more. In #197 (May 1970), reader Edward Broderick complained, "The Flash does not have any serious identity. It seems that he was spawned as a super-hero when there was a need for super-heroes." Indeed, after McCarthy's fall in 1954, the Silver Age inaugurated patriotic Cold Warriors to battle communists abroad and at home. But the industry's turn on soul-searching and characterization-heavy plots to respect the readers' intelligence—mostly from rival Marvel—spoiled DC's fans who wanted their heroes to have similar anxieties. Calling the one-dimensional, patriotic hero "shallow," Broderick asked, "*Just who is Barry Allen?*"

Editor Julius Schwarz, stumped himself, answered Broderick's question. "Who is Barry Allen? That's just what [writer] Mike Freidrich has been asking himself." Schwarz informed Broderick and others who wanted more social-issue stories to watch out for the upcoming story "No Sad Songs for the Scarlet Speedster," as evidence that DC was listening to fans. "As the 'character revolution' progresses, we'll do our best not to make it 'revolting!'" Such statements underscored DC's position between staying in tune with younger readers and not wanting to deviate too much from their traditional fan base.

This new updated Flash did not just grow out his hair. He joins the younger crowd literally in issue #198 (June 1970). In "No Sad Songs for the Scarlet Speedster," Flash has a field day at an orphanage, bonding with the parentless kids with some flashy speed tricks. The younger tots lap it up, asking him for an autograph; fully entrenched in the superhero establishment, they plan to up-trade it for Superman's or Batman's signatures. However, the supervisor asks Flash to concentrate his parlor tricks on three disgruntled teens: Rod Harris, Frankie Smith, and Betty Foster. The supervisor's sad song: "They're *orphans*—from the worst neighborhood in town. Rebels! Anti-*everything*! *I* can't get through to them!" (Kanigher, "No Sad..."). The supervisor automatically equates youth alienation to their environment. Even though they now reside in the comforts of a middle-class orphanage, signified by how wonderfully mannered the autograph-seeking younger kids are, the bratty teens' origins automatically render them antisocial and disgruntled. Nature trumps nurture, the supervisor believes, tracing their grumpiness to the "worst neighborhood" in Central City (Kanigher, "No Sad..."). Flash takes one look at these surly kids (despite their clean-cut looks, they sport love beads and bell bottoms) and knows that he's in for a tough assignment.

Indeed, the teens beat the fastest man alive to a greeting: "G'wan—buzz off!" When Flash tries to impress them with some twirls, they make it clear they have no use for anything he offers—autographs included. Their leader, Rod, snaps, "Cool it, man! We've seen that kiddy stuff before!" (Kanigher, "No Sad..."). Flash says he is open to personal requests, but Rod declines, saying they want nothing from the speedy trickster. His compatriot, Frankie, concur that Flash simply doesn't "dig" them. They walk away. The kids' rejection confuses Flash, leaving him with a question mark in a speech bubble.

As a do-gooder, Flash *does* dig the youngsters. After all, he's at the orphanage for their entertainment. But even if Frankie's statement is vague, the generation gap is clear. The caption confirms Flash is "crushed by his utter inability to communicate with the teen-agers," but the Justice Leaguer determines to unite society (Kanigher, "No Sad..."). He scoops them up in his speed lines, whisking them to their neighborhood. The police detective immediately understands the kids' attitudes as he looks at the cracked sidewalks and littered streets about him: "Looks like a meteor-blasted planet!" (Kanigher, "No Sad..."). He deduces teenage bitterness does not come from any fundamental flaw in the system he champions. Rather, they figuratively fell through the cracked sidewalks. Indeed, the kids' relatively neat and well-groomed looks signify that they are not hopeless, protesting hippies under shysters like Le Loup. Instead, these kids *try* to help their neighbors; when they're not hanging around the orphanage, they're back in their stomping grounds, trying to build a clubhouse "for the kids." These children aren't rebels, they're social justice reformers. In a flash, the Scarlet Speedster builds the club house. A stunned Rod immediately changes his mind about the superhero establishment, affirming his belief in social institutions: "Flash *is* Santa Claus, without a long white beard!" (Kanigher, "No Sad...").

This young Santa Claus does more than get the kids to believe in fairy tales. He reawakens their faith in the system thanks to some plot twists. When building the clubhouse, Santa Flash unearths a hidden satchel full of stolen money. Conveniently, gangsters spot the loot and start shooting. A bullet grazes Flash's temple and he reverts to an eight-year-old Barry. The three teens are suddenly thrust into adulthood as guardians of a kid Flash. As adult figures, they immediately appreciate the elder generation's viewpoint as they protect their young charge. At the pivotal moment, when the goons come in, the teenagers call upon a higher power to save them: God. They tell Barry he must place faith in them to heal himself. "If only you'd *believe* us, you'd overcome" (Kanigher, "No Sad..."). By referencing the Civil Rights Movement's motto, which Le Loup's brainwashed hippies had sported on picket signs thirteen issues earlier, the teens turn the call for reform into an affirmation of the status quo: superheroes and one nation's law and order under God. Their new faith inspires little Barry, who prays through teary eyes. His leap of faith restores his memory in time to punch out the bad guys.

The spiritual awakening heals the generational rift. No longer "anti-everything," the kids thank Flash by naming their new club house after him and making him an "honorary teenage member" (Kanigher, "No Sad..."). Flash accepts with glee, endorsing their club house and thankful these rebels are now on his side. Indeed, Betty, the token female, easily subscribes to a mainstream patriarchal system, calling the house a "boy's club." Flash's name emblazed on the building clearly identifies the top boy of this club. Presumably, with these norms in place, the "worst neighborhood" in Central City will be no more—Flash no longer needs to address issues of poverty, pollution, or poor road maintenance. He leaves the meteor-blasted section of town for bed, where Iris tucks in the pooped speedster, noting her husband "sleeps like a child" (Kanigher, "No Sad...").[2]

Three issues later, Flash repeats the same story of angry teenagers, although this story has a race angle. In "Million-Dollar Dream!" Flash harbors guilt because he let Central City's Spanish Village down. The residents refer to their community as a "slum," with their only hope being a teenage basketball whiz named Pablo. Dubbed the "Spanish Flash," Pablo hopes for an athletic scholarship, but Flash inadvertently makes the boy lose self-confidence when he thinks an accident leaves him crippled. His mother accuses Flash of ruining Central City's minority population: "He was out only hope of lifting us out of the slums! Of making all Spanish-speaking people proud of him!" (Kanigher, "Million Dollar...."). Her heated emotions betray her sentiment; only by reaching white, middle class standards can they be "proud" of Pablo or of themselves. Indeed, Pablo's nickname as the "Spanish Flash" renders him a pale imitation of the original, but whose connection to a gentrified superhero connotes social mobility in a mainstream establishment. Appropriately, Flash beats himself up, repeating Pablo's mom: "I ruined his life! Shattered his dreams! Crushed his people's hope of a new Spanish star rising from the slums!" (Kanigher, "Million Dollar....") Like with the teens' sad song, Pablo heals himself by restoring Flash's confidence via prayer to "Madre de Dios" and the two Flashes return to their normal selves. Flash thanks Pablo by humoring the boy's kid sister's proposal of marriage. The Spanish Flash will get his scholarship, elevate his people from the slums, and join mainstream Central City.

Flash's connecting with his inner child resonated with readers who enthused over the new DC and its focus on character angst as a means of development. In issue #199 (August 1970), longtime reader Scott Gibson evaluated the company's past year, noting how 1970 "has been a great one for human interest in comics." He noted the death of Black Canary's husband, Robin's leaving Batman's family and the Teen Titans, Green Arrow's impoverishment, Wonder Woman's severance from her Amazon heritage, and Green Lantern's identity crisis. For the Flash, his alienation and disillusionment came from his hair, wardrobe, and home life—the latter through his wife. In issue #203 (February 1971), Flash joins Superman in the Justice League's orbital satellite as the Man of Steel keeps a lonely vigil. Looking down on the Earth like a God, the Last Son of Krypton complains about being an outsider to humans. Despite his superpowers, his Kryptonian heritage alienates him by default.

An annoyed Flash rebuts Superman, asserting that he, too, endures a life of hardship, thanks to his wife. The issue flashes back as he describes how Iris learned her life was a lie. She finds an old locket with an inscription claiming she is an orphan from the year 2945. Iris immediately accepts the locket's words, returns to the future, settles down in a post-nuclear holocaust, and helplessly submits to a tyrant from Laos—apparently, Vietnam's neighbor rose to power after the U.S. and the U.S.S.R. annihilated each other—who conquered the world and wants her for a mate. The Flash, of course, dashes into this nightmarish world, deposes this yellow menace and the threat of miscegenation, and brings hope to the remaining Americans to restore their democracy. Despite this achievement, Flash clings to this wife's new origin as a legitimate reason for his emotional depth. Since his wife comes from a future society, Flash now feels he is "an alien of *Earth* ... in the *30th Century*" while Iris now feels out of place in the twentieth (Kanigher, "Flash's Wife..."). Superman silently accepts the Scarlet Speedster's tale of disillusionment and woe. The twenty-five-year-old Iris and her husband, disoriented, were not unlike Superman *or* the young people of the early 1970s.

The Allens' social life further reflected his age regression. In issue #207 (June 1971), they attend a concert, with Iris mocking her husband as a "*rock fanatic*" (Friedrich, "The Evil..."). Barry chides her: "Oh, c'mon Iris, I may be *pushing thirty*, but I'm not over the hill yet!" (Friedrich, "The Evil..."). UC Berkeley student organizer Jack Weinberg famously told reporters that the counterculture didn't trust anyone over thirty back in 1965; here, Allen shows he may be a lawman, but he's still qualifies as a youngster, made more evident by his fondness for rock. Iris herself is more of a '50s gal, saying she likes "old time rock-and-roll" like Elvis, Buddy Holly, and Fats Domino, but readers know she, too, isn't really "old" (Friedrich, "The Evil..."). Not only is she younger than her husband biologically, she hasn't even been born yet. Barry scolds her: "You're just not keeping up with the times, that's all!" (Friedrich, "The Evil..."). Eager to see his favorite band, "Washington Starship" (a riff on Jefferson Airplane, which released an album, *Jefferson Starship*, that year), Allen dashes out without bothering to change into costume. Iris laughs at the idea of her husband's green suit and pink turning him into a "mod Flash" (Friedrich, "The Evil...").

Barry Allen's favorite band, Washington Starship, confirms the Flash's countercultural turn. The lead singers, Paul and Gracie (clear references to band members Paul Kanter and Grace Slick), are determined to raise their unborn child in "a world they've [the grownups] messed up—but we're gonna fix!" (Friedrich, "The Evil..."). Their music, Friedrich's caption informs readers, was a mix of "hill-country and ghetto fury, then fused under an ever present mushroom cloud," leading to a "pulse-beat of a new age" based on "*hope*," "*love*," "*peace*," and "*joy*" (Friedrich, "The Evil..."). Friedrich also snuck in references to the Beatles and Simon and Garfunkel. Unfortunately, the evil magician Sargon crashes the concert and turns the psychedelic rock music into monsters, but Flash saves the panicking hippies. Gracie reveals that Sargon is an estranged uncle and accuses him of sending her baby "into hell and back—before it's even born!" (Friedrich, "The Evil..."). Ashamed of ruining the world and the concert for young people, Sargon disappears in a puff of smoke, leaving Iris to iron out Barry's wrinkled suit and Gracie wondering about her and her baby's mental states thanks to her uncle. The corruption of psychedelic music into monsters from hell left its mark on the next generation.

Barry Allen wasn't the only speedster trying to revive his wonder years through music. Jay Garrick, the Golden Age Flash from the 1940s, felt the years creeping up on him. In issue #201 (November 1970), a back-up story featured Garrick as an over-the-hill superhero out of touch with the modern generation; one villain taunts the oldster with "You're ob-so-lete, time's marching over you!" (Kanigher, "Finale..."). Garrick's much-younger wife assures him by using jive talk to describe his aged features: "Gray at your temples is cool!" (Kanigher, "Finale..."). To help him, she takes her husband to "Stockwood," an outdoor jam session where young people promote peace (the band "Spiked Helmets" rile the crowd with lyrics calling for sending the generals to war to duke it out themselves). An inverse of Woodstock, the gathered hippies at first reject the "over-30s" who are "stickin' their neurotic noses everywhere! Tryin' to steal our thing! When they should be in rockin' chairs!" (Kanigher, "Finale..."). But the young people quickly elevate Garrick and Williams from rocking chairs to rock concerts; once they get over their age discrimination, they call the old-timers "beautiful people" for coming "out here—at *your* age!" (Kanigher, "Finale...").

Feeling his oats, Garrick gets down to dancing and swaying. But an even greater fossil crashes Stockwood in the form of the Fiddler, a frustrated, megalomaniacal violinist whose fondness for classical music and a matching antiquated costume makes him more obsolete than Garrick's graying temples. The Golden Age Flash says as much, wondering "what he's up to in *his* old age?" (Kanigher, "Finale..."). The Fiddler tries to connect to the in-crowd; as he plays an electric violin, psychedelic colors fan out, bathing the panicking young people in a rainbow display as his goons rob the million-dollar till. The Fiddler is so giddy with his success, he uncontrollably bursts out laughing and stops playing. Garrick takes the opportunity to dash up to the stage and the Fiddler admits Flash caught him "with my bow down" (Kanigher, "Finale...").[3] The youngsters cheer on Flash with cries of "Groovy!" for his saving their concert, their ideals, and their moment in the sun. Perhaps Flash was too successful in connecting with youths; in issue #205 (May 1971), A.W. Peters complained about the jokes about Garrick's aging and slowing down, calling them a major turn-off for readers. DC quickly agreed the generation gap had to go: "The Flash-pans directed at the concept of an aging, slow-footed super-speedster hit their target! It won't happen to the original Flash again." The Golden Age Flash skipped out on his golden years.

Barry Allen's makeover met with mixed results. DC, more conservative than Marvel's angst-ridden characters, encountered resistance from readers who wanted less social relevance in their preference for straight superhero fare. In issue #200 (September 1970), reader Scott Dickerson complained about the comic's shift. "Barry and Iris's hair is getting too long," he griped. He admitted Flash needed some social consciousness to avoid being "rather blah." But he found the "big change" in the new DC that turned the Justice League into Justice Warriors mixed. Such moves "helped Batman and *some-what* helped Green Lantern, but Flash? Barry Allen is a nice-guy type who just doesn't *need* to know *why* he's a superhero. He accepts it; he has adjusted to it."[4] In issue #203 (February 1971), reader Debra Miyajima agreed, urging writers not to get carried away with sob stories: "Flash is a very refreshing break from all the super-heroes who have so many hang-ups that their problems have problems." In issue #206 (May 1971), fan Paul Emrath believed "too much emotionalism gets tiring after a while." In issue #209 (September 1971), John D. Warner singled out that writer Robert Kanigher's "slushed-over emotionalism, which he was trying to pass off as relevancy (complete with plenty of clichés for all)" didn't jive. He called for the "return of the *Scarlet Speedster* and the ditching of the *Scarlet Soap Opera*." Warner remained sympathetic to social causes, but took fans to task for criticizing the traditional superhero: "Today's young adults are more aware and concerned than most previous generations," he lectured. "These are the same young adults that were reading the EC comix in their youth. Think about it, brother!" Such concerns about bigotry and social reform were okay for shocking suspense stories and incredible science fiction, but Warner didn't want such thoughts extending to mainstream, traditional superheroes.

For Main Street heroes, the lack of outlandish, colorful supervillains was a sore spot. In issue #205 (May 1971), fan Bob Rozakis claimed the trend toward realism was too dull. Flash's rogue gallery had apparently "all retired and left town and all Flash does is have human-interest problems in each issue." In issue #215 (May 1972), fan Stephen Bunny mockingly applauded the disappearance of costumed villains: the baddies "would probably be reduced to polluting the environment, or pushing plastics, or selling out to the Russians, or holding rock festivals." While some readers found the brainwasher Dr. Lu a worthy adversary for a follow-up appearance, she didn't make the cut. The dearth of supervillains all but made the superhero superfluous for traditional readers.

While readers debated the philosophy of superheroes, they also had critiqued specific storylines. "No Sad Songs for a Scarlet Speedster" struck some as a masterpiece. The urban poor in Central City "was sad, but it told of so many truths," fan John Freienbergs argued in #201 (November 1970). The "slums, lack of communication between the generations, lack of interest in local government, it showed life like it is to so many." The spiritual aspect of the story with the kids and Flash turning to God touched another fan, who approved that "faith" allowed the teens to find redemption. However, reader Scott Dickerson found the "bare-boned" story riddled with "plot clichés." The "long-haired teens," the "mod" outfits, and the token "girl and a Negro" among the rebels showed a reliance on social stereotypes prevalent in movies, alongside the pat sermon at the end. In issue #202 (December 1970), reader Gary Kuhlmann summarized the division among fans in his evaluation of the recent trend of social issues and self-doubt plaguing superheroes in general: "Humanization of your characters is a good thing, but don't overdo it."

One long letter from Neal Martin singled out the Allens' attending a rock concert as an example of everything wrong with the series: "What happened to *Flash*? I pick up the June issue [#207] and see my favorite superhero muttering teeny-bopper clichés like 'No time to rap...' But that's not enough; I read further and find an entire page and a half devoted to Barry Allen stomping and gyrating like he's auditioning for *American Bandstand....* I read on and muddle through some more *raps, vibes, gigs, get it ons*." This countercultural turn replaced superheroics, with Flash's sole act was "whistling a group of hippies through an exit door." Like his fellow readers, Martin identified the problem: "Lately, the usual fare has been what some people call 'human-interest plots' involving everyday people. Unfortunately, this has also come to mean disappointing, uninspired adventures with little excitement and a minimum of routine super-speed action." After complaining how Flash escaped Sargon's paralyzing spell by declaring his love for Iris (emotion trumps the Speed Force), Martin urged DC to take immediate action. He wanted writers to reject the "jargon, soggy emotion, and soul-searching which are so prevalent in almost every other strip." The Flash should be a "happily-married, well-adjusted super-hero with no overwhelming problems or identity-crises. Believe me, in the current comix industry, this is UNIQUE!" In #209 (September 1971), after printing two pages of letters debating the "true" Flash, editor Julius Schwartz mused, "We wonder ... who is the typical-average reader of The Flash[...the] hard-hitting, word-slinging critic" or "the short-and-sweet fan who expresses himself," judging art and story and ignoring social relevance? The lack of a unified response among readers left DC guessing.

Conclusion: Flashing Back for the Future

The youth movement of the 1950s began with a wide-eyed enthusiasm for challenging the Man and remaking the American establishment. As the 1970s started, however, deep-rooted fissures in student movements widened as the Students for a Democratic Society splintered and died. In 1972, Alan Adelson wrote an early history of the youth movement's rise and fall, and Adelson remained upbeat about the future. "SDSers as a group have more hope and positive dedication than a whole government full of Hubert Humprhreys" and asked the reader to "join with us" to continue a peaceful approach to civil rights and the end of Vietnam (123 and 174). Humphrey lost the Democratic nomination that year to George McGovern, and McGovern's landslide defeat at the hands of Richard Nixon's Committee to Re-elect the President points to the few who joined Adelson.

Popular culture also did not have one voice, and the generation gap left various media producers torn over how to make characters relevant to all demographics. Historian Edward P. Morgan points out television shows such as The Monkees divided audiences, with old-timers unable to connect to the long-haired rockers, while the teenybopper crowd went ape over the boy band (228). Programs such as The Mod Squad tried to play it both ways, with seemingly alienated teens actually operating under the auspices of the fuzz. Fans of The Flash were also divided; in issue #210 (November 1971), reader Steve Utley approved Barry Allen allowing his "formally close-cropped hair

[to] grow wild and free," but his snappy garb to attend the Washington Starship concert "turned me completely off with his plastic attire."

As the first hit superhero of the Silver Age, the Flash set the standard for the DC universe that unfolded after him. But when the industry darted left toward progressivism, Flash stumbled. Barry Allen modernized his looks, his wife enabled him to feel like an outsider, and he inspired the downtrodden kids in Central City. At the same time, the comic toed the anti-communist line as the Justice Leaguer remained firmly patriotic, and creators depicted hippies as gullible and shallow. The revolving door of writers and artists—from Robert Kanigher to Mike Friedrich, and Ross Andru and Mike Esposito to Gil Kane and Irv Novick—left Flash's transition in the 1970s inconsistent. Indeed, reader Neal Martin's long complaint in issue #210 (November 1971), laid blame on the writers: "Kanigher dragged Flash through the bogs of human interest stories, Friedrich is too 'teen-oriented,' always trying to be relevant…. [Dennis] O'Neil, the best characterization man in the business would probably give Barry Allen a slew of hang-ups and a shaky marriage with Iris. [Frank] Robbins wrote several strocious 'camp' stories, which I haven't forgiven him for." Martin concluded by asking editor Julius Schwartz to give a hand at the scripting process. Schwartz declined.

Fans used the rocky adjustment to discuss the philosophical foundations of the American superhero. In issue #215 (May 1972), reader Scott Dickerson provided a list to creators of concepts to avoid, many of them of recent story lines: "no devil cults, no crippled athletes, no turned-off teenagers, no self-sacrificing parents, no noble nuns." In his view, the "vat of human-interest molasses" dragged the Flash down. In the same issue, reader Anthony Kowalik suggested renaming the letter column from "Flash-Grams" to "Flash-Backs" to appease nostalgic fans who prefer the traditional superhero. Editor Julius Schwartz responded by wondering the same thing.

In issue #206, several readers commented upon the Satan Circle from issue #203 (February 1971)—the cult of human-sacrificing hippies. Reader Michael Fink applauded Barry Allen's horror when he fears a dead woman is his wife. Even though the superhero stopped caring when he learns the corpse is an anonymous hippie, Fink found Allen's concern for his wife touching. "Superheroes, as these beings are called, do not exist for the sole purpose of saving the world from disaster every other day," Fink philosophized. Even though DC's legions of superheroes did just that, Fink thought they represented a higher purpose. "They must *feel*, and it is this so-called *feeling* that brings *life* into these superbeings, that brings *reality* to the adventures they are involved in." DC appreciated the support, but also noted a tug-of-war between readers. "The 'feelings' that brought Flash to life for Correspondent Fink in 'The Satan Circle' killed it for the next critic." Reader Scott Gibson took the creators to task. Even though Gibson wrote earlier in issue #199

(August 1970), describing 1970 as a good year for DC's line-up of superstars and their emotional hang-ups, the past several months overloaded his tolerance: "Whatever happened to the less realistic but nonetheless exciting days of such earth-quaking nemesis as genius gorillas and mirror-wielding screwballs? I may be severely attacked by other correspondents on my 'square' outlook, but at least you have one side of the story." For these self-described "squares," human interest tales outstayed their welcome. In a cultural-countercultural tug-of-war, the fastest man alive remained standing still, his social consciousness nothing more than a flash in the pan.

NOTES

1. The yellow, bug-eyed aliens are no relation to the Legion of Superheroes' Saturn Girl. In a blow to continuity, the editor explained to fan Jan Arrah in issue #189 (June 1969) that what happened in *The Flash* stayed in *The Flash*. Artistic license was "all part of speculative fiction—and each writer reserves the right to speculate on his own fashion on *what* or *who* may expect on other planets without being hampered by what other editors here dreamed up previously." In another instance of DC's segregating their universe from real world events, Arrah wondered why the Allens were vacationing in Paris when "for about a year now, President [Lyndon] Johnson has been discoursing Americans from traveling to European countries." To help fund the mushrooming Great Society program and the Vietnam War, Johnson hoped to keep American dollars in the U.S.

2. In #201 (November 1970), the editor noted inker Vince Colletta came up with Iris's closing quip.

3. Kid Flash did not have a crew cut; his curly locks contrasted sharply with Allen's trimmed coiffure. Wally West also participated in youth activism in his occasional back-up feature in *The Flash*; one story from #211 (December 1971) featured Kid Flash tackling corporate greed when one insensitive capitalist feeds poor people poisoned poultry. As they did with Barry Allen, some fans balked; in issue #215 (May 1972), reader Matt Graham deplored the clichés: "Hero meets rich (white, pot-bellied, of course) baddie, long-haired with it good guy finally convinces good guy and hero brings baddie to justice." Such tales contained "definite prejudice" and, even worse, were "deathly monotonous." Graham addressed writer Steve Skeates: "all good guys don't have to sling jargon and sport long hair." Julius Schwartz defended Skeates as a "Skeates stereotype."

4. In issue #207 (June 1971), Dickerson outright blamed Iris for the Flash's social awakening. Noting Allen's "haggard and drawn" face, he accused Iris of whittling her husband down. "Look at his him and his hair is creeping down over his collar (*definitely* out of character). He never mentions his police work anymore, his old friends and enemies are avoiding him…his only excitement seems to consist of eating Iris's meals—in-between rescues." Dickerson demanded the couple divorce. Editor Julius Schwartz told Dickerson to "cool it."

WORKS CITED

Adelson, Alan. *SDS,* Scribner's, 1972.

Bates, Cary (w), Irv Novick (p), and Dick Giordano (i). "Beyond the Speed of Life!" *The Flash* #209 (September 1971). New York: DC Comics.

Broome, John (w), Ross Andru (p), and Mike Esposito (i). "The Bride Cast Two Shadows!" *The Flash* #194 (February 1970). New York: DC Comics.

_____. "The Death-Touch of the Blue Ghost." *The Flash* #189 (June 1969). New York: DC Comics.

Broome, John (w), Carmine Infantino (p), and Joe Giella (a). "One Bride Groom Too Many!" *The Flash* #165 (November 1966). New York: DC Comics.

Cogdell, Christina. *Eugenic Design: Streamlining America in the 1930s,* University of Pennsylvania Press, 2004.

Friedrich, Mike (w), Gil Kane (p), and Vince Colletta (i). "Four Star Superhero!" *The Flash* #197 (May 1970). New York: DC Comics.
Friedrich, Mike (w), Irv Novick (p), and Murphy Anderson (i). "The Evil Sound of Music!" *The Flash* #207 (June 1971). New York: DC Comics.
Kanigher, Robert (w), and Murphy Anderson (p, i). "Finale for a Fiddler!" *The Flash* #201 (November 1970). New York: DC Comics.
Kanigher, Robert (w), Gil Kane (p), and Murphy Anderson (i). "Fugitive from Blind Justice." *The Flash* #195 (March 1970). New York: DC Comics.
Kanigher, Robert (w), Gil Kane (p), and Vince Colletta (i). "The Explosive Heart of America." *The Flash* #199 (August 1970). New York: DC Comics.
_____. "No Sad Songs for a Scarlet Speedster!" *The Flash* #198 (June 1970). New York: DC Comics.
Kanigher, Robert (w), Irv Novick (p), and Murphy Anderson (i). "Count 200—And Die!" *The Flash* #200 (September 1970). New York: DC Comics.
_____. "The Flash's Wife Is a Two-Timer!" *The Flash* #203 (February 1971). New York: DC Comics.
_____. "The Satan Circle." *The Flash* #202 (December 1970). New York: DC Comics.
_____. "24 Hours of Immortality!" *The Flash* #206 (May 1971). New York: DC Comics.
Luciano, Lynne. *Looking Good: Male Body Image in Modern America*, Hill and Wang, 2001.
Markstein, Don. "Brother Power, the Geek." *Don Markstein's Toonopedia*. 2014. Web. Accessed 29 August 2017.
Miller, James. *Democracy Is in the Streets: From Port Huron to the Siege of Chicago*, Harvard University Press, 1987.
Morgan, Edward P. *What Really Happened to the 1960s*, University Press of Kansas, 2010.
Robbins, Frank (w), Ross Andru (p), and Mike Esposito (i). Threat of the High-Rise Buildings." *Flash* #185 (February 1969). New York: DC Comics.
Schulz, Charles M. "Peanuts." *GoComics*, 4 February 1962, http://www.gocomics.com/peanuts/1962/02/04. Accessed 5 October 2017.
Skeates, Steve (w), Dick Dillion (p), and Dick Giordano (i). "Is This Poison Legal?" *The Flash* #211 (December 1971). New York: DC Comics.
Thompson, Hunter S. *Fear and Loathing in Las Vegas: A Savage Journey to the Heart of the American Dream*, Vintage Books, 1971.
Young, William H. and Nancy K. Young. *The 1950s*, Greenwood Press, 2004.

From Riches to Rags

The Rise and Fall of Wally West

FERNANDO GABRIEL PAGNONI BERNS

As the 1980s turned into the 1990s, comic books entered the "grim and gritty" era (Wandtke 191), in which violence escalated, art was highly stylized, and bodies sexualized. Unlike the more tame 1980s, gore ran galore and villains become even more lethal than ever. But, even as these aspects of the storytelling became heightened, there is another simultaneous issue shaping the era of grittiness: a more realistic approach to super-heroes (Klock 80). While it may seem contradictory, in this era superpowered characters were presented as human beings with their ups and downs, rather than the more traditional paragons of the Golden Age.

After *Crisis on Infinite Earths*—a fantastic event involving and reshaping the complete DC Comics' superhero universe—superheroes were reborn, their lives changed forever, often with their personal stories starting anew. The idea behind the event was to both make heroes more accessible to new audiences and DC superheroes more relevant to new generations of readers (Wolfman 6). In the case of the Flash, Barry Allen sacrificed himself in the *Crisis*, and Wally West, the former kid Flash, ascended to the role of the official Flash.

From Riches...

The new *Flash*'s adventures were initially written by Mike Baron, who made Wally West a womanizing yuppie. In the first issue, West wins the lottery and becomes a millionaire. Baron portrays Wally West as a carefree young man who lives a luxurious life-style, goes from woman to woman, and even dates a married one, Tina McGee. In Baron's run, Wally West asks for money in exchange for saving the world, the sort of behavior that would fit right in with the ethos of protagonists from the soon-to-be-released film *Wallstreet*. The sons of the hippies of the 1960s become yuppies, communism fell and young people in general were "more interested in power, money and status that at any other time" (Hayward 29) before.

William Messner-Loebs took over as writer from Baron with issue #15 and made Wally West poor again. In fact, West becomes almost homeless amidst a city that seemed always at the point of complete breakdown. Interestingly, while it may seem that Messner-Loebs was shifting completely away from Baron's interpretation of the Flash, he takes Baron's ideas and continues a harsh review on the political and economic conditions framing the last half of the 1980s. While the specificity of Wally West's life is quite different between these two runs, thematically they share much in common.

One issue permeating both Baron and Messner-Loebs' runs is the concept of instability. As the neoliberal era came to an end, and the future looks uncertain, young men like West felt that they were ultimately, "unable to reproduce the prospects and stability of their own fathers' lives" (Colin 18). The never-ending parade of girlfriends, a multicultural cast, a fragmented family, decaying cities framed by the "drugs scare," and poverty were all part of the universe of the young Wally West. The shift from richness to poverty suffered by Wally West and the circumstances around him paralleled real concerns of the era.

Interestingly, the life of Wally West in the late 1980s and first years of the 1990s seems to mirror the fortunes reigning over the ratings of national TV. One of the most successful TV shows in the history of America was *The Cosby Show* (NBC), a sitcom lead by an African American obstetrician Cliff Huxtable (Bill Cosby), the father of an upper-class family living in a luxurious neighborhood. The show had terrific ratings and revolved around a family in which every problem was resolved with patience, care and conversation. Faithful to the neoconservative politics of the 1980s and its emphasis on family values, economic problems and issues of sexuality or race were rarely mentioned (Bignell 225). Also, accurate with the backlash targeting radical feminism in the 1980s—in which feminists were depicted in popular media as lonely, angry and depressed women (Faludi 1)—the wife (Phylicia Rashad), was only infrequently seen actually working, even though audiences were told she had a job as an attorney. The series illustrated to perfection the Ronald Reagan mindset, enthroning the nuclear family in a world where anyone who works hard enough can make it to the top.

Ratings skyrocketed to the point that the supremacy of the rich, well-educated Huxtable family was considered invulnerable through the 1980s. At least, until the coming of Roseanne Barr and her successful sitcom simple titled *Roseanne* (ABC). Vulgar and flamboyant, Roseanne Conner (Barr) was the matriarch of a working-class family always struggling with payments, mortgages, and demanding jobs. Father and mother worked hard but money was always insufficient. The children fought all day and both mom and dad used sarcasm as a protective shield against a hard life. Soon, critics called the Conners a "dysfunctional" family, a complete reversal of the well-mannered Huxtables. The success of *Roseanne* tainted the clear-cut dynamics of *The Cosby Show* and already in the second season, Barr's sitcom won in ratings over the Huxtables. This fact was so huge and unexpected for audiences around America that *TV Guide* #1956 (September 1989) dedicated a cover to these "incredible" shifts of fortunes: in the cover, a montage of images which show Roseanne Barr pushing Bill Cosby away.[1] The time for upper-class families without any problems was over: all hail the struggling working-class.

This same conversion can be observed in the *Flash* series, in which the Wally West moves from his *Dynasty*-like mansion to extreme urban poverty. Arguably, this passage can be studied as a rite of maturation, with Wally West donning the costume of his mentor Barry Allen and stepping in on the big leagues after years (decades, in readers' time) of being Kid Flash. West is depicted as insecure about being capable of carrying the mantle of his mentor; so, he tries to cut any ties with the older generations. To do so, he hides himself behind a glossy image of success.

The social and cultural landscape of the late 1980s was dominated by a marked decline in the sense of community that had framed the 1960s and, in a minor way, the 1970s. By the 1980s, the Reagan/Margaret Thatcher era brought a series of new moral panics based on the vision of the New Right. Even if youth culture was far from homogeneous, there was an important shared value for many young adults: economic identification through the consumptive capacities that teenagers developed through the decade. Slowly, the countercultural image of the hippie that dominated the 1960s and part of the 1970s was transformed into a new type of youth identification: the young yuppie. The 1980s "was a decade obsessed with self-advancement, exploration, and improvement" (Berman 15). The yuppie was the epitome of this mindset.

> Traditionally, Americans gained wealth with age, as they rose through the ranks to occupy more senior positions in their chosen fields. By 1984, however, 23 percent of America's disposable income belonged to ambitious, young, upwardly mobile professionals, the so called yuppies. This segment of society found itself with high-paying jobs relatively early in life as a result of deregulation and mergers, and it was obsessed both with workplace advancement and with personal improvement. Unlike the self-improvement trends of the 1970's, however, the self-improvement goals of 1980's yuppies were often superficial, consisting largely of purchasing products that functioned as status symbols to their peers [*ibid.*].

Wally West, now "ascended" to the category of Flash (minus the "kid") is the perfect embodiment of Reaganomics and the yuppie life-style. He becomes rich after winning the lottery, thus downplaying any real effort to prove himself as capable of social mobility. The latter contradicts the yuppie's logic of meritocracy, an ideology sustained on the idea that success is bred through competition, individual talent, and hard work. However, West is interested in climbing up the social ladder already from issue one. In the first issue dated June of 1987, West differentiates himself from his predecessor, Barry Allen, who died poor, leaving many debts behind him. In fact, he died in such an economical meager state that the Justice League "paid for his funeral" (Baron, "Happy..."). The fact that Allen put the safety of the universe before his own interests is deemed heroic, and he is remembered and honored as a man who thinks first and foremost on others rather than in his welfare.

In the first two issues, West is needed to deliver a human heart for a transplant patient from New York to Seattle. Even if the person receiving the heart is Eugenie Hedstrom, a female writer of science fiction that West had read through college, he charges for the task nonetheless. He makes the doctors give him health insurance in return for his "disinterested" help. Readers and characters (within the comic book) alike surely were shocked by this attitude, as audiences had been trained to expect complete, generous sacrifice from superheroes. West, however, remains steadfast in been paid for his work. He is "heroic" as he helps people in need, but he demands financial remuneration for his acts.

Further, West insists on being called "Flash" rather than "Kid Flash" and is adamant in correcting people. It is clear that he wants desperately to differentiate himself from Allen and, by extension, from the mindset of older generations, now considered mostly as passé. There are two interesting things especially noticeable in the first two-part arc: first, the use of a renowned sci-fi writer whose work West reads. Even if he is a fan, his admiration does not mean working for free. It is interesting that Mike Baron could use any person (the character has no further weight in the story) but chose makes her a writer. West's ethos are significantly established when he does not change his mind even to help someone whose work he admires. Second, the main villain of the two-part story is Vandal Savage, not one of Barry's overpopulated gallery of rogues. Savage, as an immortal, seems to be the proper choice to sew together different generations. Vandal Savage is, in this scenario, a hard contrast against eventuality and flux, a villain forever frozen in time, now fighting the hero for the new age.

West's selfishness, hard capitalism, and individualism deepens after he wins the lottery at the end of issue one. The fruits of his new position as a rich young man can be seen in the following arcs. Rather than adopting an altruistic attitude (such as donating the money), West fully embraces the society of conspicuous consumption. As a consumer, he created a complete identity through commodities. He buys a mansion (that Tina McGee mentions is lifted directly from *The Colbys*, a TV spin-off of *Dynasty*) in Middle Hampton, a Lamborghini, a modern (at least, for the 1980s) entertainment system, and luxurious clothes. Part of the key to success in the yuppie world of the 1980s was the "power suit" (the business look) and West embraces it with gusto.

Besides all these symbols of upper status and capitalism, West's behavior reflects the political mindset of the era, fully embracing individualism, one of the pillars of the neoliberal thinking. Individualism is "rooted in the idea that each individual has inherent rights" (Ventura 10), especially right to private property. *Flash* #3, the first issue with West's new status as a rich young man, begins with a speeding ticket. West is driving his new Lamborghini, and after receiving the ticket his only thought is "I'm not going to let this ruin my day" (Baron, "The Kilgore"). On the next page, West comes to his mansion, where he finds a note from his girlfriend who is leaving him. While tearing the note, West's thought is the same: "I'm not going to let this ruin my day" (Baron, "The Kilgore"). West is steadfast in keeping people's safety and people's feelings at the margins. He would not let *other* people ruin *his* day, a phrase that epitomizes neoliberal individualism. The term "individualism" is ambiguous in neoliberal thinking. "Positively, it designates the independence, the originality, and energy of the singular, while negatively, and in modern age more prevalently, it signifies selfishness, greed and carelessness towards others and surroundings" (Mickunas 118). Here, Baron clearly uses the negative meaning of "individualism," with West violating the law and giving no consideration on people's feelings.

It is interesting that the same capitalist drive triggering Flash can be seen in others as well. In *Flash* #7, West heads to Russia searching for help in the treatment of Jerry McGee, now turned into a monster called "Speed Demon" after a prolonged abuse of drugs. In Russia, there is a scientist called Orloff working in a governmental station in Puleski who can help in curing McGee. Orloff is kept under surveillance by a trio of super-powered beings called Red Trinity, a Russian guard. Flash briefly battles against them but, to everyone's surprise, Red Trinity actually wants to go to America and indulge in capitalism. Indeed, in later issues, Red Trinity will be known in America as the Kapitalist Kouriers, a super-team dedicated to using their super-speed to help busy businessmen, carrying items for them across the entire globe (Baron, "Red Trinity"). In *Flash* #17, a depowered Flash asks the former Red Trinity to help him in tracking a lost person. However, the Kapitalist Kouriers explained him that they only work "for free" on Fridays (Messner-Loebs, "The Adventures…").

In brief, Wally West's life-style in the 1980s fits the Reaganomics' pro-business attitude in which making money is the only promising career for young adults. Baron's run is preoccupied with hedonism and family values— and the contradictory clash between these two highly appreciated aspects of neoliberal thinking—as West lives with both his new girlfriend (a mature married woman) and his mother, both of them constantly arguing. Soon enough, however, West is cheating on Tina with his new neighbor, Trudy (*Flash* #13), a new mark insinuating West's loss of a moral compass in favor of hedonism (Baron, "Savage Vandalism").

The last two issues by Mike Baron (#13 and #14) worked as a smooth transition to William Messner-Loebs's interests. In these last issues, Vandal Savage reappears to wreak havoc with a gang of junkies addicted to a drug created by the villain: velocity 9. Unlike his first appearance, Vandal Savage seems more mundane here, occupied with getting control of the city through spreading a new drug of his own concoction. Further, in *Flash* #14, West's mother informs him that all his money has been lost in a stock market crash and he has to move into an apartment in one of the poorest neighborhoods, thus starting a new set of adventures, now plagued by recession and urban decay (Baron, "Savage Vandalism").

...*to Rags*

Ronald Reagan was elected President with the promise of "fixing" the problems born from the agitated 1970s. The enthroning of family values answered, in part, this demand, and so did the neoliberal politics. Reagan's philosophy included the idea of "freeing Americans from big government," the implementation of tax cuts, and the ease of financial burdens for the rich, so money would eventually "trickle down" to the lower classes (Batchelor and Stoddart 10). These measures improved America's economy, and consumption increased in relation to previous years. "However, these gains were offset by geometrically larger budget deficits, lower levels of personal savings, and sluggish business investment. Ultimately, Reagan's supply-side economic policies weakened the foundation of the economy by relying on massive federal deficit" (*ibid.*). The death knell of the economic rise of the decade was the market crash which took place in October 19, 1987. Presumably, this was the market crash that made West lose his fortune. This crash increased the gap between the wealthy and the working-class. The first years of the 1980s were marked by a recession, especially strong in the working-class families, many which "never recovered, even after the economy rebounded" (Batchelor and Stoddart 14), and the crash of 1987 only worsened the plight of many families.

By the late 1980s, wages were growing slowly even for white-collar families. Unlike the recession which took place in Reagan's first term, this new crisis affected both young workers as well as established members of the workforce in their forties and fifties. As Frank Levy argued, "no one was safe" (54), not even ex-yuppie superheroes.

Messner-Loebs transforms Wally West into a young man facing economic instability and recession amidst a landscape of drugs scare and urban poverty. In this new scenario, West begins his new adventures almost homeless. This move can be seen now as an exaggerated one, but Messner-Loebs' concerns with poverty and the homelessness expressed real anxieties of the era.

In the late 1980s, the deteriorating labor market and economic conditions presented a landscape in which uneducated young men saw their dreams fading away. *Flash* #15, aptly titled "Hitting Bottom," opens with West moving out from his mansion to a low-class neighborhood. Chunk is there to help him moving out, and his observation mirror the cultural anxieties of the era. "You're smooth … clever. I always thought that you were better than me. But now you've lost your powers … you've lost your money … you only have enough cash to last you another month" (Messner-Loebs, "Hitting Bottom"). West's neighbors are unemployed men and old ladies hiding behind closed doors. Throughout Messner-Loebs' run, the entire secondary cast around West increases, now populated with working-class people trying to survive the ups and down of the daily economy. In fact, the entire neighborhood, a far cry from Middle-Hampton, seems to be a downtrodden place, where drugs and crime run amok.

In the last years of the 1980s, heroin and crack abuse (Velocity 9 is clearly modeled after the effects of crack) rose substantially (Lowinson 116), producing an increase in the number of deaths caused by drug use as well. In the problems related to crime and urban riots, drugs received priority. "The war on drugs that was launched in the United States in the mid–1980s and remained the central concern in this area at least from 1985 to 1992" (Zimring 3). One of the biggest drug abuse prevention strategies to come out of the 1980s was Nancy Reagan's "Just Say No" campaign, although it has been criticized as ineffective.

In Messner-Loeb's new exploration of the fears of the 1980s, individualism remains a dominant concern. West considers his girlfriend a burden in his life while cheating on her (or trying to do so) with a nurse in *Flash* #16. When the child of the man who evicted West is kidnapped in the same issue, the young hero chooses to do nothing to help him.

Flash was in desperate need for redemption, and some comes in *Flash* #20, the beginning of a turning point for the character. This issue takes Messner-Loebs' interest for reflecting the actual urban poverty, drugs scare and "the abandonment of modernity's project" (Villarmea Álvarez 6) to new heights. The cover by Greg LaRocque and Larry Mahlstedt depicts a battered Wally West, sitting in a corner, begging for money. The image that Messner-Loebs was trying to shape since he took the title, one of a world sunk on a deep economic crisis, comes to its climax with the cover and the story inside.

West suddenly (and only momentarily) loses his powers at the exact moment he is trying to borrow some money from friends. With an injured leg and with no money, completely hungry and angry, West tries to find some spare change lost in the streets, a clear reference to the figure of the unemployed and the homeless. He even begs for some money and food. To add another layer of decay and economic crisis, the city around West is one populated by those left in the margins of the capitalist system. The issue opens with a homeless man eating spinach stew with tiny shards of glass mixed in it after West's mom accidentally dropped the casserole to the floor. West and his mother try to dissuade him, but the hunger is overpowering and the pieces of glass can be spit out "like tiny bones" (Messner-Loebs, "Lost…"). This is only the first of many images of economic crisis haunting the city. People sleep in the stairways of low-class apartment buildings, there is constant looting lurking at the borders of the panels, derelicts drink from bottles wrapped in brown paper, people sleep in the streets, middle-age men scrape food from trash cans, tramps around a bonfire try to heat their bodies, entire families live in the parks, and junkies walk aimlessly in search of some money. The entire issue reflects the contemporary concerns on urban and human decay in a context of the social and economic crisis affecting the last years of the 1980s. There is even a comparison of the current situation with that of the Great Depression after the crash of 1929.

Further, there is a strong critique about the role of neoliberalism in those years. A depowered West, in need of some food to calm his hunger, begs for some money and sees "first hand" the consequences of the neoliberal political philosophy framing those years. Nobody stops to help West; for everyone, he (and by extension, every homeless person) is victim of this particular dire situation because of their own choices. West himself mirrors this kind of statement with one of his own: "anybody who's out on the streets isn't right," he says earlier in the issue (Messner-Loebs, "Lost…"). Poor people are poor because they do not want to fight hard enough. This set of prejudices against the poor turns them invisible, as West is now.

After West hits bottom, there is a pronounced "redemptive arc" running through the next issues. In *Flash* #23 West puts himself in danger to save friends without any ulterior motive. West finds a job as active member of the Justice League Europe (another successful series of the era) and, slowly but steadily, the urban stories start to change to reflect a more straightforward superheroic approach, with supervillains such as Abra Kadabra, Doctor Alchemy, and Gorilla Grodd replacing the gangs of superpowered junkies.

A new romantic interest appears, TV reporter Linda Park, who, rather than being just another date in a long succession of one-night stands, will eventually become Wally West's wife. The culmination of West's redemption comes with *Flash* #58, in which West is named one of the heirs of the deceased super-villain Icicle. As a way to come to terms with a life of crimes, the Icicle decided to give Flash some of his money (much to the dismay of the villain's relatives), a form of compensation for past felonies. West decides to use his money to build a Barry Allen Foundation to help the people who had fell out of the system (Messner-Loebs, "The Barry Allen Foundation"). The Pied Piper, an ex-villain with socialist ideas, warmly agreed with West. The issue is the perfect reverse of Flash' initial issues: there, West used his money to conform the yuppie's image of social status. Now, he wants to use his money to help people who have lost everything. Thus, the redemptive arc is complete and West's selfish image, so atone with the era, is now a thing from the past.

Conclusions

Crisis on Infinite Earths proved itself to be the perfect tabula rasa to a new breed of heroes, now more related to new readers and new times. Some readers, such as Brian Drow in the letters' section of *Flash* #17, were thankful for making young Wally West completely *human* (emphasis in the letter) thanks to his mistakes and fully "realistic" behavior.

The "realistic" approach taken with Wally West, now the new Flash, served two purposes: first, to anchor the young man into the 1980s and the neoliberal mindset of the era. Second, to create a slow redemptive act in latter issues. Still, one can question if this was really the idea that Mike Baron had in mind when delineating the new Flash. The redemption started so late in the game that it can be argued that, rather than been a complicated scheme planned by Baron and Messner-Loebs, both authors simply follow the flux of times. In fact, Vandal Savage's rants about cleaning the city of "junkies, delinquents, trash" in *Flash* #50 (Messner-Loebs, "The Fastest…") predates for some years the philosophy of Rudolph William Giuliani and his "broken windows theory"—that is to say, the idea that tolerating minor physical and social disorder in a neighborhood (such as graffiti paintings or litter) encourages violent crime. West's run to the glory is not just his coming to terms with his new status, but, also, the acknowledgment of the people around him—family, friends, girlfriends and the people turned invisible amidst a gray city.

NOTE

1. History has not been kind to these once-dominant television programs and readers may find the idea of Roseanne Barr and Bill Cosby jockeying for supremacy in popular

culture is a strange concept, demonstrating the way popular perceptions of individuals and franchises can change through time. Both shows have suffered due to the poor choices of the titular stars. At the time of this writing, Bill Cosby is standing trial for sexual assault, and Roseanne Barr was recently fired from a popular relaunch of her show due to her incendiary social media presence.

WORKS CITED

BBaron, Mike (w), and Mike Collins (a). "Savage Vandalism." *Flash* V.2 #13 (June 1988). New York: DC Comics. Print.

aron, Mike (w), and Jackson Guice (a). "The Chunk." *Flash* V.2 #9 (February 1988). New York: DC Comics. Print.

_____. "Chunk Barges In." *Flash* V.2 #11 (April 1988). New York: DC Comics. Print.

_____. "Happy Birthday Wally!" *Flash* V.2 #1 (June 1987). New York: DC Comics. Print.

_____. "Hearts of Stone." *Flash* V.2 #2 (July 1987). New York: DC Comics. Print.

_____. "The Kilgore." *Flash* V.2 #3 (August 1987). New York: DC Comics. Print.

_____. "Kill the Kilgore." *Flash* V.2 #4 (September 1987). New York: DC Comics. Print.

_____. "Red Trinity." *Flash* V.2 #7 (September 1987). New York: DC Comics. Print.

_____. "Speed McGee." *Flash* V.2 #5 (October 1987). New York: DC Comics. Print.

Batchelor, Bob, and Scott Stoddart. *The 1980s*. Westport, CT: Greenwood, 2007. Print.

Berman, Milton (Ed.). *The Eighties in America,* Vol.1. Pasadena, CA: Salem Press, Inc. 2008. Print.

Bignell, Jonathan. *An Introduction to Television Studies*. New York: Routledge, 2004. Print.

Faludi, Susan. *Backlash: The Undeclared War Against American Women*. New York: Random House LLC, 2006. Print.

Harrison, Colin. *American Culture in the 1990s*. Edinburgh: Edinburgh University Press, 2010. Print.

Hayward, Steven. *The Age of Reagan: The Conservative Counterrevolution: 1980–1989*. New York: Crown Forum, 2009. Print.

Horowitz, Daniel. *Happier?: The History of a Cultural Movement That Aspired to Transform America*. New York: Oxford University Press, 2018. Print.

Klock, Geoff. *How to Read Superhero Comics and Why*. New York: Continuum, 2002. Print.

Levi, Frank. *The New Dollars and Dreams: American Incomes in the Late 1990s*. New York: Russell Sage Foundation, 1998. Print.

Lowinson, Joyce, et al. *Substance Abuse: A Comprehensive Textbook*. Philadelphia: Wolters Kluwer, 2005. Print.

Messner-Loebs, William (w), and Greg LaRocque (a). "The Adventures of Speed McGee." *Flash* V.2 #16 (September 1988). New York: DC Comics. Print.

_____. "The Adventures of Speed McGee, part 2." *Flash* V.2 #17 (October 1988). New York: DC Comics. Print.

_____. "Channels of Love and Fear." *Flash* V.2 #37 (April 1990). New York: DC Comics. Print.

_____. "Fast Friends." *Flash* V.2 #53 (August 1991). New York: DC Comics. Print.

_____. "Hitting Bottom." *Flash* V.2 #15 (August 1988). New York: DC Comics. Print.

_____. "Like a Straw in a Hurricane." *Flash* V.2 #23 (March 1989). New York: DC Comics. Print.

_____. "Lost, Worthless, and Forgotten." *Flash* V.2 #20 (January. 1989). New York: DC Comics. Print.

Messner-Loebs, William (w), and Jim Mooney (a). "Rogues Reunion." *Flash* V.2 #19 (December 1988). New York: DC Comics. Print.

Messner-Loebs, William (w), and Gordon Purcell (a). "The Barry Allen Foundation." *Flash* V.2 #58 (January 1992). New York: DC Comics. Print.

_____. "The Clipper Returns." *Flash* V.2 #23 (February 1989). New York: DC Comics. Print.

_____. "The Comfort of a Stranger." *Flash* V.2 #31 (October 1989). New York: DC Comics. Print.

_____. "The Fastest Man Alive." *Flash* V.2 #50 (May 1991). New York: DC Comics. Print.

_____. "Nobody Dies." *Flash* V.2 #54 (September 1991). New York: DC Comics. Print.

Mickunas, Algis. "Globalization, Neoliberalism, and the Spread of Economic Violence: The Framework of Civilizational Analysis." *Neoliberalism, Economic Radicalism, and the Normalization of Violence.* Ed. Vicente Berdayes and John W. Murphy. New York: Springer, 2016. 107–126. Print.

Rossinow, Doug. *The Reagan Era: A History of the 1980s.* New York: Columbia University Press, 2017. Print.

Shary, Timothy. *Generation Multiplex: The Image of Youth in Contemporary American Cinema.* Austin: University of Texas Press, 2002. Print.

Ventura, Patricia. *Neoliberal Culture: Living with American Neoliberalism.* New York: Routledge, 2012. Print.

Villarmea Álvarez, Iván. *Documenting Cityscapes: Urban Change in Contemporary Non-Fiction Film.* London: Wallflower Press, 2015. Print.

Wandtke, Terrence. *The Meaning of Superhero Comic Books.* Jefferson, NC: McFarland, 2012. Print.

Wolfman, Marv. "Introduction." In *Crisis on Infinite Earths.* New York: DC Comics, 2000. Print.

Zimring, Franklin. *American Youth Violence.* Oxford: Oxford University Press, 1998. Print.

Wrestling with Legacy

How "The Return of Barry Allen" Shaped DC Superheroes in the 1990s

Tom Shapira

> "So you see, I became the super-fast Flash on my Earth much as you became the Flash on yours. Indeed, reading of your Flash adventures inspired me to assume the secret identity of the Flash."—Gardner Fox, "Flash of Two Worlds," The Flash #123 (September 1959)

> "Weaker talent idealizes; figures of capable imagination appropriate for themselves."—Harold Bloom, *The Anxiety of Influence*

Superhero comics are a unique artifact in their relation to the dimension of time. As Umberto Eco noted—"[...] a confused notion of time is the only condition which makes the story credible" (19). This is something that has become so inherent to the genre within the medium that fans learned to take as a given that time moves for the fictional world but not for its inhabitants. Spider-man, for example, has been fighting crime since the 1960s and yet Peter Parker has aged barely a decade (from teenagehood to semi-adulthood), and his acquaintance, Flash Thompson, served in the U.S. military in both the Vietnam War and in the Iraq War—both times as a fresh recruit.

Try to imagine other genres operating in the same manner—how odd it would seem if detective fiction was still ruled, to this day, by Sherlock Holmes, whose adventures are now written by people who were not yet born when Arthur Conan Doyle died and who would operate in 21st century England as if they had not lived through a century's worth of events. Even though there have been many further adventures of Sherlock Holmes, written by fans and professionals and even family (*The Exploits of Sherlock Holmes* collection was co-written by Doyle's youngest son, Adrian Conan Doyle), none of them come close to displacing the original stories. It is not simply Sherlock Holmes that is revered, it is Sherlock Holmes as written by Sir Arthur Conan Doyle.

For many years when it came to superhero comics, it was the characters rather than specific creators or plots that have been the selling point. The publishers are encouraged to keep the same characters in circulation, and to keep these characters in the same status quo that represents them at their highest commercial value. Thus Superman cannot be killed (without getting better), nor can he be allowed to grow old, or retire, or lose a limb or even grow a mustache. Anytime a company or a writer tries to change something fundamental about Superman the readers know it's only a matter of time before things revert to the way-it-has-always-been. Comics Critic Douglas Wolk refers to this as "the illusion of real and lasting change" (103). A superhero character is like a rubber band, you can only stretch him so far before he either returns to his original state or breaks entirely.

In his "The Myth of Superman" (1972), Umberto Eco recognizes Superman (and by extension, all superheroes) as part of the mythic structure once reserved for the gods of old:

> The mythological character of comic strips finds himself in this singular situation: he must be an archetype, the totality of certain collective aspirations, and therefore, he must necessarily become immobilized in an emblematic and fixed nature which renders him easily recognizable (this is what happens to Superman); but since he is marketed in the sphere of a "romantic" production for a public that consumes "romances," he must be subjected to a development which is typical, as we have seen, of novelistic characters [15].

Another appropriate title to Eco's article, if it had not been already taken, might have been "The Myth of Sisyphus": like the Greek hero of old Superman is bound to relive the same life unto eternity. When Superman first made the transition to the silver screen in the form of animated shorts his adventures began with the apt tagline "fighting a never-ending battle for truth and justice."

The problem of allowing change within a fictional structure that is antithetical to the concept of growth is exactly the subject of "The Return of Barry Allen"—a six issue storyline, taking up issues #74–79 of The Flash Volume 2, by writer Mark Waid, penciler Greg La Rocque and Inker Roy Richardson. It is a work which was highly regarded at the time and now, in retrospect, is seminal. Waid and La Rocque's story set the tone and theme for much of the content of late 1990s and early 2000s DC Comics. Without "The Return of Barry Allen" storyline there is no Starman, Hourman, Stars and STRIPE, JSA and many other revivals of long forgotten characters—revivals that put new names and faces behind old masks and mantles.

After an encounter with the recently resurrected Barry Allen, Wally West laments, "He accused me of usurping his legacy… replacing him in the hearts and minds of the public. I tried to reassure him. I told him we were a team. He spat in my face… and left me to die" (Waid, "The Once…"). West, the third man to carry the identity of "The Flash" *idolizes* Barry, but Barry seems to hate West, and also hates the idea that someone would try and replace him.

There's a metafictional quality to the line, the "hearts and minds of the public." The people West is talking about are the fictional citizens of the DC Comics Universe, but he might as well be talking about the very real readers of *The Flash* comics series who were still grappling with Wally West starring in the title. After all, Barry Allen carried the Flash name and costume for almost thirty years; generations of comics readers grew up on his adventures. Putting Wally West in the crimson tights, even though he served as Allen's sidekick Kid-Flash for decades beforehand, must have felt *wrong* somehow. So when issue #73 hit the stands it seemed like an attempt to fix an obvious misstep. In a Christmas story dubbed "One Perfect Gift" readers got what they begged for: Barry Allen was back, entering through the front door with a warm smile and the light of the moon giving his head a near-halo effect, a resurrection worthy of Christ. Breaking from the ever present first person caption boxes, an omnipresent narrator informs the readers "Sometimes you do get what you wish for!" (Waid, "One Perfect…").

It's an interesting assumption that even after 73 issues with Wally West as the lead most readers still harbored a secret (or even not-so-secret) desire to see Barry Allen back in the book. Many of the issues since Mark Waid took over as a writer dealt with West's insecurities in the role, with his self-perceived inability to fill Barry's boots. Waid and La Rocque's vision of Barry Allen, filtered through the eyes and words of star-stricken Wally West, was that of a saint. Of course he should return, Wally West kept telling the readers that he was not fit to wear that costume.

But that story-arc turned out to be something else entirely. Alan Moore once said that "it's not the job of the artist to give the audience what the audience wants…. It is the job of artists to give the audience what they need." (*The Mindscape…*) If the audience claimed what they *wanted* was for Barry to return what they *needed* was to accept that he wouldn't, he couldn't (at least for now). The returned Barry quickly turns angry and violent, at a certain point lashing out at his former protégé before leaving him for dead in a deadly trap and starting a terror campaign against his own city for daring to allow other Flashes beside himself.

Wally West tries to stop Barry Allen's unexpectedly villainous turn, but he cannot. At first it seems that the problem is merely physical, that Allen is faster, but as the storyline progress it becomes clear that West's problem is a mental one; it's not that he is unable to run as fast Barry, it's that he does not (on a subconscious level) wish to diminish his hero/father figure. To see Barry turn into a villain is one thing, but to see him as someone *lesser* is something else entirely. In a dialogue with older speedster Max Mercury, West is forced to grapple with his own unwillingness to transcend his former mentor:

> WALLY WEST: No One can tell me that I'm afraid of speed! I love what I do!
>
> MAX MERCURY: But you love your uncle Barry even more. That's why you took his name and costume, isn't it? In a sense you did it so the world won't forget him… or his heroism. You keep saying you don't want to replace Barry but the moment you become as fast as him… that's exactly what you'll have done [Waid, "Blitzkreig"].

As the story draws to a close the now demented "Barry Allen" is revealed to have been the time traveling supervillain Professor Zoom, The Reverse Flash, the only enemy Barry Allen has ever killed (Bates). Zoom was originally a fan of Barry Allen from the far future who traveled to the past in hopes of meeting his hero. But he missed his mark and arrived after Barry's death, learning that he is destined to become not the Flash's partner but his greatest enemy. The shock of the time travel along with the psychological shock of realizing what he is destined to become sent him over the edge and made him believe that he is Barry Allen.

Despite being a villain, Zoom's admiration for Barry Allen is an honest one; he truly does believe him to be the greatest man to carry the mantle of the Flash. Zoom broke the very borders of time to be with Allen. The subject of "The Return of Barry Allen" is the way this reverence for something good can be so easily perverted, how with zealously towards something, good can itself become evil. By putting Barry Allen on a pedestal Zoom effectively closes the lid on any possibility of change. In a telling early scene, the seventh page of issue #74, Allen reacts with a sneer to the discovery that one of his former villains, The Pied Piper, has reformed and that West doesn't actually bother with keeping a secret identity. It's a small moment—La Roque does not overplay the gesture—but we can see a hint of the sneer remains on the second panel after West explains to the older Flash that "times change, Barry…. And so do people" (Waid, "Trust"). The sneer is aimed not so much at a former villain (one of the recurring themes of the various incarnations of *The Flash* comics is that he often has a rather friendly relation with many members of his "rogues gallery") but at the very idea of change.

In the story Zoom becomes a mirror image of the type of fan who would not accept Wally West as the Flash simply because he is not Barry Allen and thus can never be *their* Flash—the type of fan who sees change as inherently bad. It is fitting that West defeats him not by simply beating him up physically, but by sending Zoom back to his own time, erasing his memory of the last few days, so that he will one day go back to past and die by (the real) Barry Allen's hand. Zoom's true destiny is history—he has no place in the present—because things must change. To hammer the point home the Green Lantern Hal Jordan (himself destined to be replaced by a young upstart in a few years' time), a longtime friend of Allen, tells West—"I used to say [Barry Allen] was the greatest hero I'd ever known. But that was before I saw a man put his life on the line... just to preserve his legend" (Waid, "The Once...").

In case the readers didn't fully comprehend the authorial intent, the letters page of that issue also contained an afterword for the storyline by Mark Waid: "...in the end we came to realize that "The Return of Barry Allen" wasn't about Barry Allen at all. It was about Wally West, a good man who Brian [Augustin, the book's editor] and I both believed is capable of equaling [...] his uncle's legacy" (Waid, "The Once..."). It is not a story about the importance of the father, but of the ascendance of the son.

Born of Darkness

It is important to put things in context, and the context of superhero comic books in the early 1990s was an odd one: the timeless nature of these characters, of that genre, caught up with them. Throughout the 1980s came a series of works that deconstructed either specific titles or the medium as a whole—*Watchmen*, by Alan Moore and Dave Gibbons is the most prominent one in public memory—but there were also others (*Miracleman*, *The Dark Knight Returns*).

While "deconstruction" became an overused terms in comics criticism it's important to recall the original meaning, as coined by Deridda in his *Positions*:

> To "deconstruct" philosophy, thus, would be to think—in the most faithful, interior way—the structured genealogy of philosophy's concepts, but at the same time to determine—from a certain exterior that is unqualifiable or unnamable by philosophy—what this history has been able to dissimulate or forbid, making itself into a history by means of this ... motivated repression [Derrida].

Derida speaks of trying to form new philosophy from an old one, without rejecting or re-writing its forefather utterly. In the case of superhero comics, to "deconstruct" is to write a story that operates within genre while exposing its weak points.

One can read the deconstructionist movement in comics as a representation of Harold Bloom's theory of *Anxiety of Influence*. While someone like Bloom has little interest in the field of comics, especially the inherently derivative work of superhero comics, we can see in the works of Moore, Miller and Milligan a strong desire to not only reject but to destroy their (literary) fathers: Moore wrote *Whatever Happened to the Man of Tomorrow* which was meant as "the last Superman story" (clearing the ground for the then upcoming reboot of the character under John Byrne) while Miller made Batman into an old man. If they could, just maybe, force the characters out of the way, it would free them from the shackles of the older generations.

When *Watchmen* concludes the godlike Doctor Manhattan, until then a prisoner of the narrative (able to conceive his own existence in a comic book like form—knowing the fate of the story yet unable to change it), leaves the world of super heroes to create life. He is the reader of superhero comics who had grown tired of them, who went on to create something new and different, just as Moore later did (although Moore's attempt at non-superhero work turned out not to be as financially successful and he found himself returning to the genre several years later). It is just as Bloom said of the poet—forever in debt for the past yet eternally seeking to escape it, to create something free of its influence: "for every poet begins (however "unconsciously") by rebelling more strongly against the consciousness of death's necessity than all other men and women do" (Bloom, 10).

The comic books and graphic novels mentioned above "deconstruct" the notion of superhero by bringing up uncomfortable truths that fans and creators have been conditioned for years not to notice. After *Watchmen* it was hard not to see the underlying misogyny and fascism in the heart of the heroic fantasy. After *Miracleman* it was impossible not to think about all the censored violence that was probably the byproduct of superhero battles in the heart of major metropolitan areas. After *The Dark Knight Returns*, with its greying Batman that looked like he actually lived the fifty years since the character's 1939 origin, the dimension of time came into sharp focus.

These characters grew old without growing up, without changing. They had become static. *Dark Knight Returns* is often read as the triumph of Batman: He stands over the beaten Superman, gloating about his superiority and "letting" the Man of Steel appear as the winner in the public's eye (Miller). But to read it like that is to ignore that Bruce Wayne wins by letting "The Batman" die. He sheds the cape and cowl to start a new world underground—a world intentionally populated by the young who will replace him.

Being replaced by the young and accepting change is also the subject of the other famous Mark Waid written comics of the 1990s, the four issue miniseries *Kingdom Come*, drawn in the recognizable photorealistic style of Alex Ross. Like "The Return of Barry Allen" the series also begins as a simple act of reverence for the past. The new breed of superheroes that has replaced the old guard are presented as dangerous lunatics and the return of Superman is seen as something akin to the rebirth of Jesus. But once the old guard *does* come back, establishing domination over the young, we see that they to do not possess all the answers—just like their predecessors, they also surrender to eternal bickering (Waid, *Kingdom Come*).

Kingdom Come ends with Superman, Batman and Wonder Woman sitting in a diner talking, except it's not Superman, Batman and Wonder Woman, it's Bruce, Clark and Diana that sit down to eat and chat. They have each given up the costume and mantle. Furthermore Bruce even notes that the ageless Diana actually shows signs of physical change for the first time in a millennia: she is pregnant with Clark's child—"for an ageless amazon of perfect physique, you've put on a pound or two" (Waid, *Kingdome Come*) notes Bruce in the first panel of page 210. The next panel focuses on Diana's hair, showing several grey streaks. All of them have gotten out of the "fixed nature," as Eco called it, of superhero comics.

That is not to say that there will be no more superheroes, for that is the end of *Watchmen*, but that they will be new superheroes for a new world. *Kingdom Come* is not as successful in its task: partly because the writing, which seek to humble the gods of old, sometimes feels at cross purposes with the art, which constantly elevates them, and partly because the story often feels over excited with itself. Taking effort to cram in every possible character in the foreground or background, *Kingdom Come* can often feel more like a character catalogue than a story, with hundreds of new heroes and villains. Even with its faults its influence is undeniable; the story was massively popular, receiving multiple collected editions, and remains in print to this day. Together with "The Return of Barry Allen" it positioned Mark Waid as a writer who tries to find a "solution" to the problem of post–*Watchmen* superheroes.

While *Watchmen* was busy changing the way superheroes were understood another 12 issue series running through 1986 was changing the way the fictional universe they inhabited was operating. *Crisis on Infinite Earths* (written by Marve Wolfman, with art by George Perez, Dick Giordano, Jerry Ordway and others) was about the destruction of the DC "multiverse" (a fictional structure of all possible variations of the company's various superheroes) and its replacement by a single, supposedly more coherent, universe. This was done, at least partly, as an exercise in house cleaning—stemming from the belief that having several different versions of Superman and Batman confuses the readers. This streamlined universe would, hopefully, allow DC to overtake their across town rivals Marvel Comics in the sales department.

Crisis on Infinite Earths may have been a cynical exercise, but it did offer something that seemed impossible before: a blank slate, a chance to update the universe that had become old and stagnate. As Wolfman wrote in his introduction to the collected edition, "Every generation of comic book readers deserves to have the comics belong to them, not to their older siblings and parents" ("Introduction"). Critic Mark Sobel noted that Alan Moore did not share Wolfman's optimism, instead seeing *Crisis on Infinite Earths* as something coarse, paving over the bones of the past to make room for some vulgar new generation. In response to that bloated crossover he wrote a short story called "In Pictopia" with artist Don Simpson (originally published in 1986 in the short lived anthology *Anything Goes* and later republished fully in Sobel's book *Brighter Than You Think*). "In Pictopia" follows the inhabitant of a fictional town which represents the history of comics, a Mandrake the Magician type, who sees his home destroyed and is farther horrified when one of his old friends gets "rewritten" as an edgy, punk-ish, superhero type—"It wasn't Flynn, I thought, "this is Flynn's replacement!" (Moore, "In Pictopia").

Ignoring Moore's own influence on the creation of that type of superhero, even if unintentionally, Sobel's interpretation of Moore puts him as one of the old superheroes from *Kingdom Come* looking from above at the younger generation, sneering at how far they have fallen. But the grotesqueries of Moore's old magician might as well simply be a new norm. As the superheroine Harbinger notes towards the end of *Crisis on Infinite Earths*: "...we should never forget the past, but we should always look to the future... because that's where we're going to spend the rest of our lives" (Wolfman, "Final Crisis").

But if Wolfman and Perez intended to usher a new age of heroes they seemed to have missed their mark. In the wake of *Crisis on Infinite Earths* the reading public mostly got rehashed versions of the characters they already knew. The characters were tweaked to a lesser or greater degree, but still essentially the same. One exception was the Flash, who was replaced by his own sidekick. Waid's long run on the character is essentially about growing up. His first story-arc, *Year One*, was an exploration of West's childhood, and later issues saw him grapple with the weight of adulthood. *The Flash* #88, "Mean Streak," has Flash confronted by a woman who suffered horrific injuries during his fights with a supervillain weeks before, which began a long streak of West learning that for all his powers he cannot save everyone (Waid, "Mean Streak").

It is a familiar trope for superhero comics—this is one of the cornerstones of too many Spider-Man stories to count—but with *The Flash* title it ties back to the idea of post–*Watchmen* comics: West learning to deal with his own limitations serves as a metaphor for the superhero genre accepting the lessons of deconstruction, realizing its own faults. *Watchmen* charged that, at least partially, the superheroes black-and-white morality no longer holds in a complex world. *The Flash* then becomes a story about trying to reconcile the faults of oneself, and therefore one's fathers, without forgoing all their positive qualities.

As the series progressed Waid introduced several of West's possible future replacements, such as Impulse and Jesse Quick, and kept him interacting with previous speedsters like Jack Garrick and Max Mercury. The point of all these meetings and team-ups was to show that West himself was not expected to keep the role permanently—one day he will be replaced by a newer Flash. The subject of legacy remained at the forefront of the title as long as Waid was helming it and, as he explained in a retrospective interview, it was something that was essential to the series even before he came in. "I think there's something about the idea that power that ability runs in the family. No pun intended. A little bit of a pun intended. I think that's also because the Flash as a character has a bit of a legacy of heralding a new age in comics" (Salvatore).

Waid speaks here about Barry Allen's own introduction in *Showcase #4* (October 1956)—which is considered, unofficially, as the beginning of the Silver Age of comics. In Allen's origin story he is inspired by the adventures of the first Flash, Jay Garrick (here presented as just a fictional character in a comic book), to become a superhero himself after a freak lab accident gives him similar superpowers. There is no family connection between the two Flashes and they would only meet each other three years later in *Flash #123*, but one is still considered a worthy heir to the other. Barry Allen, as Waid argues, was meant to signify a progression, a move forward from the old icons (while never forgetting they existed). The only proper way to show respect to his spirit is not by keeping him alive forever, but rather by keeping that legacy moving ever forward.

A Family Affair

Wrestling with one's legacy became one of the leading themes within the DC Universe throughout the late 1990's. Reading throughout that decade one could almost see a slow wave building, as the critical success of "The Return of Barry Allen" got translated into the macrocosm of the DC Universe. *Starman* (1994), written by James Robinson, was all about family and legacy and how these two things intermingle. The series starts with Jack Knight, the son of the original Golden Age Starman, Ted Knight, taking up the identity of his father—after his brother was killed on the job.

Unlike Wally West, Jack Knight's journey is a reluctant one, done at first out of necessity (his life and the fate of the city being in danger) and later as a form of family therapy with the father he didn't want to know. Along the way he discovers hidden connections to other characters that also bore the name "Starman" including a blue-skinned freak locked in a circus for the strange, an alien prince of a faraway empire, a future member of The Legion of Superheroes and others.

If "The Return of Barry Allen" was about helping fans to accept the importance of change, *Starman* approaches the problem from the other end. *Starman* is about learning to appreciate the old things. It is no mistake, and might be too blunt of a choice, that Jack Knight's civilian identity is that of a junk dealer, a man who can always find value in what others discard. It's a series-long letter to the fans who only want their comics to be hip and modern, who are embarrassed about the gaudy bright costumes, telling them that they can find great things in the past.

In its way, *Starman* is also a response to "In Pictopia." If Moore feared that a new breed of heroes meant the destruction of what came before, that from now on they will only exist as a bastardized version of their former self, *Starman* seeks to connect all versions into a grand tapestry. The main difference between the 1990's series of *The Flash* and *Starman* is that the former assumes reverence to the past while the latter believes it must be earned.

It's interesting to compare both "The Return of Barry Allen" and *Starman*, with the 1994 version of *Green Lantern*. In *Green Lantern*, the established main character, Hal Jordan, turns evil and is swiftly replaced by the young Kyle Rayner, who is given the ring of power by the last Guardian of the Universe in an act of desperation. "You shall have to do" Jordan tells the surprised Rayner as he hands over to him one of the most powerful weapons in the universe (Marz 31). This new version of the character quickly earned the ire of many of the older fans. The grand irony of it all is that Hal Jordan himself was introduced in a similarly callous manner, in *Showcase #22* (October 1959) with a brand new origin story and no pretense that there ever was a Golden Age Green Lantern before him (Broome).

In part the rage directed towards Rayner as Green Lantern likely has to do with the timing. The World Wide Web was becoming more common and fans that would've previously simmered alone were able to share their frustration with like-minded fans in AOL Chat rooms. There was even a website for the pro–Hal/anti–Kyle movement called HEAT (Hal's Emerald Advancement Team), a site which still functions to this very day at glheat.tripod.com. But the hostility towards Kyle was also, at least somewhat, tied to the context of his appearance in DC Comics. Rayner was narratively linked not only to the degradation of the previous holder of the title (Jordan turned into a supervillain in order to clear the way) but also to the wholesale destruction of the Green Lantern Corps as a concept. It wasn't simply that Kyle was not a legacy character; he is in essence anti-legacy. He was younger than Hal, his hair was spiky (as was the fashion at the time), the classic eye-slit mask was replaced by a thick visor, the costume was different and the attitude was different. He was that thing the old Magician was dreading in Moore's "In Pictopia"—"The costume was similar, but with slight modifications. The visor looked more sinister somehow" (Moore, "In Pictopia").

If the superhero is meant to represent something to which the reader can aspire one can almost understand the anger towards Kyle Rayner. He represented, to the older fans, not only the replacement of the past but the full erasure of it. As O'Brien tells the helpless Winston in George Orwell's *1984*: "Nothing will remain of you: not a name in a register, not a memory in a living brain. You will be annihilated in the past as well as in the future. You will never have existed" (Orwell).

Attempts to placate older fans were made, if not in the *Green Lantern* book itself, then in other titles. In a 1996 issue of *Green Arrow*, itself having recently replaced the original archer Oliver Queen with his son Connor Hawk, the two younger emerald heroes allow themselves a short bonding session over the difficulties of carrying on their shoulders such a mighty burden.

> GREEN LANTERN: You're Oliver Queen's son?
> GREEN ARROW: Guilty. The whole Green Arrow thing is kind of in my blood.
> GREEN LANTERN: The only thing [Hal Jordan] and I had in common is this ring. And maybe the desire to do what's right [Dixon, "Bad Blood"].

As written by Chuck Dixon and drawn by Rodolfio Damaggio this short scene focuses on the similarities between Hal and Kyle rather than the differences; it is an attempt to give the new character legitimacy fans thought he lacked. It is *not* the blood that counts, it's the actions. Connor Hawk himself, despite being the son of the previous title holder is a bastard, a child born out of wedlock without the father's knowledge. Similarly, Wally West is also not a blood kin to Barry Allen (being merely the nephew of his girlfriend at the time of his introduction).

That Kyle was as uncertain about his own worthiness just as much as the fans became a cornerstone of his characterization within the 1990's *JLA* (Justice League of America) run, written by Grant Morrison and drawn by Howard Porter. Green Lantern was portrayed as a newbie among a cast of seasoned professionals who never quite felt himself up to the task until issue #41 (which sees Morrison and Porter leave the series). In a scene that feels like a mirror of "The Return of Barry Allen," it is now Wally West who gives his blessing to the young Kyle Rayner, telling him that he is indeed worthy of the name and legacy:

> WALLY WEST: You Look rough, Kyle, but…. I can't believe I'm saying this… you look like Green Lantern, man.
> KYLE RAYNER: Yeah. Finally starting to feel like him too [Morrison, "Mageddon"].

In both scenes the outside validation also serves to enforce what the characters already knew about themselves. As Bloom noted: "Though all such discovery is a self-recognition, indeed a second birth, and ought, in the pure good of theory, to be accomplished in a perfect solipsism, it is an act never complete in itself…. For the poet is condemned learn his profoundest yearnings through the awareness of *other selves*" (Bloom, 25–6).

Morrison carried the themes of legacy introduced by *The Flash* forward with the Justice League–centered crossover event *DC One Million*. Various DC heroes are visited by their doppelgangers from the 853rd century (not a million years in the future, rather—the century in which monthly DC titles will reach their one million issue if they continue regular publication). While other characters of the future JLA (Justice Legion Alpha) are from the 853rd century and appearing in the crossover for the first time, their version of the Flash is actually John Fox, a future speedster from the 27th century who made his first appearance in the Mark Waid scripted "Flash Special #1" in 1990. Morrison acknowledges that there's something unique about the connection between the various Flashes as established by Waid.

Though Jack Knight is in space at the time *DC One Million* takes place, his father gets to make the subtext explicit, and make it in a conversation with the original Flash Jay Garrick. Featuring the Golden Age Flash and Starman together ties together the two family-obsessed titles. The Golden Age Starman says, "It validates everything we fought for, Jay. Whatever happens, we now know that good prevails in the end. That dream we had, that stupid idea when we were young, that we could make things better… it all comes true, Jay" (Morrison, "Riders").

The true impact of "The Return of Barry Allen" and of Mark Waid's *Flash* run as a whole was not felt fully until 1999. In that year DC began publishing new series rooted in the Golden Age legacy of DC Comics. These included titles focused on Hourman, Doctor Mid-Nite, JSA and even the Star-Spangled Kid. *Stars and STRIPE,* the series that focused on the Star-Spangled Kid, is an especially interesting case in that context, as it was written by Geoff Jones (who would become one of the most prominent writers of DC in the 2000s—helming runs on Superman, Green Lantern, the Flash and the Justice League), and it resurrected a legacy not many cared, or even knew about. The Star-Spangled Kid was a mostly forgotten Golden Age character only notable in being co-created by Jerry Siegel of Superman fame and in being a rare case of a child character with an adult sidekick, "Stripesy."

Rarer still is the fact that the sidekick became the linking chain between the original and the resurrected version. *Stars and STRIPE* follows the adventures of the older Stripesy, Pat Dugan, and his adopted daughter, Courtney Whitmore, who takes on The Star-Spangled Kid name. In issue #12 Mike Dugan, the real son of Pat Dugan, wants to claim the title of the Star-Spangled Kid for himself. According to Mike, he deserves to hold the title because he is a direct blood descendent of a heroic legacy, while Courtney has just lucked into it by adoption. "This is about blood. About family. […] I deserve it. You don't" (Johns, "Dragon Food").

Stars and STRIPE makes the claim that legacy is something to be earned, not given, that blood is not enough. Courtney works hard for the legacy while

Mike Dugan simply expects to have it handed over, which is why she ends up with name. Note that, unlike Zoom, Mike learns to accept Courtney. That is a watershed moment, and it signifies the full acceptance of the philosophy behind "The Return of Barry Allen"—that change is necessary for the survival of the title, that superheroes need to adapt to their time.

Johns, transferring to the *JSA* (Justice Society of America) title as *Stars and STRIPE* and *Starman* were winding down, added a link to the chain by inserting a brief appearance from the future Courtney as Starwoman, showing that the concept of legacy is evolving. Johns, after Waid, is not trying to introduce a canonical "final" version of the character. Johns expects that the character would one day move beyond its current role, that the legacy might change in unexpected ways. Starman becomes Stargirl becomes Starwoman becomes Starboy becomes Starman again; all versions are equally valid. Legacy becomes not a chain but a net cast both far *and* wide into the future and deep space, beyond family, beyond blood.

Comics' critic Chris Sims referred to the unique sensation of that period—"In the '90s, the entire DC Universe felt like it was moving forward, and a lot of that had to do with what was going on in the Flash" (Sims). For decades comics fans *knew* with certainty that some things cannot, will not, change. But after "The Return of Barry Allen" it felt like that fictional world could finally move forward. The children were allowed to grow up.

End of an Era

That version of the DC Universe was abandoned in the late 2000s. Ironically, it was the work of Geoff Jones which possibly did more than any other to reverse the tides of changes he helped to engineer. The 2004 series *Green Lantern: Rebirth*, written by Johns and drawn by Ethan Van Sciver, brought back Hal Jordan, dead for over a decade, as *the* Green Lantern. Five years later Johns would write *The Flash: Rebirth* which re-established Barry Allen as the Flash (the character having been resurrected following the *Final Crisis* storyline). Legacy began to move backwards with the younger generation giving in to their predecessors.

When Batman "died" in *Final Crisis*, just as Barry Allen was being brought back, there was no pretense that his replacement, Dick Grayson (the first Robin), was going to be permanent. Grayson had been allowed to "graduate" from Robin into the more adult identity of Nightwing, but it was made clear to the readers that while Grayson would don the cowl for a time, Batman is, was, and always will be Bruce Wayne.

Writer Grant Morrison, the man behind both *Final Crisis* and the *Batman* series at the time, inserted an oft repeated reference that "Batman and

Robin will never die!" into his stories (Morrison, "Midnight"). But when Waid wrote about the Flash legacy stretching for eternity he wrote about a role, not about a man. These new-old versions took characters back to the Eco model, back to the "fixed position." Batman and Robin will never die because Bruce Wayne will never be *allowed* to die. He is too big, too important. Thus it was decided, even if only subconsciously, that what works for the biggest icons, Batman and Superman, must work for all other characters. All DC superheroes must revert to what the creators at the time believed to be their "classic" mode.

And so change was averted. But for an unexpected period it felt, against all expectations of the genre and medium, that it was possible. That in the future lies not only the same old characters but also something new.

WORKS CITED

Bates, Cary (w), and Carmine Infantino (a). "The Slayer and the Slain!" *The Flash #324* (August 1983). NY: DC Comics.

Bloom, Harold. *The Anxiety of Influence: A Theory of Poetics.* 2nd Edition. New York, Oxford: Oxford University Press, 1997.

Broome, John (w), and Gil Kane (a). "SOS Green Lantern." *Showcase #22* (October 1959). New York: DC Comics.

Derrida, Jacques. *Positions.* Alan Bass, trans. Chicago: University of Chicago Press, 1981.

Dixon, Chuck (w), and Damaggio Rodolfo (a). "Bad Blood." *Green Arrow #104* (January 1996). New York: DC Comics. 13.

Eco, Umberto. "The Myth of Superman." *Diacritics, Vol. 2, No. 1* (Spring, 1972), pp. 14–22.

Fox, Gardner (w), and Carmine Infantino (a). "The Flash of Two Worlds." *The Flash #123* (September 1959).

Johns, Geoff (w), and Lee Moder (a). "Dragon Food." *Stars and STRIPE #12* (July #200). New York: DC Comics.

Marz, Ron (w), and Darryl Banks (a). "The Future." *Green Lantern #50* (March 1994). New York: DC Comics.

Miller, Frank (w & a). *The Dark Knight Returns.* New York: DC Comics, 1986.

The Mindscape of Alan Moore. Directed by DeZ Vylenz. Shadowsanke Films. 2005.

Moore, Alan (w), and Don Simpson (a). "In Pictopia." *Brighter Than You Think: 10 Short Works by Alan Moore.* Marc Sobel, ed. Minneapolis, MN: Uncivilized Books. 2017. 22–35.

Morrison, Grant (w), and Howard Porter (a). "Mageddon." *JLA #41* (May 2000). New York: DC Comics.

Morrison, Grant (w), and Tony S. Daniel (a). "Midnight in the House of Hurt." *Batman #676* (June 2008). New York: DC Comics.

Morrison, Grant (w), and Val Semeiks (a). "Riders on the Storm." *DC One Million #1* (November 1998). New York: DC Comics.

Orwell, George. *1984.* New York: Signet Classic. 1961.

Salvatore, Brian. "Interview with Mark Waid." Multiversity Comics. February 11, 2016. <http://www.multiversitycomics.com/interviews/mark-waid-tells-us-why-he-loves-the-flash/>.

Sims, Chris. "Ask Chris #151." *Comics Alliance.* April 26, 2013. <http://comicsalliance.com/the-flash-wally-west-barry-allen-mark-waid-silver-age-dc/>.

Waid, Mark (w), and Greg La Rocque (a). "Blitzkrieg." *The Flash #78* (July 1993). New York: DC Comics.

_____. "Mean Streak." *The Flash #88* (March 1994). New York: DC Comics.

_____. "The Once and Future Flash." *The Flash #79* (August 1993). New York: DC Comics.

_____. "One Perfect Gift." *The Flash #73* (February 1993). New York: DC Comics.

_____. "Trust." *The Flash #74* (March 1993). New York: DC Comics.

Waid, Mark (w), and Alex Ross (a). *Kingdom Come.* New York: DC Comics. 1997.

Wolfman, Marv. "Introduction." *Crisis on Infinite Earths.* New York: DC Comics. 1998.

Wolfman, Marv (w), and Georg Perez (a). "Final Crisis" *Crisis on Infinite Earths #12* (March 1986). New York: DC Comics. 41.

Wolk, Douglas. *Reading Comics; How Graphic Novels Work and What They Mean.* De Capo Press, 2007. 103.

Flash Back to the Future

Mark Waid's Counter-Narrative
to the Superhero Dark Age

JOHN DAROWSKI

The 1990s was a decade of extremes. Following the entropic end to the Cold War, the United States should have entered a prosperous future with unencumbered enthusiasm. Instead, the baby boomer's triumph was met with seeming apathy by Generation X as society vacillated between pessimism and optimism during the inexorable march towards the new millennium. America was uncertain how to fulfill its role of sole superpower as the world fragmented into competing ideologies rather than cohere into secure stability. Domestic disharmony focused on the social ills of crime and scandal, which both threatened moral corrosion and highlighted disenfranchised minorities. The U.S. entered a national identity crisis, driven by the dilemma of how the country should define itself and its mission. Superheroes, through their uncanny ability to reflect the cultural climate, answered with an identity crisis of their own. Costumed crusaders began to question their principal morals and to explore alternative values, either through the replacement of traditional characters or the introduction of violent anti-heroes. Jeffrey K. Johnson sums up the quandary in *Super-History*:

> Many comic book readers and creators asked if a superhero should be a positive role model and ethical symbol of good citizenship or a hero adopt a relativistic ethical standpoint? Should heroes serve as an example of what readers could strive for or should these supermen and women provide violent wish fulfillment to readers burdened by an often dangerous and discouraging world? [163].

For the third Flash, Wally West, the answer is emphatically the former. Under the pen of Mark Waid, who wrote most of series during the decade, *The Flash* served as a positive counter-narrative to the grim-and-gritty excesses of the superhero Dark Age. It reassured despondent readers of the ability to recover idealism and recuperate heroism in discouraging times. Wally West faced the future (often literally) by combining the legacy of his speedster predecessors and his individual determination to forge his own authentic identity as the Flash.

Mark Waid took over writing duties on *The Flash* with Volume 2 issue #62 (cover date May 1992),[1] having earned his first writing credits on *The Flash 50th Anniversary Special* #1 (1990) and *The Flash* Annual #4 (1991). He would continue to pen the adventures of the Scarlet Speedster for the rest of the decade, ending his run one hundred issues later with #162 (July 2000).[2] Wallace "Wally" West graduated from Kid Flash to the Flash after the second Flash, Barry Allen, sacrificed himself to save the multiverse in *Crisis on Infinite Earths* #8 (November 1985). Given the comic book speculation boom of the early nineties, Wally soon became the definitive Flash for many readers, as he was the one to whom they were initially introduced and portrayed in popular media such as the *Justice League* animated series.

The first sidekick to fulfill the promise of taking up the mantle to honor his predecessor, Wally proved a likeable lead. He had an Everyman quality, funnier and more outgoing than his uptight, bow-tie wearing uncle, with a singular superpower to which anyone could relate. Unlike flight or x-ray vision, there is a primacy to speed as a natural extension of the human experience. Mark Waid explains: "I think there's a thing about the Flash's power that is a very relatable element in that nobody knows what it's like to run clearly in a Mach 6, but everybody knows what it's like to just miss the bus and wish they could have caught it, or feel like just miss it by this much." Waid continues: "Everybody wants to feel faster and everybody knows what that runner's high feels like when you get moving" (Salvatore). But Wally could also be unsure how to live up to the legacy of his uncle, much as America was uncertain how to fulfill its new role in the world. When compared to the more experienced Barry Allen, Wally West, coming into his own during Generation X, could read as a copy of inferior quality (Berns and Lando 136). Waid helped Wally moved out of his uncle's shadow and even exceed those expectations in executing his responsibilities to safeguard the United States and the world. Many of the threats would come from various futures (twenty-fifth, twenty-seventh, thirtieth, and sixty-fourth centuries), adding a unique dimension to the Flash's mission of securing peace and tranquility. As the protector of Keystone City and as a member of the Justice League Europe, Wally West was well positioned to reflect the uncertainties of the 1990s.

Throughout the proceeding four decades of the Cold War, the United States was guided by a consensus ideology that the American way of life would create a utopia, as long as nuclear Armageddon could be avoided. The collapse of the Soviet Union proved that grand narrative to be a fiction; the promised utopia a two-dimensional simulacrum propped up more by what it was not, not-Communist and not-totalitarian, than by any substance of what it was. This freed the world to consider new and exciting possibilities, many of which were not previously conceivable. But the resultant lack of agreement, internationally or domestically, on what form a secure and peaceful future should take fragmented the world into competing narratives. A Pandora's Box of woes opened through unending regional and ethnic strife and international terrorism (Smith 165; Costello 164). The United States' military might, compounded with weak policy from the European Union, pressured the country to assume the leadership of western hegemony as the world's policeman, at least when American interests were involved (Berns and Lando 131). But unchecked authority could become an exercise in moral relativism, resulting the U.S. becoming as totalitarian as the U.S.S.R. had been characterized (Darowski, "Searching for..." 172). The lack of clear direction is evident in the first Iraq war (August 1990–February 1991), wherein the U.S.-led coalition managed a swift victory but failed to remove a dictator that threatened to destabilize the region. The search for new governing values formed part of the crucible of this national identity crisis.

As the world splintered into diverse ideologies, there was no stable external Other against which the United States could define its national self-identity. Citizens displaced their anxiety over international concerns by turning inward to focus on domestic discord and civil disruption. The beginning of the decade was marred by deep recession, with an accompanying rise in poverty, and social division. Reports on the increase in crime, drug use, and the AIDS epidemic, along with the continued dismantling of the nuclear family, threatened the unitary hegemony by calling attention to those disenfranchised from the American Dream by race, class, and/or sexuality (Costello 163). The 1992 L.A. riots demonstrated that violence was one way for the marginalized to make their voices heard (Mercer 6). Many viewed the crises as the result of the country's own actions (or inactions), with little trust that the institutions of authority could rectify the situations. Neither political party offered a new policy that captured the mandate of the majority; their growing fractiousness frequently devolved into internecine squabbling (Costello 163, 166). The thriving technological revolution, brought on by decreased size and cost, increased mobility, and the introduction of the World Wide Web, proffered a promising new path of unifying progress. But anxiety about the ubiquity of technology in daily life with its potentially dehumanizing effect, coupled with overly optimistic estimates of the profitability of the tech bubble and paranoia concerning Y2K to render such tech as inoperative, failed to unite public opinion at the time (Costello 198; Darowski, "Searching for...," 173–4). Americans did not look to the oncoming millennium with hope but with uncertainty.

Anxiety about the future is a theme woven throughout Waid's run on *The Flash*, either through battling foes from the future, such the Reverse Flash Professor Zoom or Abra Kadabra, or traveling to those centuries. Time travel has been a recurring element for the Flash since the Silver Age, the period when Waid first began reading comics. The motif is reintroduced in Waid's first writing credit, *The Flash 50th Anniversary Special* #1, in which John Fox of the twenty-seventh century must travel back to visit the three previous Flashes (Jay Garrick, Barry Allen, and Wally West), before taking up the legacy in his own time. Waid even introduced a new sidekick for the Flash in Impulse (Bart Allen), Wally's first cousin once removed from the thirtieth century.[3] But these futures are frequently dystopic, indicating a failure of the democratic experiment. For Professor Zoom, the twenty-fifth century had become a "cold and sterile place" without heroes as technology had eradicated crime and disaster (*The Flash* #79 384). The xenophobic Earthgov of the thirtieth century had tried to exploit Impulse before his grandmother Iris rescued him and they escaped to the twentieth century (*The Flash* #92 309–10). And Abra Kadabra, whose sixty-fourth century technology is indistinguishable from magic, was exiled to the twentieth for rejecting collectivism. As a policewoman from the future explains: "The being you call Abra Kadabra was an aberrant personality—who denied the groupmind and sought individuality. For his crime he was exiled through time. Sending him here seemed the humane thing to do" (*The Flash* #67 279). The skepticism concerning the future reflected the discouragement of the national identity crisis and the dour mindset of the contemporary generation.

The failure of the ephemeral promise of the utopian dream in contradistinction to the fear and precarious prospects of reality resulted in a jaded disenchantment with society by the post–Baby Boomers: Generation X. Described alternatively (and alliteratively) as ambivalent, apathetic, or angst-ridden, Gen Xers were cynical due to a sense of social alienation brought on by growing up during the sociopolitical turbulence of a culture that had seemingly already failed (Freim 163; Hammontree 143). A general lack of purpose, deriving from not only cultural ennui but a dearth of economic opportunities, led the media to label many teenagers and twenty-somethings as "slackers." This bleak worldview would seep into several aspects of popular culture.

The dreary outlook was well represented in the Dark Age of superhero comic books (1986–2000).[4] While works of popular media can reflect the contemporary culture, they do so by constructing and defining a shared imagination rather than the complexities of factual truth, and in doing so legitimize popular wisdom through a simplified narrative (Berns and Lando 132). The deconstruction of the superhero mythos initiated by Alan Moore and Dave Gibbon's *Watchmen* and Frank Miller's *The Dark Knight Returns* ushered in a grim-and-gritty ethos which echoed the tumultuous zeitgeist of the late eighties and early nineties. The legitimization of these works as high art brought new attention to the medium, which helped to fuel a speculation boom. Superhero publishers churned out content, emphasizing quantity over quality and experimenting with characterization to see what would resonate. An extreme tone accompanied by flamboyant artwork that accentuated style over substance, particularly hyper-muscular men and impossibly proportioned women, proved particularly popular. This trend is best illustrated by Image Comics, a company created by seven superstar artists who wanted more creative control as well as rights over their creations. Additionally, issues would often feature some gimmick, typically a specialty cover, to give the illusion that it was more valuable as a collector's item.

Another way to make an issue valuable was to utilize one of several storytelling tropes of the era, some only permissible by the final revision of the Comics Code in 1989.[5] These conventions include (i) the multipart event, forcing collectors to buy all issues to get the complete story and usually ending with dramatic repercussions. Said repercussions could be: (ii) a makeover which updates the costume, frequently integrating technology in some armored form, to brings the character more in line with the new visual and thematic aesthetic; (iii) re-invention, seeing an established hero lose their position and a new younger and sometimes diverse character claiming the mantle; or (iv) the death of a superhero, which simultaneously capitalizes on the ambient pessimism of the decade and gives remaining characters a reason to be angry.[6] Anger leads to the last cliché, (v) the anti-hero, a vigilante who embraces moral ambiguity to justify their ruthlessness and violence.[7] All of these elements appear in the defining storyline of the era, the Death of Superman. Told through multiple events over the course of a year, the saga saw the death of the greatest superhero at the hands of the epitome of nineties extreme, Doomsday, only to be replaced by four potential supermen: the armored Steel; the reinvention of Superboy as teenager with a Generation X attitude; the technological makeover as the Cyborg Superman; and the Last Son of Krypton, a remorseless anti-hero. Ultimately, none of the four can replace Superman, as the original returns to save the day. The story works well as an allegory for contemporary societal fears, but as a publicity stunt it marked the beginning of the end of the speculation boom. Comic book fever faded by mid-decade as fans tired of the altering of classic characters for shallow commercialism and speculators realized that market glut meant more supply than demand and that their issues could only depreciate. The publishers who survived the bursting of the bubble scrambled to again reinvent characters to maintain relevancy in a rapidly changing world.

Wally West would seem perfectly poised to embody the extremes of the Dark Age. He is a re-invention of the Flash following the death of his mentor, Barry Allen, which, when coupled with his younger, Gen X age among the established heroes, would have provided ample reason to be resentful and cynical. But Wally always seemed to race ahead of the curve of the era's excesses. His re-invention came out of the earlier event *Crisis on Infinite Earths* (April 1985–March 1986), DC Comics' first attempt to streamline its continuity and rebrand its heroes. Even just a few years later in the nineties, many of DC's established heroes, like Superman, were feeling outdated and in need of reinvention. Part of this stems from the fact that their mission and meaning emerged from the ideological system of the Cold War, which was now undergoing intense scrutiny. The Flash's identity, while built on legacy, was at liberty to develop greater meaning through individualism and personal freedom without feeling alienated from society (Darowski, "Cold Warrior" 176). This was undoubtedly helped by the fact that Wally West was an established character, first appearing as the sidekick Kid Flash in *The Flash* #110 (January 1960). Other reinventions of the period featured new, relatively unknown characters taking up the mantle; when Batman's back was broken by Bane, it was not Robin (Time Drake) or Nightwing (Dick Grayson) who replaced him, but the recently introduced Azrael (Jean Paul Valley). Such characters were often created expressly to deconstruct a hero or the genre itself, but as such were a novelty tied to a specific moment in time and failed to create lasting change. Revisionism became the more common tool in the second half of the decade, reinterpreting classic characters through reconstruction of traditional virtues modified with reevaluated ethics. Kid Flash's graduation to the Flash serves as a precursor to such revision by modelling how to synthesize core super heroic beliefs with modern characterization. In doing so, *The Flash* became a counter-narrative to the clichés of the Dark Age.

A key aspect of revisionism centered on the mission of the superhero, itself an indicator of national character. According to Richard Reynolds in *Super Heroes: A Modern Mythology*: "The superhero by his very existence asserts American utopianism, which remains a highly potent cultural myth" (83). But by the end of the Cold War, there was a disturbing questioning of what superheroes were fighting for. The search for a new American identity revealed significant doubt as to whether such a utopia could exist; the turn to the anti-hero indicates a more likely dystopia. If the potential for utopia remained, the question then became what form it should take and what values it should be built on.

A key myth of the Cold War consensus ideology was already built into the United States' founding principles of virtue, progress, and individualism (Costello 228). Rather than needing reform, American exceptionalism only needed to be reclaimed. This is expressed by John Shelton Lawrence and Robert Jewett in *The Myth of the American Superhero*, wherein they establish the following form of the superhero social contract:

A community in harmonious paradise is threatened by evil; normal institutions fail to contend with the threat; a selfless superhero emerges to renounce temptations and carry out the redemptive task; aided by fate, his decisive victory restored the community to its paradisiacal conditions; the superhero then recedes into obscurity [6].

What is then needed for the nation to move forward is not revolution but restoration. *The Flash* recognizes this by not only having Wally honor the legacy of his predecessor but learn from the speedsters of the greatest generation: the first Flash, Jay Garrick; Johnny Quick, who gains speed through a mathematical formula; and Waid's creation Max Mercury, the Zen master of speed.[8] Max Mercury learned how to access the Speed Force, the mythical source of all super speed, from a shaman in the 1840s, and has leapt through time after entering it. Wally frequently consults and trains with these heroes. In particular, it is by combining Johnny Quick's formula and Mercury's spiritual knowledge that Wally is able to access the Speed Force and become the fastest Flash of all. But the Golden Age heroes also realize that they are not able to keep up with the speed of the modern world and their values, though beneficial, will not answer all the problems of a changing society. Likewise, the values that had led the Baby Boomers to victory through the Cold War had resulted in a less than prosperous or virtuous present in the nineties, leading many Americans to resent their elders for not providing a stable society (Duncan 130). As Matthew J. Costello states: "Without a common language of progress and virtue, only individualism remained as an American value to be asserted" (228). This is evidenced in the iconoclasm of anti-heroes, who insist on following their own morally-challenged brand of personal ethics.

This theme is explored in a storyline from *The Flash* #88–90 (March–May 1994), wherein American exceptionalism is put on trial. Allison Armitage sues the Flash for negligence after he failed to save her during a battle with a supervillain, resulting in her disfigurement and the loss of her legs. But the trial is less about whether the Flash could have saved Armitage from suffering and more about whether Wally West is virtuous enough to be a hero. When Wally attacks a lawyer, believing him to be Abra Kadabra, the court legally forbids him from using his powers or costume. Without a common consent validating his mission, Wally is forced to rely on his individualism to prove that Abra Kadabra was manipulating the trial. Even though Wally is cleared to act as the Flash again, the trial placed doubts in his mind as to whether he was exceptional enough to save everyone.

In trying to protect all the citizens of Keystone City, as Wally attempts following the trial in issue #91 (June 1994), the Flash is enacting a different form of the superhero social contract. Richard Reynolds presents an alternative mission for the superhero; instead of restoration, the superhero fights to preserve the status quo. He states:

A key ideological myth of the superhero comic is that the normal and everyday
enshrines positive values that must be defended through heroic action—and
defended over and over again almost without respite [...] The normal is valuable and
is constantly under attack, which means almost by definition the superhero is battling on behalf of the status quo [77].

This responds at least in part to Lawrence and Jewett's version, in that the
superhero is not allowed to "recede into obscurity" but stay ever vigilant.
Additionally, it rebukes the idea that the present is fallen and the danger of
misplaced nostalgia. Danny Fingeroth sums up the need to protect the present
in *Superman on the Couch* as: "It ain't a perfect system, but it's the best we've
come up with so far" (157). But for many in the nineties, it wasn't the best
system. The paradigm shift after the Cold War finale left the country seemingly directionless with few values to uphold. The radical changes many
heroes underwent illustrated that the status quo was not static but undergoing
a dramatic transformation. The trend of anti-heroes revealed that the state
of the world wasn't worth preserving, but it was worthwhile to prevent society
from getting worse. And Wally knew how bad it could get from seeing
dystopian futures.

The recurring theme of fighting the future provides a third direction
for the social contract, one that may allow the versions by Lawrence and Jewett and Reynolds to be synthesized. Contrasted with a fallen dystopia, the
present becomes a more harmonious paradise worth preserving in its status
quo. The policewoman from the sixty-fourth century states that "according
to out records, the late 20th century was a renaissance of reckless behavior"
(*The Flash* #67 279). But choice to engage in reckless behavior is built on
personal freedom, which is a far cry better than Abra Kadabra's future, where
individuality is the antithesis of order and people are programmed like
mechanical timepieces (*The Flash* #68). Freedom is also why Impulse and
Iris West escape from the thirtieth century. While dystopian futures may
reinforce the pessimism of the early nineties, it also meant the present was
the best of times, not the worst.

All of these ideas are explored in one of Waid's most well-regarded storylines, "The Return of Barry Allen." In *The Flash* #74–79 (March–August
1993), the second Flash returns from the grave and takes up his mantle again.
But Barry, in a desire to be the only Flash, grows increasingly jealous of Wally
and lashes out at his former sidekick, shattering Wally's confidence. Becoming
unhinged, Barry declares that Keystone City has forgotten about him and
therefore deserves to be destroyed. Jay Garrick, Johnny Quick, and Max Mercury team-up to stop him, but they are not powerful enough. By now, Wally
has realized the truth and confronts Barry in the Flash Museum, revealing
that this returned Barry is actually Professor Zoom (Eobard Thawne), the
Reverse Flash from the twenty-fifth century. In a twisted desire to protect

the legacy of Barry Allen, Zoom would destroy all others who call themselves the Flash. Wally is now able to overcome his doubts, become the fastest man alive, and return the Reverse Flash to his proper time. For Zoom, the twentieth century was a paradise of heroes compared to his twenty-fifth century, but this type of romanticized nostalgia, that everything was better in the past, proves toxic. Zoom's later decision to destroy everything that came before his arrival reflects the Dark Age's rejection of what came before to search for a completely new identity, which proved untenable. Wally modelled a better path, learning from the past heroes to create an ethical foundation and modifying valid values to suit contemporary circumstances. The mixture of timeless and timely avoids the inadequacies of moral relativism while still allowing compromise for a changing world. This served as an ideal as superheroes moved away from experimentation and returned to classic characterization in the second half of the decade.

Which is not to say *The Flash* avoided all the tropes of the Dark Age. The Flash was temporarily reinvented when John Fox replaced a time-displaced Wally in issues #113–117 (May–September 1996). And Impulse is introduced as a reinvention of Kid Flash, albeit it one representing certain aspects of Generation X. Instead of pessimism, Impulse expresses unbounded exuberance to the point of ADHD, which is compounded with his immaturity. Contributing to this is the fact that Bart Allen grew at an accelerated rate. Unable to control his speed powers, by the time Bart was two, he was physically twelve (*The Flash* #92 310). To compensate, Impulse was raised in a virtual reality that could keep pace while providing information. Though echoing concerns about the influence of video games, Impulse promulgated the idea that the rising generation could handle the responsibility of safeguarding the world.

Additionally, Waid introduced Argus in *The Flash* Annual #6 as part of the 1993 Bloodlines event, an attempt to create a batch of new heroes in the mold of the new aesthetic. Argus fit the bill as a morally ambiguous character, a police officer who infiltrated the mob, before gaining super-strength, infrared vision, and the ability to become invisible in shadows. Argus's costume is a pastiche of the nineties style: armored; big shoulder pads; extraneous belts and pouches. Argus would help the Flash battle secret organizations like the Combine and Kobra, now defined as terrorists rather than totalitarians seeking world domination as they would have during the Cold War (Costello 165). The fact that the Flash and Argus did not get along serves as a counterpoint to Wally's secure characterization against the extremes of the Dark Age.

Mark Waid's last storyline on *The Flash* serves as a commentary on the themes of the Dark Age by offering a vision of the Flash who embraced the hard-edged characterization of the era in "The Dark Flash Saga." After entering the Speed Force to defeat Cobalt Blue (secretly Barry Allen's long-lost twin brother Malcolm Thawne) in issue #150 (July 1999), a different Flash emerged. From *The Flash* #152–159 (September 1999–April 2000), this grim-and-gritty version brought brutal enforcement against criminals. It is eventually revealed that this is Walter West from an alternate dimension. After seeing his girlfriend killed, Walter became ruthless and violent in his pursuit of his form of justice. Abra Kadabra is behind this switch and his defeat restores Wally and Walter to their appropriate dimensions. Walter serves as a Jungian shadow-self to Wally, their contrast showing how far Wally has come as a hero.

The nineties ended on a positive note. Having weathered the Clinton scandal, the economy was robust and crime was down. The national identity crisis was resolved as traditional values reasserted themselves, though not as powerfully as in previous generations. For superheroes, there was a retreat from the vagaries of the extreme to the tradition of the mythic (Hammontree 149). The revisions of the early nineties were replaced by a return to the conventional characterizations that reasserted the myth of the American Way. And while Barry Allen did not actually return at this point,[9] Wally West earned his place among the mythic heroes. In *The Flash* #100, he enters the Speed Force and becomes faster than ever. In doing so, Wally achieves an authentic identity as the Flash, by becoming the archetype for all speedsters in the DC Universe.

The end of the Cold War was a paradigm shift whose fallout American society wrestled with throughout the 1990s. While the United States acknowledged that changes were now possible, perhaps even necessary, to move forward, there was little consensus on what the way forward should be. The deconstruction and reconstruction of the superhero illustrated how hard lasting change can be to achieve (Johnson 157). Mark Waid's tenure on *The Flash* served as a precursor to the shift from ambition to reiteration by building consistent characterization that reified traditional superhero values. Doing so tapped into the mythic qualities of the genre to not only reflect but shape society (Duncan and Smith 78). Wally West embodied optimism during a period of pessimism and served as a reminder of what superheroes should be in the face of revisionism. In doing so, the Flash recuperated American values for Generation X and led the way to the new millennium.

NOTES

1. The cover date does not necessarily indicate the month of publication. When comic books were primarily sold on newsstands, the issues were postdated with the month the vendor should remove unsold copies. The discrepancy between actual month and the cover date could range from one to three months. With the advent of the direct market, wherein publishers sold to specialty stores instead of newsstands, the system was further modified the cover date matched the month of publication for some publishers, while others maintained

the time shift. As such, it is often much easier to track the cover date than the publication date and will be done so here.

The volume number of comic books is one way to track continuity. Despite ten-year gap between *Flash Comics* #104 (February 1949) and the Silver Age reboot with *The Flash* #105 (March 1959), it is all considered to be Volume 1. Following *Crisis on Infinite Earths* in 1986, DC Comics streamlined their continuity and restarted *The Flash*, now starring Wally West, with Volume 2 #1 (June 1987).

2. In addition, Mark Waid wrote several *The Flash* annuals (#4, 5, 6, and 8) and ancillary specials, as well as the initial issues of *The Flash* spin-off series *Impulse*, from #1 (April 1995) through #27 (July 1997). Though his tenure is lengthy, it was not an uninterrupted run. In addition to co-writers and the occasional fill-in, Waid was notably interrupted for 12 issues, #130 (October 1997) through #141 (September 1998), by writers Mark Millar and Grant Morrison. Waid would also return to write *The Flash* #231 (October 2007)–#236 (March 2008).

3. Wally West's aunt Iris, who married Barry Allen, was sent from the thirtieth century to the twentieth as an infant, when she was adopted by the West family. Upon her murder by Professor Zoom, Iris's birth parents brought her life force back to the thirtieth century and placed it in a cloned body. She was reunited with Barry and gave birth to the Tornado Twins, Don and Dawn. Don fathered Bart Allen (Impulse) while Dawn became the mother to Jenni Ognats, who became XS of the Legion of Super-Heroes.

4. The Dark Age lasted from approximately 1985 to 2000. Some prefer the term Iron Age, to more closely link to the proceeding Bronze Age, while others will insert a Copper Age from 1986 to 1992. I prefer Dark Age as it suits the overall tone of the period, from content to publishing history.

5. Facing criticism over the violence in crime and horror comics, The Comics Code Authority was created in 1954 to self-censor and regulate material in comic books. Any comic book without the seal of approval from the CCA would not be sold on newsstands. Societal changes and the shift from the newsstand to the direct market lead to revisions of the code in 1971 and 1989, though by 1989 the seal has lost most of its relevance.

6. Women, be they girlfriends, wives, or family, were also a frequent target of violence to motivate the male heroes to act. One of the most infamous examples of this came when Green Lantern Kyle Rayner found his dead girlfriend stuffed in a refrigerator, leading Gail Simone to coin the term for this, "women in refrigerators."

7. Most heroes at DC Comics experienced some form of these tropes. Top tier characters, like Superman, Batman, and Wonder Woman, could be temporarily replaced, usually by an anti-hero, but quickly return. Lower tier characters would see seemingly more permanent changes. Perhaps the best example of this is Green Arrow (Oliver Queen). In 1988, writer/artist Mike Grill transformed Green Arrow from a liberal social activist known for his gimmicky trick arrows to an urban vigilante who used real arrows to maim and kill violent criminals. Queen sacrificed himself stopping a bomb in 1995 and was replaced by his son, Connor Hawke. Oliver Queen would return from the dead in 2001.

8. During the Silver Age (1955–1970), the Golden (1938–1954) heroes had been relegated to the Earth 2, a separate dimension from the rebooted superheroes in DC Comics multiverse. *Crisis on Infinite Earths* collapsed the multiverse into one universe, rewriting DC's history. The Flash I (Jay Garrick) and the Justice Society of America returned from an extra-dimensional space in 1991.

9. Barry Allen would return *The Flash: Rebirth* (2009).

WORKS CITED

Berns, Fernando Gabriel Pagnoni, and Leonardo Acosta Lando. "Lacking Leadership: The Justice League Europe's Place in the DC Universe." *The Ages of the Justice League: Essays on America's Greatest Superheroes in Changing Times,* edited by Joseph J. Darowski, McFarland, 2017, pp. 131–141.

Broome, John (w), and Carmine Infantino (a). "Meet Kid Flash!" *The Flash* Vol. 1 #110. DC Comics, 1960.

Costello, Matthew J. *Secret Identity Crisis: Comic Books and the Unmasking of Cold War America.* Continuum, 2009.

Darowski, Joseph J. "Cold Warrior at the End of the Cold War: John Byrne's 'War Games' in an Era of Transition." *The Ages of Iron Man: Essays on the Armored Avenger in Changing Times,* edited by Joseph J. Darowski, McFarland, 2015, pp. 171–180.

_____. "Searching for Meaning in 'The Death of Superman.'" *The Ages of Superman: Essays on the Man of Steel in Changing Times,* McFarland, 2012, pp. 166–176.

Duncan, David Allen. "*Generation X*: Mutants Made to Order." *The Ages of the X-Men: Essays on the Children of the Atom in Changing Times,* edited by Joseph J. Darowski, McFarland, 2014, pp. 128–144.

Duncan, Randy, and Matthew J. Smith. *The Power of Comics: History, Form, and Culture.* 1st ed., Continuum, 2009.

Fingeroth, Danny. *Superman on the Couch: What Superheroes Really Tell Us About Ourselves and Our Society.* Continuum, 2006.

Freim, Nicole. "The Dark Amazon Saga: Diana Meets the Iron Age." *The Ages of Wonder Woman: Essays on the Amazon Princess in Changing Times,* edited by Joseph J. Darowski, McFarland, 2014, pp. 174–183.

Hammontree, D.R. "Extreme Transitions: Trends and Trepidations from 1992 to 1996." *The Ages of the Justice League: Essays on America's Greatest Superheroes in Changing Times,* edited by Joseph J. Darowski, McFarland, 2017, pp. 131–141.

Johnson, Jeffrey K. *Super-History: Comic Book Superheroes and American Society.* McFarland, 2012.

Lawrence, John Shelton, and Robert Jewett. *The Myth of the American Superhero.* William B. Eerdmans Publishing Company, 2002.

Mercer, Kobena. *Welcome to the Jungle: New Positions in Black Cultural Studies.* Routledge, 1994.

Reynolds, Richard. *Super Heroes: A Modern Mythology.* University of Mississippi Press, 1992.

Salvatore, Brian. "Mark Waid Tells Us Why He Loves the Flash." *Multiversity Comics,* 11 February 2016, http://www.multiversitycomics.com/interviews/mark-waid-tells-us-why-he-loves-the-flash/. Accessed 10 March 2018.

Smith, Matthew J. "The 'Triangle Era' of Superman: Continuity, Marketing, and Grand Narratives in the 1990s." The Ages of Superman: Essays on the Man of Steel in Changing Times, edited by Joseph J. Darowski, McFarland, 2012, pp. 156–165

Waid, Mark (w), Brian Augustyn (w), and Paul Pelletier (a). "Convergence," *The Flash* Vol. 2 #156. DC Comics, 2000.

_____. "Dimensionally Challenged," *The Flash* Vol. 2 #154. DC Comics, 1999.

_____. "Finish Line," *The Flash* Vol 2 #150. DC Comics, 1999.

_____. "The Folded Man," *The Flash* Vol. 2 #153. DC Comics, 1999.

_____. "New Kid in Town," *The Flash* Vol. 2 #152. DC Comics, 1999.

_____. "Payback Unlimited," *The Flash* Vol. 2 #155. DC Comics, 1999.

_____. "Reverse Flash," *The Flash* Vol. 2 #158. DC Comics, 2000.

_____. "Setting the Stage," *The Flash* Vol. 2 #157. DC Comics, 2000.

_____. "Whirlwind Ceremony," *The Flash* #159. DC Comics, 2000.

Waid, Mark (w), and Phil Hester (a). "Undercover Angel," *The Flash Annual* #6. *The Flash by Mark Waid Book Two,* DC Comics, 2017, pp. 288–351.

Waid, Mark (w), and Greg LaRoque (a). "Beat the Clock," *The Flash* Vol. 2 #68. *The Flash by Mark Waid Book One,* DC Comics, 2016, pp. 287–309.

_____. "Blitzkrieg," *The Flash* Vol 2 #78. *The Flash by Mark Waid Book Two,* DC Comics, 2017, pp. 352–374.

_____. "Identity Crisis," *The Flash* Vol. 2 #76. *The Flash by Mark Waid Book Two,* DC Comics, 2017, pp. 230–252.

_____. "Misdirection," *The Flash* Vol. 2 #67. *The Flash by Mark Waid Book One,* DC Comics, 2016, pp. 261–285.

_____. "The Once and Future Flash," *The Flash* Vol. 2 #79. *The Flash by Mark Waid Book Two,* DC Comics, 2017, pp. 375–430

_____. "Running Behind," *The Flash* #75. *The Flash by Mark Waid Book Two,* DC Comics, 2017, pp. 207–229.

_____. "Suicide Run." *The Flash* Vol. 2 #77. *The Flash by Mark Waid Book Two,* DC Comics, 2017, pp. 274–296.

_____. "Trust," *The Flash* Vol. 2 #74. *The Flash by Mark Waid Book Two,* DC Comics, 2017, pp. 183–206.

Waid, Mark (w), Carlos Pacheco (a), and Salvador Larroca (a). "Terminal Velocity Redline: Ultimate Rush," *The Flash* Vol. 2 #100. DC Comic, 1995.

Waid, Mark (w), and Mike Parobeck (a). "Generations," *The Flash 50th Anniversary Special* #1. *The Flash by Mark Waid Book One,* DC Comics, 2016, pp. 10–82.

Waid, Mark (w), and Kris Renkewitz (a). "Swift Decision," *The Flash* Vol. 2 #89. *The Flash by Mark Waid Book Three,* DC Comics, 2017, pp. 223–246.

Waid, Mark (w), and Mike Wieringo (a). "Mean Streak," *The Flash* Vol. 2 #88. *The Flash by Mark Waid Book Three,* DC Comics, 2017, 199–222.

_____. "On the Run," *The Flash* Vol. 2 #90. *The Flash by Mark Waid Book Three,* DC Comics, 2017, pp. 247–271.

_____. "Out of Time," *The Flash* Vol. 2 #91. *The Flash by Mark Waid Book Three,* DC Comics, 2017, pp. 273–296.

_____. "Reckless Youth Chapter One: Speed Kills," *The Flash* Vol. 2 #92. *The Flash by Mark Waid Book Three,* DC Comics, 2017, pp. 297–320.

Wolfman, Marv (w), and George Pérez (a). "A Flash of Lightning!" *Crisis on Infinite Earths* #8. DC Comics, 1985.

Impulsive Students, Speedster Teachers and Education in the 1990s

Daniel J. Bergman

The 1990s saw American education explode into a prominent topic among national politicians and federal leaders. "This has never happened in the nation's history. Education is now a major, high priority national concern, as well as a state and local responsibility" (Bell 595). Before then, schools and standards had mostly been left to state and local policymakers. Following multiple reform efforts in the 1980s (Firestone et al. 349; Kaplan K5; Murphy 3), both presidents George H.W. Bush and his successor Bill Clinton took the mantle of "Education President."

Based on work during his previous Arkansas governorship, President Clinton advocated for school accountability and nationwide standards. These efforts, now at the federal level, culminated in the Goals 2000: Educate America Act (H.R. 1804). "Emphasis shifted from educational inputs to educational outcomes and from procedural accountability to educational accountability" (Goertz 62). Referred to as "Goals 2000," this legislation targeted eight objectives to reach "by the year 2000." Topics included early childhood school readiness, high school graduation rates, academic achievement, global eminence, school safety—each of these adopted from the National Governors' Association. Two additional items joined the Goals 2000 list: teacher education and parental involvement (Webb 332). President Clinton signed Goals 2000—the first national education goals—into law on March 31, 1994. During his signing in front of school children in San Diego, Clinton remarked, "We insist that it's time to abolish the outdated distinction between academic learning and skill learning. [...] We can teach our young people to learn in the way that best suits their own capacities and the work they have to do."

A Teen Hero for the 1990s

A few months later in July 1994, DC Comics presented a potential poster child for 1990s adolescence: Impulse. Although Impulse (a.k.a. Bart Allen) actually came from the future—30th century, to be exact—his attitude and behaviors reflect many teenage notions from the last decade of the 20th century. The very name "Impulse" evokes stereotypical characteristics of Generation X adolescents: short attention span, entertainment-first obsession, disregard for adult instruction, and a general leap-before-you-look disposition. With regard to the workforce, "Generation X" individuals are described as "good at change ... comfortable with technology ... independent ... not intimidated by authority ... creative" (Raines 8). Interestingly, Bart Allen shares first names with another prominent Bart in the 1990s—Bart Simpson, the rebellious son of *The Simpsons,* whose name is a stand-in for that of creator Matt Groening (Groening and Jean) and is an anagram of "brat" (BBC).

The attitude of DC's spunky and speedy teenage hero is conveyed succinctly in a pre-release advertisement for the new ongoing *Impulse* series (DC Comics). This one-page ad features a massive traditional green chalkboard at the front of a classroom, and echoes Bart Simpson's "chalkboard gag" of writing different messages in opening sequences of *Simpsons* episodes (Turner 71). In the print advertisement (drawn by series regular artist Humberto Ramos), Impulse moves so quickly across the page that there are three images of him—a common method to show lightning fast super-heroes in comic book panels. The first figure of Impulse zips onto the page to reach for a piece of chalk; in the second image he holds the chalk to the board; the third image is only Impulse's foot and hand, tossing the chalk behind as he zooms off the page. On the chalkboard are 54 copies of the same sentence: "I won't run in the hall." The advertisement includes a tagline for the new series: "Sometimes you just gotta go with your IMPULSE."

Before getting his own solo series, however, Bart Allen first appeared in *Flash (Vol. 2)* #92 (July 1994), by writer Mark Waid and artist Mike Wieringo—credited as co-creators of Impulse. According to *Flash* and *Impulse* editor Brian Augustyn, "Mark is the perfect guy for Impulse because, in so many ways he *is* Impulse—brash, goofy, but absolutely fearless in his pursuit of his craft." ("Follow Your Impulse" 5, emphasis in original). The initial approach in writing the *Impulse* comic series reflects this creative spontaneity. In a 1996 interview with *Wizard Guide to Comics* magazine, Waid shares his method: "With *Impulse,* I'm just making it up month to month. I have no grand plan" (Russo 52). Editor Augustyn describes this attitude he and Waid agreed upon in writing the series: "Stop worrying and overthinking the story and it will come," and using a "jump-first-worry-later method" which mirrors the title character's personality and behaviors (4).

Privately, Waid and Augustyn considered "that *Impulse* wasn't a super-hero comic at all, but rather a situation comedy in tights.... [S]tructure, character interplay, conflict and resolution are all out of 'Must-See TV.' And there are lots and lots of jokes. Mark and I love great sitcoms, and we set out to intentionally try to create a comic that blended the sitcom structures with our familiar four-color medium" (4). DC Comics executives quickly expressed support for a solo *Impulse* series—mere months after Bart's first appearance—which made its creators search for a unique voice. Waid explains in a 2016 interview (Salvatore) how he approached the title, including how to make it stand out compared to the main *Flash* series, which starred Wally West at the time:

> Bart had been in the comics for 6 months and he got his own book, so we had to really think hard about, "Okay, young Wally is a cute idea but it needs to be deeper than that if it's going to carry its own series." What do we do with that? Like I said, we came up with the idea of making it more about his naivety, more about his relationship with Max Mercury, and more about the idea that a genuine kid is a superhero doing kid stuff and being involved in kid level threats.

Like many heroes introduced in 1990s, Bart Allen's background is somewhat convoluted and continuity-laden. Born with full super-speed, he is the grandson of the Silver Age Flash, Barry Allen, and "cousin" to Wally West, the main Flash in the DC Universe from 1986 to 2009. In *Flash (Vol. 2) #92* (July 1994), Bart's grandmother Iris explains how "Unlike Wally, Bart can't shut down. Since birth, his hyper-metabolism has been burning non-stop, aging him more and more rapidly. At age one, he looked two. At two he looks twelve." By the time Wally saves Bart from "hyper-metabolism," the young hero looks fourteen physically but is only two chronologically. As Bart himself reveals in a school-assigned autobiographical essay in *Impulse #1* (April 1995), "I'd still be two years old in the head if the scientists hadn't plugged it with virtual reality. So my world was unusual. Who could tell? All I knew was that I made the rules (and learned whatever I needed to feel kind of normal)."

In essence, Bart's abridged upbringing in the future 30th century made him a true "digital native." Grandmother Iris describes Bart's origin in *Flash #94* (September 1994):

> Bart grew up in isolation, aging at hyperspeed. His contact with the outside was minimal. He was fed virtual reality to keep him entertained, but that did more harm than good. Now that he's free, he thinks everything is the same fantastic game as in VR. That's why he's so impulsive—he doesn't know that in the real world, he can get hurt.

As labeled in the opening narration of *Impulse #1* (April 1995), Bart Allen is a "poster child for the judgement-impaired." He has an overstimulated toddler's mind in a teenager's body, and acts accordingly. During his first non-action scene in *Flash #94*, Bart zips back and forth in a kitchen with constant demands and complaints: "Where's the holo-vision?" "I'm bored!" "Can I have this?" "I want an omnicom!" "I'm really bored!" "Where's the matter converter?" "Come on, people—let's move!" Such hastiness becomes hazardous during super-heroic adventures. Hence Iris comes to Wally with her request: "Bart has no concept of danger ... and that terrifies me. I can't teach him how to survive, but you can. You must ... and soon."

Such is the basic premise of Bart Allen's narrative—a hyper-active, super-fast teen hero in need of an education. While this scenario provides entertaining and humorous stories, a similar situation—and more sobering struggle—existed among millions of American students in the 1990s. During this decade, as many as 10 percent of all U.S. school-aged children were diagnosed with attention-deficit/hyperactivity disorder, or ADHD (Centers for Disease Control and Prevention). Other estimates are lower, but the number of diagnoses has risen over the years (Holland and Riley). Between 1990 to 1995, for example, office-based visits with ADHD diagnoses for children ages 5 through 18 increased from 947,208 in 1990 to 2,357,833 in 1995 (Robison et al. 212).

The only official diagnosis Bart Allen receives is from his cousin Wally West, who attributes Impulse's behavior to "Single Synapse Theory." In *Impulse* #1 (April 1995), this behavior is described as "from thought to deed in one electric leap, with never a pause to ponder consequence." Elsewhere in *Impulse* #4 (July 1995), narration describes Bart as "the boy with the Danger Deficit Disorder." Augustyn writes, "Bart drove Wally crazy by establishing what would become his primary method of operation: do now, think *never*" (63, emphasis in original).

While Wally West/Flash is the most famous super-hero to mentor Bart/Impulse, other heroes and characters filled this teaching role. The following paragraphs feature various teachers of Impulse—including both super-heroes and "normal" civilians and school faculty. Included is an analysis of each teacher's methods and motivations, along with relative effectiveness on Bart Allen's education and development as a hero and young man. Two primary teachers emerge, which reflect two primary approaches to teaching in the 1990s, as framed by Fenstermacher and Soltis (4).

For the purposes of this chapter, the names Bart and Impulse will be used interchangeably, referring to the former in most cases and the latter when he is in his masked persona among the public or enemies. Since multiple heroes have worn the Flash mantle, Wally's name will be used to refer to his then-status as the primary Flash in the DC universe. The focus is content written by Impulse co-creator Mark Waid, beginning with Bart's early appearances in issues of *Flash (Volume 2)* and later in the solo *Impulse* series, following Waid's stories from issue #1 (April 1995) to issue #27 (July 1997).

The Executive Teacher: Flash (Wally West)

Waid's issues of *Flash* are typically narrated in first person by Wally, which provides information from the teacher's perspective, including hopes, fears, struggles, and more. Right from the start, readers gain insight into Wally's thoughts about this "new Kid Flash in town," as hyped on the cover of *Flash* #92 (July 1994). The first encounter between these two speedsters is a matter of life and death, literally, as Wally must save Bart from pre-mature aging and perishing. Their initial meeting is a blurred brawl, with the two trading punches at super-speed. Wally narrates the action in *Flash* #93 (August 1994):

> [Bart's] Grandma—my Aunt Iris—brought him back to my time, praying that I could teach Bart to control his hyper-metabolism. How am I doing so far? Not great. Separated from Iris—disoriented—Bart ran halfway around the world before I could catch him. Can't blame him for cutting loose. Iris says his life's been spent in scientific confinement. Problem is, he's not used to exercising his power. Pupils are dilated, blood overoxygenated. He's got the world's worst case of runner's high. Got to snap him clear, however I can.

Wally's solution is a fist to Bart's face, which knocks the inexperienced speedster to the ground. Bart pauses to blurt, "What … what'd you do that for?" before sprinting away. Wally narrates self-criticism of his instructive abilities: "Nice going, Teach. So much for calming him down. Now he's fleeing in terror."

As Wally chases Bart across the globe, the latter rapidly ages from 12 to 14 years old. Wally narrates, "This kid doesn't realize what he's doing to himself! I'd love to explain it to him, but it's kind of hard to hold a conversation at Mach Twenty. By the time my voice gets heard in Paris, I'm already in Philadelphia." Before Bart can "die an old man within the hour," however, Wally manages to give Bart a boost and stabilize his powers. Wally explains that Bart "may not be completely cured, but he's on the fast track to recovery."

This sort of "quick fix" is representative of Wally's approach to teaching Bart. Immediate issues are addressed as they arise, with little attention given to long-term planning or lasting impact. Of course, Wally has a lot on his mind, making Bart's rescue and training one issue among many. Subsequent issues in *Flash's* "Terminal Velocity" storyline feature the heroes' investigation and struggle against the evil Kobra shadow cult. Wally must protect his reporter girlfriend Linda Park from ongoing threats and attacks, with added pressure from a premonition of her future demise (#95, November 1994). At the same time Wally appears to be approaching a destined trip into the mysterious Speed Field with no hope of returning (#97, January 1995).

All of these issues turn out okay for the heroes at the end. But in the meantime, Wally's drama unfolds alongside the incessant tutelage of new-comer Bart, who is not the most obedient or attentive student. An additional strain is Wally's reluctance to fulfill the role of teacher and mentor. As he narrates to himself in *Flash* #94 (September 1994), "I'm not about to shoulder that responsibility.... I don't do sidekicks." Nevertheless, Wally does try to teach Bart through various lessons and conversations.

Similar to how Wally fights off wave after wave of enemy threats, American teachers faced repeated attacks in this era of education. Educators had experienced three distinct waves of reform in the 1980s, and barrages continued into the next decade. Throughout the 1990s, teachers encountered various campaigns focused on school choice (Metcalf et al. 4), including private school vouchers, charter schools, and for-profit school contractors (Webb 336). Emphasis on standards and accountability increased—which added more stress to a teacher's typical workload. "Pressure resulting from the assessment of pupils' performance is not new, but it is now taking new forms. External examinations were introduced largely in an attempt to control teachers and teaching and this is still one of their major purposes: their existence exemplifies a lack of trust" (Howson and Wilson 80). When teachers perceive increased pressures (from curriculum mandates, standards, colleagues, students, and more), their instructional impact weakens and students have less intrinsic motivation and self-determination (Pelletier et al. 186).

In many ways, Wally's circumstances reflect those of American teachers during the same time in history. Perhaps due to so many burdens, his instructional work with Bart features an underlying emphasis on immediate results and performance. Wally's approach to teaching aligns with that of "executive," as articulated by Fenstermacher and Soltis: "The executive approach views the teacher as an executor, a person charged with bringing about certain learnings, using the best skills and techniques available" (4).

Several episodes between Wally and Bart reveal elements of the executive approach. Fenstermacher and Soltis note that executive teachers use "cues," described as "maps and signposts; the teacher employs them to alert students to what is to be learned and how to go about learning it" (14). During an early reconnaissance mission into enemy Kobra headquarters (*Flash* #95, November 1994), Wally delays Bart long enough to explain the objectives: "If we want to stay alive.... If we want to learn Kobra's goals, we take names before we kick butt, understood? No screwing around. Follow instructions. Do what I tell you to do and no more—and learn!"

Another aspect of the executive approach to teaching is corrective feedback, defined by Fenstermacher and Soltis, "wherein teachers quickly remedy errors in written and oral work" (14). Wally is typically quick to address Bart's shortcomings. In the above scene inside the enemy base, Bart ignores Wally's instructions and instead attacks unsuspecting Kobra henchmen with a cry of "Down with espionage! Up with carnage! Yee-haa!" Chaos ensues with Wally repeatedly saving Bart from hazards. During their escape, Wally provides verbal correction multiple times: "Cork it, Bart. Concentrate on staying alive ... and on finding an exit!" Bart's poor choices continue however, resulting in more verbal reprimands from Wally: "What was that? A prank? That won't scare Kobra out of Keystone! It'll just make him mad.... You didn't listen! We needed a decisive victory!" In this case, Wally's feedback is disparaging as well as corrective, but such heroics are much more "high-stakes" than a typical school classroom. Wally's pattern of rebuking Bart via "corrective feedback" continues throughout their relationship, including the following year's "Dead Heat" storyline. During a battle in *Impulse* #11 (February 1996), Wally scolds him repeatedly: "Why aren't you ever on the same page as the rest of us?" "This isn't about pranking, kid!" "No more joking around!"

The executive approach to teaching also features reinforcement. "Reinforcement, ranging from a fleeting smile through marks on report cards all the way to such tangible rewards as food, toys, or money, is also quite powerful as an instructional technique, although it requires experience and insight into the learner to employ it well" (Fenstermacher and Soltis 14). Although not as frequent as reprimands, Wally does provide reinforcement to Bart in the form of praise and positive feedback. After witnessing Bart vibrate through a solid wall, Wally says, "That was amazing! Pure instinct propelled you through that wall!" (*Flash* #94, September 1994). Wally provides a tangible reward, too, much later when Bart is about to return to his future "home" 30th century: a costume-changing ring. During the gift-giving and momentary farewell (*Impulse* #24, April 1997), Wally admits to Bart, "I probably could have been more patient with my own cousin, but here, maybe this'll make up for it."

As noted by Fenstermacher and Soltis, effective use of positive reinforcement requires the executive teacher to possess perceptive abilities and expertise. In Wally's case, his relative inexperience with teaching results in a noteworthy motivational misfire. In an early attempt to spur Bart to hone his skills and take training seriously, Wally decides to name another young speedster—Jesse Quick—as his successor (*Flash* #97, January 1995). Wally's true intent is revealed a few issues later (*Flash* #99, March 1995), when the battle with Kobra reaches its climax. Jesse realizes the miscalculated strategy, telling Wally: "[This] wasn't what you had in mind, was it? I know what you were up to, Wally. I think I've known all along.... You pretended to give me the suit to provoke Bart into getting serious about the gig. You played me like a piece of chess." Bart's reaction is more succinct: "What a jerk!" The heroes eventually triumph, but not without hurt feelings, resentment, and distrust directed toward Wally.

To his credit, Wally readily admits his pedagogical limits. Many times his narrative thoughts reveal a critical self-assessment of his teaching abilities: "Not great" (*Flash* #93, August 1994); "I'm doing a lousy job" (#94, September 1994); and "The job gets harder every minute.... What does it take to get through to this kid?" (#96, December 1994). During a moment of downtime, Wally consults with fellow speedster Max Mercury, whom he calls the "Zen Master of Speed." Their discussion in *Flash* #96 resembles similar conversations heard in teachers' lounges nationwide:

> MAX: Let's talk about Bart. He really does need a leg up on destiny.
> WALLY: And yet I cannot teach him. God he makes me furious!
> MAX: So you know this.
> WALLY: He's impatient, he's arrogant, he's obstinate.
> MAX: You know this, too. You know his nature, and every time you try to change it, you get run over.
> WALLY: Exactly. So what am I doing wrong?
> MAX: You're blaming the wreck on the train. You can't get angry with him for being who he is. Maybe you can't teach him. Maybe all you can do is let him learn. Will he listen to anyone else but you?
> WALLY: Let's find out.

In the subsequent scene, Wally tries his revised approach, introducing Bart to "the faculty." In addition to Wally and Max, this teaching staff includes Golden Age Flash Jay Garrick, Johnny Quick and his daughter Jesse Quick.

Despite this new collaborative teaching approach, Bart's development continues to stumble along. This lack of progress may be due, in part, to the accelerated curriculum. Wally narrates the lesson in *Flash* #97 (January 1995): "All afternoon we've been teaching him what we know, cramming years of super-speed education and training into hours." Such a rapid pace of instruction undermines the executive teaching approach, and ultimately student learning:

> Sometimes teachers embark on complex topics or ideas but allow too little opportunity for students to become involved in these topics to the extent that the topics demand. The material is covered too quickly, without adequate background preparation, or is misrepresented in order to cover it in the short time allowed. Any of these factors denies the student adequate opportunity to learn the material [Fenstermacher and Soltis 15].

Additional drawbacks of the executive approach arise with Wally's limited impact on Bart's education. Although Wally tells Bart they both have things to learn, he mostly remains on the "outside" of the process. "The teacher is not so much an actual part of the process as a manager of it. The teacher is not, it seems, 'inside' the process of teaching and learning but 'outside,' where he or she regulates the content and the activities of the learner" (Fenstermacher and Soltis 16). Another criticism of the executive approach is the focus on results at the expense of other key considerations, "such as the nature and interests of individual students, the special characteristics of different subject matters, and the varying demands that differences in geography, economics, and culture make on what takes place in school" (Fenstermacher and Soltis 16).

Despite these weaknesses, the executive approach was commonly found in classrooms during the 1990s, and its presence continues into the 21st century in the era of accountability (Webb 359). "[T]here is a marked emphasis on student learning outcomes based on fixed conceptions of what students should know and be able to do. These outcomes are precisely what state and federal educational policy are promoting as the twentieth century comes to an end" (Fenstermacher and Soltis 66). All the while, criticism continues from various realms of thought, not the least are constructivists who view learning as an active process enacted by individual students' cognitive change, supported through research by Jean Piaget, Lev Vygotsky (39), and others. Even Wally sees the limits of this executive approach (and his own teaching), agreeing to pass on the responsibility of mentoring Bart to Max Mercury, resulting in the ongoing *Impulse* comic book series.

The Therapist Teacher: Max Mercury (Max Crandall)

Over the course of his super-hero career, Max Mercury has held several different names: Ahwehota, Windrunner, Blue Streak, Quicksilver, and others (*Flash* #97, January 1995). Wally calls Max the "Zen Master" or "Guru" of Speed, and editor Brian Augustyn refers to him as "the fastest mentor alive" (*Impulse* #4, July 1995).

Through an educational lens, Max most closely resembles the "therapist" approach to teaching. Interestingly, like Max this approach has undergone several name changes: therapist, fostering, and facilitator. Fenstermacher and Soltis admit this approach is the most difficult to describe (68). "Therapist" implies giving isolated attention to a mentally unhealthy student. In actuality, a "therapist teacher" is someone who helps every student in the classroom with his or her personal development. The term "fostering" aligns with the image of teacher as a cultivator or nurturer, but some may assume "foster" teacher refers to a type of substitute teacher (Fenstermacher and Soltis 69). In the Fourth Edition of *Approaches to Teaching*, Fenstermacher and Soltis introduce "facilitator" to label this teacher (5). Regardless of title, this approach "views the teacher as an empathetic person charged with helping individuals grow personally and reach a high level of self-actualization, understanding, and acceptance" (4). For the purposes of this chapter, "therapist approach" will be used since it was the initial term presented by the authors, including the editions published before (1992) and after (1998) Bart Allen's introduction in DC Comics.

While education in the 1990s received nation-wide attention, *Impulse* sidesteps large scale super-heroics and instead plays on a smaller stage. In fact, the majority of the comic series takes place in Manchester, Alabama, described as "a place that moves considerably more slowly than [Bart]" (Augustyn, "A Flash of Inspiration" 24). Writer Mark Waid was born in Hueytown, Alabama, and this personal background adds a layer of authenticity to *Impulse's* setting. The real Manchester is an unincorporated community six miles north of Jasper, the county seat of Walker County (Foscue 90). The fictional community of Manchester is a stereotypical small town, and the *Impulse* comic features multiple locations in this area: Applegate Park, Griffin's Hill, Minhota Reservation Casino, Technodyne Industries, Junior High School and Homewood High School (a real one does exist in a suburb of Birmingham).

Although Bart is new to the entire 20th century, the relatively remote setting of Manchester provides both a fresh start and an ideal location for growing up. When Bart asks Max about their new home in *Impulse* #1 (April 1995), the Zen mentor responds, "It's peaceful is what it is. With wide open spaces and a relaxed atmosphere. In other words, it's a prime place to teach you about power … and patience." Editor Bryan Augustyn explains how Max relocates Bart to Manchester to enroll him "in a middle school—and in real life" ("Follow Your Impulse" 64). This holistic perspective aligns with the purpose of the therapist approach to teaching, which is "to enable the learner to become an authentic human being, a person capable of accepting responsibility for what he or she is and is becoming, a person able to make choices that define one's character as one wishes it to be defined" (Fenstermacher and Soltis 27).

Max's focus on personal development appears throughout the *Impulse* series, mostly made of single- or double-issue length stories. At the end of *Impulse* #2 (May 1995), Max tells Bart he has plans for him in the "years to come," revealing a long-term perspective necessary for developing true wisdom and skill mastery, as opposed to mere content memorization and mimicry. Or, as narrated in *Impulse* #23 (March 1997), "Since being appointed Bart's guardian, Max's job has been to engineer the world's biggest attitude adjustment."

In addition to refining superpowers and battle tactics, Max provides multiple opportunities for Bart to grow socially and spiritually. In *Impulse* #3 (June 1995), Max explains his role is to "teach Bart Allen how to act and think like an ordinary 20th century boy, not a 30th century wild man." He then tells Bart, "Your assignment today is to make some friends at school," which becomes an issue-long adventure involving a quick trip to France, a cafeteria food fight, dodgeball attacks, and an epic after-school rumble. In other *Impulse* issues, Max introduces Bart to numerous experiences beyond the scope of core academic or super-hero topics, such as attending a magic show (#17, September 1996) and playing various team sports (#20, December 1996). One of the longest sustained discussions between Bart and Max occurs in *Impulse* #14 (June 1996), dealing with the topic of faith and religion.

During the religion conversation—which occurs over several panels and pages—Bart asks Max to tell him what to believe in. Max responds that it "doesn't work that way. I can't give you an order." Later he elaborates: "In the end, where you place your faith is something you have to decide for yourself…. I want you to think long and hard about your convictions. Even though faith is very personal and takes many forms, I think everybody needs something to believe in." This emphasis on encouraging student choice reflects the therapist approach to teaching. Fenstermacher and Soltis write, "the teacher as therapist does not accept responsibility for moving specific knowledge and skills from some outside source into the mind of the learner; rather the teacher accepts responsibility for helping the student make the choice to acquire knowledge of a given kind and for supporting the student as she acquires that knowledge and uses it to advance her sense of self" (27).

Max gives Bart the opportunity to act on his choices, including difficult decisions with uncertain outcomes. For example, in *Impulse* #6 (September 1995) Bart suspects a classmate's parent of child abuse. Max listens to Bart's concerns, and cautions him that incorrect accusations could harm an entire family's reputation and relationships. Probing further may also expose Bart's secret identity. Even so, Max uses a therapist teaching approach by allowing Bart to decide how to proceed in his investigation. Providing his student freedom to choose is ultimately apparent when Max lets Bart decide to leave Manchester and return to the 30th century with his mother (*Impulse* #24, April 1997), despite unfinished lessons in the present and potential dangers in the future.

Along with choice is the student's firsthand experience with events before, encounters during, and effects following each decision. The therapist approach to teaching is informed by the work of humanistic psychologist Carl Rogers, who believes teaching is generally overrated and promotes the practice of "experiential learning" (103). Fenstermacher and Soltis elaborate that such learning "is filled with personal involvement; the whole person is *in* the learning event, not a passive absorber of whatever the teacher dispenses" (33, emphasis in original). Throughout the *Impulse* comic series, Max allows Bart to run headlong into mysteries (#1, April 1995), heists (#4, July 1995), catastrophes (#8, November 1995), and rescue missions (#13, May 1996). Compare this approach to an executive teacher who must have control over content, scheduling, and evaluation. Wally, for example, tries to manage these aspects and more during his time with Bart. The youngster's impulsive tendencies, however, typically result in bypassing any such barriers.

Even with an experience-centered curriculum based on student choice, the therapist teacher still fulfills a critical role in the learning process: "guide, suggest, encourage, and maybe even, when the occasion is appropriate, warn" (Fenstermacher and Soltis 33). The latter teacher action—warn—is especially important in life-or-death heroics found in comic books. Nevertheless, Max's therapist approach rarely involves direct commands or warnings as he releases Bart to adventure. When he does give specific instructions, it is often after Bart has first experienced a challenge, completed a task, or failed in an attempt. For example, at the end of *Impulse* #5 (August 1995), Bart mopes at home following the escape of a crafty thief, and sarcastically tells Max to "Let me have it! … I did everything wrong! Lecture away!" Max gives a calm, consoling response: "You want words of wisdom? Here are six. Sometimes the bad guys get away." His answer actually continues, although never in the tone of a stern lecture: "You went towards her with a plan. Granted, it was only half thought out, but that's half more than your last plan. You tried. No one was hurt. She won't come back soon. Those are good things."

One may consider Max's response to be "corrective feedback" or reinforcement used by an executive teacher. The difference, though, is in the relationship between student and teacher. "These relationships are founded on care, trust, concern, and nurture" (Fenstermacher and Soltis 70). As the student develops self-identity, this growth occurs through experiences and decisions involving others—peers and mentors alike.

Max also reveals his role as therapist teacher through purposeful lesson design. This includes a sense of "controlled freedom" in the learning environment. In their discussion of relabeling "therapist" to "fostering" teacher, Fenstermacher and Soltis note, "While it may be the case that emphasis on relationship leads to more open classrooms, with greater degrees of choice, fostering teachers may also exercise care for their students by limiting their choices and confining the options available to them" (70). Through seemingly subtle ways, Max creates prompts and activities to safely scaffold Bart's development, such as designing an obstacle course with a surprise ending to teach alertness (*Impulse* #8, November 1995) or slowly selecting a necktie to instill patience (#17, September 1996). Other times, Max is more explicit in his role. During a hockey arena hostage situation (*Impulse* #23, March 1997), Bart asks if Max will join him or not. Max answers, "If I'm needed, I'll jump in. Until then, you handle it. I want to see what you do."

With super-heroes, "jumping in" involves more than a verbal cue or correction. Max, for example, rescues Bart and a friend from a cliff-diving car in *Impulse* #5 (August 1995) by creating an air cushion with his super-fast legs. Max makes it a collaborative technique with Bart, working together to save the car and Bart's unconscious friend. This promotes the "relational bond between teacher and student," a primary goal in the therapist approach (Fenstermacher and Soltis 71). Max also uses the experience to teach Bart about choices impacting collateral damage and secret identities, again keeping a long-term view of holistic development.

Any worthwhile super-hero story features conflict and calamities of all kinds, including interpersonal drama among both friends and foes. Max's mentorship of Bart is not without struggles and setbacks. During the car rescue of *Impulse* #5, for example, Bart first argues with Max about who is to blame for driving off the cliff in the first place. Even after Bart frees hostages at the hockey arena in issue #23 (March 1997), Max is nonplussed that his apprentice still prefers to fight criminals over saving bystanders because "there's more points for busting up the bad guys."

Although building relationships is a noble endeavor, one would argue a super-hero still needs to protect the innocent and overcome evil. Likewise, the therapist approach's focus on relationships and self-actualization leaves some educational goals unaddressed. An executive teacher would expect content competency; others would demand that students become critical thinkers and change agents in particular disciplines. Another drawback to the therapist approach is the focus on individualized personal development. Fenstermacher and Soltis note that "a difficult problem for the therapist approach to teaching" is that "each person is unique" (37).

While Max may be able to focus on Bart as his lone pupil, the typical teacher works in a classroom and school full of different students. As addressed earlier, the preeminence of the executive teaching approach in the 1990s (and beyond) can be attributed to the desire to efficiently provide content delivery for a large population of students. "In the United States it has long been accepted that the maintenance of democracy and national identity requires a common education. This is generally made manifest as a common core of studies for all students" (Fenstermacher and Soltis 37). Note how the authors address attention toward widespread student impact, even foreshadowing Common Core State Standards, which do not appear for another decade (National Governors Association Center for Best Practices, Council of Chief State School Officers). Such standards of any sort are absent in Bart's education from both Wally and Max. Before examining the impact of such instruction, attention should focus on one more group of educators in the pages of *Impulse*.

Non-Speedster Teachers

In addition to speedy mentors Wally and Max, Bart encounters non-powered, "regular" teachers during his time at Manchester Junior High

School. All of these "normal" instructors are supporting characters and fall mostly into stereotypical roles depicted in Hollywood film or television.

Bart's English teacher is Mrs. Dalrymple, a middle-aged woman with round eyeglasses, tied-back hair, and the same outfit in every scene she appears: high heels, black skirt, black suit jacket, white blouse. She also wears the same look of shock or indignation at unexpected student behavior, sending Bart to the principal's office for any perceived mockery. Mrs. Dalrymple's classroom instruction consists of traditional assignments such as student autobiography papers (*Impulse* #1, April 1995) and pop quizzes (#10, January 1996).

Some teachers appear once or twice as "bit parts" in the larger storyline. The gym teacher is known simply as "Coach." This title is stamped on the front of his ball cap, topping off an outfit of sweatpants, sweatshirt, and tennis shoes. Coach continually scowls under a pronounced mustache, getting in students' faces to yell insults as often as instructions. He repeatedly calls students in the all-boys gym class "girls" (#3, June 1995), and makes them run laps for losing dodge ball matches, which is the only activity ever depicted (*Impulse* #3, #10). Coach aligns with cinematic representations of gym teachers, "without the benefit of any particular curricular value framework because most of them are not depicted in the process of teaching" (Dalton, 74).

Mr. Graham is found only in *Impulse* #3 (June 1995), and presents a reasonable assignment while emphasizing an attempt to expand students' learning: "This is not your parents' study hall, students. In this library class, you will learn study skills." He then assigns them a "pop quiz" to look up three specific facts about France, adding "I don't care where you find the answers. Just find them before the end of class." Mr. Graham doesn't expect Bart to leave the library and actually travel to Paris to find the answers (and stop a bank robbery). Nor does he notice Bart's temporary absence or subsequent return. Aside from the pop quiz, Mr. Graham teaches no specific study skills, and shows little interest in his students beyond assignment completion.

All of these teachers reflect traits of Hollywood's "bad teachers," as described by Dalton: "typically bored by students, afraid of students, or eager to dominate students" and who "follow the standardized curriculum, which they adhere to in order to avoid personal contact with students" (61). Moreover, "[t]he bad teacher is generally presented neither liked nor disliked (by other teachers) but as part of the system embedded so deeply into the structure of the school as institution that he or she must be accepted or at least tolerated."

The only "good teacher" featured at Bart's middle school is actually the assistant principal, Randall Sheridan. The area where Mr. Sheridan has greatest association with Dalton's analysis of Hollywood teachers is in personal connections with students: "The good teachers in the movies are frequently more closely aligned with their students than with other adults in the school" (30). When they first meet (*Impulse* #2, May 1995), the assistant principal tells Bart to call him by his first name Randy, just like "all the kids do." Mr. Sheridan then advises Bart to write "extra dry" English papers to appease Mrs. Dalrymple ("Give her the paper she wants"), but encourages him to continue his creative work, even offering collaboration. Elsewhere, Mr. Sheridan's personal involvement ranges from helping one student exposed to domestic violence (#6, September 1995) to hosting a rock band concert in the school gymnasium (#12, March 1996). The latter case puts Mr. Sheridan in a precarious situation between the expectations of his student body and safety concerns of the head principal. Although he himself is an administrator, Mr. Sheridan's "good teacher" approach to serving students reflects "tension between the teacher and administrators" commonly found in Hollywood films (Dalton 34).

Evidence of Student Learning

Bart's teachers resemble a diverse collection of super-heroes and licensed educators. Even though Wally and Max share similar speed-based powers, they teach Bart using two distinct approaches. As an "executive" teacher, Wally stresses immediate action through direct instruction, cues, and corrective feedback. Using a "therapist" approach, Max emphasizes long-term results, student choice, and personal development of his individual pupil. Although more attention goes to Max's instruction throughout the ongoing *Impulse* comic book series, both approaches have merit. Writing in 1998, Fenstermacher and Soltis conclude, "The executive and therapist approaches are needed for successful teaching in systems of schooling as they now exist. Both offer perspectives and methods that permit teachers to practice effectively and humanely in the complex, highly differentiated classrooms of today" (60).

The staff and faculty at Manchester Junior High do not receive as much attention, but this is understandable since their work is not the main focus of the comic books. In a sociological study of school-based Hollywood movies, Bulman notes, "What matters most in these films is not academic achievement, but the achievement of one's independent identity" (86). The same can be said for Bart's adventures as Impulse and as an adolescent.

The ultimate evidence of educational impact is the student's application of instruction. To that end, Bart shows hints of his learning beginning in the second year of *Impulse*'s run. In issue #13 (May 1996), a classmate named Roland attempts dangerous feats to gain school-wide fame. Bart spends the first half of the story behind the scenes as Impulse, rescuing Roland from each death-defying venture. The accolades grow along with the hazards of each new challenge, and an exasperated Bart complains to Max that Roland "bolts headlong into the most ridiculous danger without even thinking! ... His stupid stunts are getting riskier and riskier! ... He just won't learn!" Max responds with a smile: "Maddening, isn't it?" Bart forgoes his super-hero identity and approaches Roland directly to point out the difference between fame and true friendship. Roland finally sees Bart's point and—before one last, unexpected rescue—gives up his daredevil antics.

In addition to classmates, Bart teaches adults—starting with his mentor. After his past offenses resurface in *Impulse* #16 (August 1996), Max sprints away at super-speed—so fast that he is on the verge of traveling decades forward in time. Before Max can make the one-way trip, Bart catches up to explain his own error in letting their secret identities slip. More than admitting a mistake, however, Bart models how to correct things, telling Max: "I guess I wanted to let you know that I'm not going to run away from it. I'm going to go back ... and take responsibility for anything I did wrong." Max learns from Bart's example, returning to make amends.

Bart also "shows what he knows" during a trip to the future with his mother Meloni (*Impulse* #25, May 1997). Throughout their adventures in the 30th century, Bart repeatedly talks through his decisions and vocalizes a thought-process taught by his mentor: "Max always said to take care of people in trouble!" "At this point, Max would wait and find out more!" As they try to outwit the enemy, Meloni asks her son what Max would do, and Bart quickly answers with a plan for the next step. Although Bart is reviewing his mentor's teaching, he himself has assumed the role of teacher. At the end of the issue, Bart must return to the 20th century—part of a truce agreement, and also so that he can continue his tutelage with Max. Much to Bart's chagrin, his mother admits that "Max is a better parent than I am.... He's teaching you well. Better than I could." Heartbroken but hopeful, Bart leaves his mother in the future. Even though they spend mere hours with one another, Meloni expresses fond familiarity: "I know you, Bart. You're someone who'll put his heart aside to do the right thing.... That's my son."

Evidence of Bart's learning arises one final time during Mark Waid's tenure as *Impulse* writer. In issue #27 (July 1997), the teens of Manchester stage an all-night sit-in at the shopping mall to protest a proposed town curfew. Bart joins the event as Impulse in order to help calm and contain the crowd. For the rest of the issue, he races around the mall to stop restless kids from damaging property and injuring themselves. As the narration puts it: "Traditionally Impulse is less babysitter than babysat. Tonight, however, it's up to him to be responsible for others. It's the longest night of his life." In addition to protecting the stores and his friends, Bart manages to thwart a trio of thieves and clean the entire mall by morning. The event is a success because of Impulse, sitting in the shadows and exhausted from his thankless work. Many teachers can relate.

New Century, Ongoing Learning

Although creator Mark Waid left *Impulse* after co-writing issue #27 in July 1997, the comic book series continued five more years with the final issue being #89 in October 2002. In addition to adventures and education with Max Mercury, Bart teamed up with other super-heroes, took more time-traveling trips, and even spent some time as the Flash. At the direction of different writers and editors, Bart has assumed several identities, grown up, died, and returned to life young again. Overall, however, the "fastest teen alive" has never returned to the level of prominence he once had with his own solo *Impulse* series in the 1990s.

Like Bart Allen, education continues moving forward and transforming at the whims of various stakeholders. In January 2002, President George W. Bush signed the No Child Left Behind Act into law (Webb 360). Like its predecessor Goals 2000, "NCLB" stated optimal achievement targets and deadlines. In the case of NCLB, every student should perform at grade level proficiency by 2014. That year has come and gone, along with additional educational initiatives. Of course, idealized objectives found in legislation like Goals 2000 and NCLB are never fully reached. Nevertheless, the purpose of education—regardless of teaching approach—is to promote ongoing student learning and school improvement. Similar growth and changes occur for any ongoing comic book character, Bart Allen among them. The process is a marathon, not a sprint.

WORKS CITED

Augustyn, Brian. "A Flash of Inspiration, a Reckless Impulse … and You." In *Impulse* #1 (April 1995). New York: DC Comics.
_____. "Follow Your Impulse! Simple Entertainment, or Metaphor for Life?" In *Impulse: Reckless Youth*. New York: DC Comics, 1997, pp. 3–6, 63–4.
Bell, Terrel. "Reflections One Decade After a Nation at Risk." *Phi Delta Kappan*, vol. 74, 1993, pp. 592–7.
Bulman, Robert C. *Hollywood Goes to High School: Cinema, Schools, and American Culture.* Worth Pub., 2005.
Centers for Disease Control and Prevention. "ADHD Throughout the Years." Attention-Deficit/Hyperactivity Disorder. 7 February 2017, www.cdc.gov/ncbddd/adhd/timeline.html.
Clinton, William J. "Remarks on Signing the Goals 2000: Educate America Act in San Diego." The American Presidency Project. 31 March 1994, http://www.presidency.ucsb.edu/ws/index.php?pid=49895.
Dalton, Mary M. *The Hollywood Curriculum: Teachers in the Movies.* P. Lang, 2007.
DC Comics advertisement. Impulse. *Wizard Magazine*, 1995.
Fenstermacher, Gary, and Jonas Soltis. *Approaches to Teaching.* 3rd ed. New York: Teachers College Press, 1998.

_____. *Approaches to Teaching.* 4th ed. New York: Teachers College Press, 2004.

Firestone, William, et al. "An Overview of Education Reform Since 1983." In *The Education Reform Movement of the 1980s: Perspectives and Cases.* Ed. Joseph Murphy. Berkley, CA: McCutchan Publishing, 1990, pp. 349–64.

Foscue, Virginia. *Place Names in Alabama.* Tuscaloosa: The University of Alabama Press, 1989.

Goertz, Margaret. "Redefining Government Roles in an Era of Standards-Based Reform." *Phi Delta Kappan,* vol. 83, 2001, pp. 62–6.

Groening, Matt, and Al Jean. *The Simpsons Movie: A Look Behind the Scenes* (DVD). Distributed by The Sun, 2007.

Holland, Kimberly, and Elsbeth Riley. "ADHD by the Numbers: Facts, Statistics, and You." *Healthline,* 4 September 2014, www.healthline.com/health/adhd/facts-statistics-infographic.

Howson, Geoffrey, and Bryan Wilson. *School Mathematics in the 1990s.* ICMI Study Series. Cambridge: University Press, 1986.

H.R. 1804 Goals 2000: Educate America Act. March 1994. www2.ed.gov/legislation/GOALS 2000/TheAct/index.html.

Kaplan, George. "TV's Version of Education (And What to Do About It)." *Phi Delta Kappan,* vol. 71, 1990, pp. K1–K12.

Metcalf, Kim, et al. *School Choice in America: The Great Debate.* Bloomington, IN: Phi Delta Kappa International, 2001.

Murphy, Joseph. "The Education Reform Movement of the 1980s: A Comprehensive Analysis." In *The Education Reform Movement of the 1980s: Perspectives and Cases.* Ed. Joseph Murphy. Berkley, CA: McCutchan Publishing, 1990, pp. 3–55.

National Governors Association Center for Best Practices, Council of Chief State School Officers. *Common Core State Standards.* Washington, D.C.: Author, 2010.

Pelletier, Luc, et al. "Pressure from Above and Pressure from Below as Determinants of Teachers' Motivation and Teaching Behaviors." *Journal of Educational Psychology,* vol. 94, no. 1, 2002, pp. 186–96.

Piaget, Jean. *Construction of Reality in the Child.* London: Routledge & Kegan Paul, 1957.

Raines, Claire. *Beyond Generation X: A Practical Guide for Managers.* Menlo Park, CA: Crisp Publications, 1997.

Robison, Linda, et al. "National Trends in the Prevalence of Attention-Deficit/Hyperactivity Disorder and the Prescribing of Methylphenidate Among School-Age Children: 1990–1995." *Clinical Pediatrics,* vol. 38, no. 4, 1999, pp. 209–17.

Rogers, Carl. *Freedom to Learn.* Columbus, OH: Charles E. Merrill, 1969.

Russo, Tom. "The Wizard Q&A: Mark Waid." *Wizard Magazine,* vol. 55, March 1996, pp. 48–54.

Salvatore, Brian. "Mark Waid Tells Us Why He Loves the Flash." *Multiversity Comics,* 11 February 2016, www.multiversitycomics.com/interviews/mark-waid-tells-us-why-he-loves-the-flash/.

The Simpsons: America's First Family (6 Minute Edit for the Season 1 DVD). BBC. UK: 20th Century Fox, 2000.

Turner, Chris. *Planet Simpson: How a Cartoon Masterpiece Documented an Era and Defined a Generation.* Toronto: Random House Canada, 2004.

Vygotsky, Lev. "Thinking and Speech." In *The Collected Works of L.S. Vygotsky, Volume 1: Problems of General Psychology.* Ed. Robert W. Rieber and Aaron S. Carton. New York: Plenum Press, 1987. 39–285. (Original work published 1934.)

Waid, Mark (w), and Anthony Williams (a). "Faith." *Impulse* #14 (June 1996). New York: DC Comics.

Waid, Mark (w), Ruben Diaz (w), Sal Buscema (a), and Craig Rousseau (a). "Fight for Your Right to Party." *Impulse* #27 (July 1997). New York: DC Comics.

Waid, Mark (w), and Salvador Larroca (a). "Terminal Velocity, Mach One: The Dead Yet Live." *Flash (Vol. 2)* #95 (November 1994). New York: DC Comics.

_____. "Terminal Velocity, Mach Three: The Other Side of Light." *Flash (Vol. 2)* #97 (January 1995). New York: DC Comics.

_____. "Terminal Velocity, Mach Two: All the Wrong Moves." *Flash (Vol. 2)* #96 (December 1994). New York: DC Comics.

_____. "Terminal Velocity, Redline: Ultimate Rush." *Flash (Vol. 2)* #99 (March 1995). New York: DC Comics.

Waid, Mark (w), and Carlos Pacheco (a). "Reckless Youth, Chapter Three: Just Do It!" *Flash (Vol. 2)* #94 (September 1994). New York. DC Comics.

_____. "Reckless Youth, Chapter Two: Quick Study." *Flash (Vol. 2)* #93 (August 1994). New York: DC Comics.

Waid, Mark (w), and Humberto Ramos (a). "Bad Influence." *Impulse* #4 (July 1995). New York: DC Comics.

_____. "Crossfire." *Impulse* #2 (May 1995). New York: DC Comics.

_____. "Dead Heat—Fifth Lap: Breaking the Barrier." *Impulse* #11 (February 1996). New York: DC Comics.

_____. "Dead Heat—Second Lap: Disaffected Youth." *Impulse* #10 (January 1996). New York: DC Comics.

_____. "First Base." *Impulse* #20 (December 1996). New York: DC Comics.

_____. "How to Win Friends and Influence People." *Impulse* #3 (June 1995). New York: DC Comics.

_____. "Lessons Learned." *Impulse* #23 (March 1997). New York: DC Comics.

_____. "Lightning Strikes." *Impulse* #5 (August 1995). New York: DC Comics.

_____. "Quicker Than the Eye." *Impulse* #17 (September 1996). New York: DC Comics.

_____. "Reunion." *Impulse* #24 (April 1997). New York: DC Comics.

_____. "Running from the Past." *Impulse* #16 (August 1996). New York: DC Comics.

_____. "Secret Identity." *Impulse* #6 (September 1995). New York: DC Comics.

_____. "The Single Synapse Theory." *Impulse* #1 (April 1995). New York: DC Comics.

_____. "Smart Men, Foolish Choices." *Impulse* #8 (November 1995). New York: DC Comics.

_____. "Sonic Youth." *Impulse* #12 (March 1996). New York: DC Comics.

_____. "Water Rat." *Impulse* #13 (May 1996). New York: DC Comics.

_____. "You and Me Against the World." *Impulse* #25 (May 1997). New York: DC Comics.

Waid, Mark (w), and Mike Wieringo (a). "Reckless Youth, Chapter One: Speed Kills." *Flash (Vol. 2)* #92 (July 1994). New York: DC Comics.

Webb, L. Dean. *The History of American Education: A Great American Experiment.* Upper Saddle River, NJ: Pearson, 2006.

An Impulsive Teen from the Future

Imagining Youth, Virtual Reality and the Digital Future at the Turn of the Millennium

Louie Dean Valencia-García

A Reckless Youth

Two households, not quite alike in dignity, in the 30th century, where we lay our scene. From ancient grudge break to new mutiny, where civil blood makes civil hands unclean. From forth the fatal loins of these two foes, Thawne and Allen. A pair of star-cross'd lovers spawn a child born with super-speed who grows-up believing life is but a video game—with a reset button. Born a thousand years in the future, the birth of Bart Allen, son of Meloni Thawne and Don Allen, and the grandson of the Silver Age Flash, Barry Allen, and reporter Iris West-Allen, and Thaddeus Thawne, the president of Earthgov and descendent of the Silver Age speedster's arch enemy, the Reverse Flash, could have been the symbolic merger of rival families. However, this was not the case. Debuting in the summer of 1994 in the pages of *The Flash*, in a story titled "Reckless Youth," Bart would become the teenage superhero code-named "Impulse." Later, he would become known as the second Kid Flash, and, eventually, albeit briefly, taking up the mantle of the Flash from the third bearer, his cousin Wally West.

As most issues of his titular, monthly comic—which ran from 1995 to 2002—restated in some variation, Impulse was born with uncontrollable hypermetabolism as a result of his connection to the so-called "Speed Force." Introduced the month before Bart's first appearance, the Speed Force was an extradimensional power that gives speeders their power and has since become part of Flash canon and a major element of the Flash mythos (Waid, "Out of Time"). As a temporary fix to Bart's accelerated aging, a side-effect of his hypermetabolism, the authoritarian future government, Earthgov, placed Bart in a virtual reality (VR) program intended to keep up with his super-speed and accelerated growth. In this way, the two-year-old boy was able to mentally keep up with his rapidly aging body—looking around age fourteen when introduced in in 1994 (Waid, "Reckless [...] Chapter One"). Only by breaking Bart out of Earthgov's VR program was Iris Allen-West able to escape to the past so that her nephew, Wally West, the third Flash, could save Bart from the degenerative nature of that hypermetabolism. However, as a side effect of living the equivalent of fourteen years in a virtual reality, as Iris explains, "Now that [Bart's] free, he thinks everything is the same game as in VR, that's why he's so impulsive—he doesn't know that in the real world, he can get hurt" (Waid, "Reckless [...] Chapter 3," 10).

Although Iris traveled to the past so that her deceased husband's former sidekick could save her grandson, Bart would not become a protégé to the third Flash, as might have been expected a generation earlier. In fact, toward the end of the story that introduces Bart, Wally thinks to himself, "Oh, man, what a handful he's gonna be. I'm not looking forward to telling Iris that I'm not about to shoulder that responsibility. I know she means well, but she thinks too retro. I don't do sidekicks" (*ibid.*, 12). By rejecting the role of mentor, a particular dynamic is created between the third Scarlet Speedster and the "reckless youth." If the previous generation of superheroes adopted their sidekicks as part of an attempt to present a more heteronormative family,[1] the generation of teenaged superheroes who came up during the 1990s, came from more complicated (and arguably more realistic) familial backgrounds. This new generation of heroes found great success in the pages of the comics and among their fans. By looking at Bart Allen, a teen from the future, who is raised by an adoptive father-figure/mentor and his estranged daughter, and later the extended Flash family, including the Golden Age Flash, Jay Garrick and his wife, Joan, we can better understand the super-teen as a prototype for what it meant to be a young person at the turn of the millennium.

Infamously, pop historian-sociologists Neil Howe and William Strauss codified the term "millennial"—the "generation" born between 1982 and 2004—into the American consciousness in 2000 with the publication of the book *Millennials Rising: The Next Great Generation*. In that work, the authors contended that the millennial persona is: (1) Special; (2) Sheltered; (3) Confident; (4) Team-oriented; (5) Achieving; (6) Pressured; (7) Conventional (Howe and Strauss). While their claims had little basis on scientific data, and was released some five years after *Impulse* debuted, it is not hard to see the obvious ways in which Bart Allen fell into such faulty stereotypes of what it meant to be a teenager at the turn of the millennium. Bart was indeed special because of his super-speed, grew-up sheltered in a VR world, which caused him to be overly confident when confronted with real danger. Bart helped form a team, Young Justice, did not like to be bested, was constantly pressured early on by his mentors to be better, and at the same time had, somewhat conventionally, entered into the family business of crime-fighting. Of course, such stereotypes are problematic, inherently; yet, still, because of Bart's characterization, which fit so perfectly into those stereotypes, we can also understand him as sort of an Ur-millennial figure sent from the future. Simultaneously, because of these depictions as a teenager from the future, the writers also used his character as a vehicle to understand a more connected society and the ways young people were interacting with their communities through new technologies.

Being a Teenager (and Superhero) in the 1990s

Dubbed "Impulse" because of his trigger-quick impulsive nature, Bart Allen joined the Flash family with a bang, quickly spinning off into his own self-titled series, *Impulse*, just a year after his introduction in the pages of *The Flash*. The series, written by acclaimed author Mark Waid, who also wrote *The Flash*, followed the refugee from the future and heir to the Flash dynasty as he learned to be a teenager living in the late 20th century world of the fictional hamlet of Manchester, Alabama, under the guidance of Max Mercury, who posed as Bart's uncle. Mercury was a mysterious, yet trusted, speedster "guru" from the past, who had moved to Alabama to be closer to his middle-aged daughter, Helen, who chronologically was not much younger than Mercury due to his time travel.

To understand the character of Bart Allen, it is helpful to compare him to his young superhero contemporaries of the 1990s. Bart, although from a far future, embodied what a "millennial" superhero could be. In that period, numerous young, mostly male, heroes were given their own (often short-lived) series, namely: *Ray* (February 1992), *Robin* (November 1993), *Damage* (April 1994), *Superboy* (February 1994), *Supergirl* (a miniseries in 1994 and regular series in 1996), *Anima* (October 1994), and *Impulse* (April 1995). Of those characters, Superboy, Impulse, and Robin were both the closest in age and were launched in the pages of A-list heroes Superman, Flash, and Batman. Toward the end of the decade, in 1998, the three would form the team "Young Justice" along with Wonder Girl (Cassie Sandsmark), Arrowette (Cissie King-Jones)—a character first introduced in the pages of *Impulse* but loosely associated with Green Arrow—and "the Secret," a phantasmal girl of mysterious origins. The gender-balanced teenaged team followed a long tradition of successful teenaged superhero groups in the DC Universe, a tradition going back to the Legion of Super-Heroes and the original Teen Titans. Curiously, with the exception of Batman who was a more hands-on mentor to Robin, the superheroes who would have been their adult mentors, Superman, Wonder Woman, Flash, and Green Arrow took a more hands-off approach with this new batch of teenage heroes, often finding separate mentors for each of the teens. In this way, this younger generation of heroes differed from their Gen-X counterparts, the original Teen Titans, claiming more autonomy early on in their superhero careers.

Impulse was placed under the care of Max Mercury, a hero who first was introduced in 1940 as "Quicksilver," but only reappeared in the modern comics in 1993. Wonder Girl was raised by her mother, Helena Sandmark, a Harvard-trained archeologist who had an affair with the Greek God Zeus. Wonder Girl was trained by Amazons, including Wonder Woman, and was given mythical accoutrements that gave her strength and flight, until she developed her own powers. Superboy was a clone of Superman and arch-enemy Lex Luthor (originally thought to be the also villainous Cadmus director Paul Westfield), and was mentored by a genetically engineered "DNAlien," named Dubbilex. Arrowette was raised by her mother, who might be considered something of a "stage mom" for the superhero circuit. Robin, Tim Drake, at least in the mid–1990s, was a teenager who lived at home with his father, an international business man, who was recovering from the death of his wife, but eventually fell in love with his physical therapist, who becomes a loving step-mother to Tim. Tim was brought into the Batman family through his own investigation discovering Batman's secret identity. Comparatively, Bart Allen's origin was the most straightforward—grandson of Barry Allen and cousin to Wally West. Nevertheless, despite the potentiality of living with his immediate family, Bart was sent to live with pseudo-uncle, Max Mercury, in an effort to keep the timeline intact (other alternatives included his grandmother and his mother, who were potential risks because of their knowledge of the future.) Each of these young characters, and especially Impulse, demonstrated that familial structures had certainly changed from the 1960s to the 1990s. The sort of hybrid "superhero families" that were created in the 1960s comics, by the end of the millennium had expanded into what were large extended family groups which interacted regularly among each other. Arguably, the 1990s generation of young superheroes entered into more complicated family trees and dynamics than could have been imagined for the 1960s heteronormative nuclear family.

Generally, the tone of these new younger superhero comics was much lighter than what had been prevalent in the pages of Superman, Batman, Wonder Woman, and the Flash. *Robin* was a series about a young detective and tech genius; *Superboy* was a sci-fi beach serial; and *Impulse*, was a high school student teenaged superhero obsessed with video games, cursed with short attention span, and who had no desire to plan for the future. Bart was popular at school, if only accidently, and had little interest in girls. *Impulse* did address many issues that teenagers of the time dealt with, particularly surrounding responsibility and popularity, and always did so with a keen sense of wit and humor—with an awareness that seemed to acknowledge both genre and audience. One long-time reader of comics described *Impulse* in a letter written to the comic's letter column, still popular as a way for readers and comic creators to communicate in the 1990s:

> Feeling a little down? Have too many of your heroes gone dark and gritty on you? Have the high numbers of senseless deaths in your various comics got you wondering what you ever saw in comics to begin with? I have the perfect cure for you. *Impulse* #1 is no more and no less that pure fun! I have been needing a comic that is not so dark, and Impulse is it. This is one of the best reads I have had in a long while. This book is a refreshing change from all the angst-ridden books being published today. Even with the new generation of heroes, Robin, the Ray, Anima, Damage, etc., there is entirely too much darkness for my taste. Impulse proves you can tell a good story without having to wipe out cities, destroy the lead characters' faith in themselves, cause irreparable harm to those closest to them and other disasters. Yes, you can have fun in comics again. This is truly why I began reading comics 25 years ago: for enjoyment [Waid, "Bad Influence," 23].

   Curiously, one might imagine that the adventures of a teenage old boy from the future would mostly appeal to teens and children, however, from the start, *Impulse* also had an adult fan base, which gave space for humor in comics that was both appealing to adult and younger audiences. Still, while appealing to adults, *Impulse* certainly was appreciated by young readers:

> Dear Guys,
>
> MORE! I want more! I just finished my copy of *Impulse* #1 for about the fourth time and I cannot wait for the next issue! You guys are incredible! I would kill to have your jobs and be able to take a new, relatively untouched, teenaged male superhero and just write to my heart's content! I love Impulse as a character and can't get enough of Bart Allen! I love to read heroes in high school, and I can really get into the setting. I want more Impulse, more Bart, more school, team-ups galore and some girls thrown in to show Bart what speed is really about.[2]
>   Throughout my in-depth studies of the DC Universe, I have noticed how incredibly current you guys stay with teenage lingo. How do you do it, I'm not sure. I've come up with three possible answers; choose the best on:
>   a) *All DC writers have teenage children and learn the language through constant environment.*
>   b) *DC writers pull a Jane Goodall and travel into the depths of public high schools to study the linguistics of a most perplexing species, the American teenager.*
>   c) *You guys are all so incredibly current that you know the language and use it in your daily conversations and vocabularies.*

Keep up the great work and I hope someday to join your ranks in the comic-book industry. Dare to Dream [*ibid.*, 24].

If those letters are any indication, the teenage superhero from the future certainly marked a change of tone in DC Comics contemporary line of comics, and instantly attracted a fan base. In publication until October 2002, with a total of 90 issues, *Impulse* received much fanfare. The comic resonated with younger and older audiences because of a perceived authenticity of the character. While other comics of the era had decidedly gone darker—Batman had recently had his back broken and Superman killed—the kid from the future helped to bring back lightheartedness to the comics of the 1990s.

Just Another Kid Flash at the Turn of the Millennium

In part three of "Reckless Youth," the story in which Bart debuts, the teenager speeds around the Flash's house, introducing his personality to readers for the first time, pronouncing while running around Wally West's kitchen at super-speed: "Where's the holovision? I'm bored! Can I have this? I want an Omnicom! I'm really bored! Where's the matter converter?" (Waid, "Reckless […]" Chapter 3, 9). In a blur, the boy is simultaneously eating a sandwich, drinking a soda, and investigating a toaster. Wearing a white and red suit and yellow goggles, Bart holds a power not possessed by Wally—the ability to vibrate through solid matter, moving faster than molecules. It is made clear that Bart requires the type of attention that Wally West is not prepared to give, prompting the decision to hand over the boy to Max Mercury.

The choice of the fictional Alabamian town of Manchester was a personal one for writer Mark Waid. At the end of the first issue of *Impulse*, editor Brian Augustyn writes a short essay for readers titled "A Flash of Inspiration, A Reckless Impulse…. And You" to situate the author, character, and audience. In that essay, the reader learns that Waid is from Alabama himself—a small town called Hueytown. Augustyn writes, "[Mark Waid] knows the environs of this book firsthand and remembers it all with great fondness. From Richmond to Memphis to Dallas, our scribe has wandered through more of the south than most tractor-pull touring shows and has a wealth of experience that should serve stories for years to come" (Waid, "The Single," 24). The images of the town were inspired by photographs taken by a "junior high chum" of Waid's, Nick Patterson, a then reporter for the Birmingham Post-Herald (24). While Barry Allen and Wally West came from the American midwest, Bart's setting in Alabama only heightened the juxtaposition of a teenager from the future being raised in the past.

Once Bart moves from Keystone City to Manchester, Alabama readers get to know him better. Physically, he's a 15-year-old boy. He has hazel eyes and an impossibly full head of hair with bangs that go down to his nose. Bart's large head and feet are disproportional to his small-framed body. The boy has a big imagination—with the creators of *Impulse* often depicting his thoughts as drawings, rather than the standard text-based "thought bubbles" still common in the era. In one early story, Bart writes himself to be a "monster hunter from the planet Korbal" in an autobiographical assignment for school (Waid, "Crossfire," 10). When sent to the office for his insubordination, the hip school assistant principal, Randy, tells Bart he might have "quite a future in video games" (10). The administrator asks Bart to write the dry paper that was requested, but encourages the teen to continue writing his fantastical stories for him so they could work on developing his talent. When Bart goes back home, after solving a weapons espionage case, Max attempts to tether the hero to reality, telling Bart that he needs to be "grounded in the real world." Bart returns to his autobiographical essay, writing himself as a 15-year-old from Keystone City, who was liberated from the dungeons of Mercury—certainly a swipe at "uncle" Max Mercury. This vignette is particularly significant in that it demonstrates two fundamental qualities about the character: 1) Bart doesn't believe in blind obedience to his elders—having grown up largely independent in his virtual reality world; and 2) the character's impulsiveness is intrinsic to his personality—demonstrating an inability to see the repercussions of his actions—a driving plot device for the series. Somehow, despite chaos ensuing because of that impulsiveness, Bart always walks away unscathed—at least in the early run of the series. In a sort of vicious circle, the series sets itself up to require that these two defining characteristics be resolved in order for the character to evolve. Any sort of evolution would require that Bart escape the influence of his VR childhood, and would, essentially, redefine the character.[3] To escape that influence, would make the character no longer "impulsive"—effectively destroying the character as he was initially introduced.

The decision to write a character from the future in rural Alabama is significant, as Bart became one of the few D.C. Comics superheroes starring in his own title that was based in the United States' south.[4] His setting is both atypical in the period for its location and for its setting in a seemingly normal high school—which regularly featured a multiracial cast, as well as strong female characters that were portrayed as more than love interests—often subverting expectations. In Bart's first adventures he gained a reputation as being willing to stand up to bullies, take on ridiculous dares, and started to build friendships with two other students in school, Carol Bucklen and Preston Lindsay. The first "heavy" story line in the series surrounded Preston coming to school bruised. Assistant Principal Randy was particularly unnerved by the bruising. One of many people (including Max) encouraging Bart to make friends, Randy asks Bart to watch out for Preston. Preston was a bit of an outsider, blond, and fan of film, often with camera at hand. After a run-in with Preston's father, and then seeing Preston bruised in the locker room, Bart goes to Max to figure out how to deal with an abusive situation. Max suggests that Bart be aware that false accusations can destroy a family, but after seeing Preston bruised, Bart decides to investigate as Impulse. In that investigation, Impulse confronts the father, only to find out that Preston's mother was the one who is abusing the boy—shocking both Impulse and the father. Not only does this story subvert expectations by showing Preston's mother as the abuser, but the story subverts itself by showing Preston desiring that his mother get help with her anger (Waid, "Secret Identity"). By taking on a rather weighty subject early in the series, while still delivering comic relief, *Impulse* created a place for itself in a crowded market. While many stories hinged on Bart's impulsive nature, in many ways that impulsiveness was a metaphor for youth—a negotiation of experience, learning, and adapting.

A Kid from the Future: Sci-Fi Adventures, Technologies and the Internet

In the summer of 1995, readers are introduced to White Lightning, a teenage super villain who inspires teenage boys to join in on her heists—searching out her recruits online (Waid, "Bad Influence"). Carol describes White Lightning as the "bandit legend of the internet," explaining:

> Since local boys follow her around like puppy dogs, she uses them to help pull thefts. No one gets hurt, no one gets caught... generally... and so everybody wants the status of being part of the legend. Whoever helps her walks away with an insignia jacket and reflected glory. They think that makes them cool [Waid, "Bad Influence," 16–19].

Bart is invited by a group of teenage boys from his high school who are auditioning to be a part of the White Lightning's crew. One boy tells Bart: "You're just the piece she cruises for, man! You're an ace..." Another chimes in, "You're quick." And another adds, subtly subverting gender expectations, "...and you're really good looking!" The other boys look at the third surprised, and the boy recovers himself, "That's what my girlfriend says! I dunno!" Bart agrees to audition for the crew, initially getting rejected, but eventually finding his way in. This issue demonstrated a rising awareness of the internet as a tool for both building communities, and for criminality. Moreover, it showed a tacit projection of queerness—albeit one that is quickly qualified (although unconvincingly).

Coincidentally (or not?), it was also in this issue that "DC Comics Online" was first promoted in the pages of *Impulse*. DC Comics Online was part of

America Online, a subscription-based dial-up internet service that gave users access to exclusive content provided by mostly well-known media outlets, including ABC, Discovery Channel, Business Week, etc., as well as access to what was then called the "World Wide Web." Fans, with a computer and a modem, could request a "DC Comics Online starter kit with no obligation." Upon calling a 1-800 number, America Online would send out a diskette that featured a long-haired, "modern" Superman prominently on purple packaging. The mailer also promoted a collection of "hundreds of full-color images of your favorite characters," access to the "DC Comics archives," the ability to "[t]alk directly with artists, writers, and editors," previews of new comics, and chatrooms and forums where fans could interact with each other.[5] While it is difficult to say whether or not the internet-related story had anything to do with the release of the new platform, the story does certainly reflect the rise of the internet in the mid–1990s. Moreover, both the disk sent out to DC Comics fans and the White Lightning story demonstrated two popular features of the internet that were recognized early: the ability to directly interact with celebrities (both White Lightning and comic book producers, respectively), and the ability for fans to interact with each other online.

In an era where video games and social media—instant messaging, message forums, and chatrooms—were becoming more common, Max decides to take Bart on a camping trip. Max bans Bart from bringing his handheld videogame, horrifyingly disconnecting Bart from his virtual world—what the teen speedster calls "sensory deprivation." The trip was motivated by Bart's decision to act impulsively during a hostage situation at an ice rink. Max wanted to understand Bart's impulsive behavior and the boy's inability to strategize during the hostage situation. Specifically, Bart failed to try and rescue the bystanders in that rescue situation. Rather than saving the hostages first, as Max would have liked, Bart goes after the gunmen with a Zamboni—placing the hostages at risk (Waid, "Lessons Learned"). For Max, this is a cardinal superhero sin.

At the campsite, as a sort of test for his young protégé, Max vibrates, causing a minor earthquake, intentionally lodging his foot into a crevice—calling to Bart for help. Again, rather than extricating Max from falling rocks, Bart goes after the rocks, individually pulverizing them one-by-one. After smashing the rocks, Bart exclaims, "Game over." When again confronted with the question of why the teen went after the gunmen and the falling rocks, instead of attempting to simply remove the endangered parties, Bart replies, "Because there's more points for busting up the bad guys," leaving Max completely horrified, believing all his training being useless (Waid, "Lessons Learned," 16–19). One reader, Stacey Hogan, wrote in response to that story:

> If I were Max, I would be upset too, but Max knew, or should at least have had a clue that Bart's mind is not going to immediately erase all its prior knowledge and experiences simply because Max is giving it new information.... The VR experiences has

dominance. It will never, ever, ever completely go away, and I doubt that anything short of actually losing someone or even indirectly being the cause of another's death will make the seriousness dominate the impulsiveness ... then again, at the rate Bart's going now, that may not be too far away [Waid, "Scorched," 24].

Readers like Hogan, both had a clear idea of who the character was and what his limitations were. They did see potential for an evolution of the character, to move past his impulses, but recognized that to change Bart's core, something drastic would indeed have to happen.

Shortly after that camping trip, Bart's mother travels to 1997 to bring Bart back to the future, where in their adventure they encounter an artificial intelligence (AI) intent on keeping them captive. The AI lets them know that it is programmed by "the most inventive escape artists in the galaxy" to predict any strategy. Bart and his mother, who both have an impulsive streak, quickly defeat the AI because of their *lack* of plan or strategy—something that was not predicted. The AI proclaims, "This unit finds no linear method to-to-to-to—your mad-mad-madness," eventually crashing (Waid, "You and Me"). This episode demonstrates the belief that an AI would be incapable of understanding human randomness, and further demonstrate popular fears that although artificial intelligence technology could be forthcoming, there would still be some sort gap between computers and people—questioning the relationship between technology and people.

While Mark Waid had a clear idea of what the internet's potential was in his 1995 *Impulse* run, William Messner-Loeb, who later took on the series, on the other hand, viewed technology differently. In fact, one 1998 Messner-Loeb story feature Max Mercury installing a fax machine so that to keep up with the latest news. One scene, from the story "The Devonian Age," highlights Bart's impatience, but also indicates the role of the fax machine in the 1990s. For some, like Max Mercury, the fax machine was a new form of technology still at the end of the decade; for Bart, and probably many young people like him, the device was already passé. The fax machine, for Max, was a way for the older hero to be connected to the world outside of Manchester, Alabama. When news broke, all Max had to do was wait for instructions to come in on his brand-new fax machine. Bart, on the other hand, was more interested in finding trouble himself, arguing "I don't even see why we need a fax machine, Max." Max retorts: "Because we have to keep in touch. The JLA, the JSA, Arkham Asylum, Oracle.... They're all sources of detailed information, and we need to receive and pass on that information easily and quickly. Now where does the wall wire plug in?" Bart replies, "It says here, 'after installing paper, run the line wire into module A and the phone wire into module B. Then program your Fax-O-Gen 9000 by first holding down the mode key, while typing...' This is never gonna work, Max. It's broken." With a sigh, Max pleads, "It's not broken. We just need a little patience. Just once I'd like to hear you say, "What a good idea, Max!" "You were right, Max!" In a flash, Bart gives up, "'Bye, Max! I gotta get to school" (Messner-Loebs, "The Devonian Age"). Both Waid and Messner-Loeb indeed had different understandings of technology. Waid understood that technology had potential to build communities—even if for ill. Messner-Loeb, although discussing the fax machine, also saw potential benefits of the technology—although Waid certainly better understood the potentiality for the internet. For some, even in 1998, the fax machine certainly did seem to be a remarkable technology in and of itself. Even in a series about a boy from the future, the use of technology within those comics depended largely upon the writers' own capacity to understand the use of that new technology.

Messner-Loeb certainly had his reservations about the use and so-called progress of technology. Another Messner-Loeb story, "Virtual Pets, Virtual Heck," highlights an underlying fear of the increasing presence of digital technology. In the story, computerized digital pets, "Binkatoochies"—named after toymaker Bandai's "Tamagotchis," which had become popularized contemporarily. The story features a boy, Herbie Jameson, who in 1941 imagined futuristic cities with moving sidewalks, in 1952 that young man imagined easy, global communication, in 1963, smaller computers, in 1972 personal computers, in 1982, small, fast computers with an easy interface, and in 1992, a digital pet with artificial intelligence—culminating with the Binkatoochies in 1998. While seemingly all his high school peers are impressed with the crude digital key-chain creatures, Bart is sarcastically ambivalent about the device. It is soon discovered that the digital animal pets programming was based on an artificial intelligence created by Jameson's own consciousness, which goes awry, creating disillusioned digital beings in search of domed cities and floating cars. Jameson and Impulse discover that the program was encoded with the scientist's dream of a more perfect world through science, as well as his frustrations having moved from being a computer scientist to a maker of digital toys (Messner-Loeb, "Virtual Pets"). This story in particular demonstrated a fear of what could happen in a world in which technology went awry. While Messner-Loeb demonstrated a fear the destructive potential of AIs, and Waid a belief that there inevitably would be something intrinsically human missing, both writers were thinking about young people's relationship to the technology.

Several Steps Ahead of His Time

In later stories, Bart develops photographic memory and the ability to duplicate himself, faces an evil clone, and even stars in a reality show. With much consistency, *Impulse*, for most of its run, reflected many of the trials and dilemmas that young people at the turn of the millennium would have experienced in their everyday lives. Moreover, the comic also demonstrated that normative understandings of familial structures at the end of the millennium had drastically changed from the more heteronormative ones depicted just a generation earlier. While the comic did deal with issues of popularity, bullying, peer pressure, and child abuse, it avoided dealing with issues of race, gender, sexuality, and class head-on, but did use a diverse cast in which girls could play baseball, boys could avoid toxic masculinity, and readers (young and old) could imagine what the future might bring—both technologically and for young people. A genre which had been imagining rocket ships and futuristic technology since its inception in *Action Comics* #1, *Impulse* was well on the forefront of imagining what a youth of the future might be.

NOTES

1. See: Valencia-García, Louie Dean. In Joseph J. Darowski, ed., *The Ages of the Justice League: Essays on America's Greatest Superheroes in Changing Times* (Jefferson, NC: McFarland, 2017), 18–32.

2. This comment by the letter-writer about "some girls thrown in to show Bart what speed is really about," is, indeed, vague and unclear. However, given that readers would not see any development in Bart's love life for several years, the fan's expectations might have come up somewhat short. In fact, in *Impulse* #20, Bart and Carol Bucklen have their first kiss after a baseball game, and simultaneously break out laughing hysterically at the ridiculousness of that kiss. This kiss, subverts expectations for a relationship between the two teenagers, and indicates that neither one of them, at that time, were ready for such a relationship. See: Waid, Mark (w) and Mike Wieringo (a). "First Base" *Impulse* (December 1996). New York: DC Comics. Print.

3. This evolution does, indeed happen much later, after a knee injury leads him to take time off, re-emerging as "Kid Flash" after the events of the mini-series *Titans/Young Justice: Graduation Day* (July–August 2003.)

4. Of course, famously, Superman grew up in the fictional Smallville, Kansas. Other contemporary DC Comics heroes based in the south include Starman (Jack Knight), who was based in the fictional Opal City, South Carolina, as well as Resurrection Man (Mitch Shelley), who was also based in South Carolina.

5. This was seen in an America Online diskette that was sent to interested fans of DC Comics. The front of the mailer featured an image of Superman. On the back, other DC Comics imprints were also featured, including Mad Magazine, Vertigo, Milestone, and Paradox Press.

WORKS CITED

Howe, Neil, and William Strauss, *Millennials Rising: The Next Great Generation*. New York: Vintage Books, 2000.

Messner-Loebs, William (w), and Craig Rousseau (a). "The Devonian Age." *Impulse* #34 (February 1998). New York: DC Comics. Print.

_____. "Virtual Pets, Virtual Heck." *Impulse* #42 (October 1998). New York: DC Com.

Valencia-García, Louie Dean. In Joseph J. Darowski, ed., *The Ages of the Justice League: Essays on America's Greatest Superheroes in Changing Times* (Jefferson, NC: McFarland, 2017). 18–32.

Waid, Mark (w), Sal Buscema, and Craig Rousseau (a). "Scorched." *Impulse* #26 (June 1997). New York: DC Comics. Print. 24.

Waid, Mark (w), and Carlos Pacheco (a). "Reckless Youth, Chapter Three: Just Do It!" *The Flash* #94 (Sep. 1994). New York: DC Comics. Print.

Waid, Mark (w), and Humberto Ramos (a). "Bad Influence" *Impulse* #4 (July 1995). New York: DC Comics. Print.

_____. "Crossfire." *Impulse* #2 (May 1995). New York: DC Comics. Print.

_____. "Lesson's Learned." *Impulse* #23 (March 1997). New York: DC Comics. Print.

_____. "Secret Identity." *Impulse* #6 (September 1995). New York: DC Comics. Print.

_____. "The Single Synapse Theory." *Impulse* #1 (April 1995). New York: DC Comics. Print.

_____. "You and Me Against the World." *Impulse* #25 (May 1997). New York: DC Comics. Print.

Waid, Mark (w), and Mike Wieringo (a). "Out of Time." *The Flash* #91 (June 1994). New York: DC Comics. Print.

_____. "Reckless Youth, Chapter One: Speed Kills." *The Flash* #92 (July 1994). New York: DC Comics. Print.

Restraining Deconstruction

Geoff Johns' Reframing of The Flash

CHRISTIAN JIMENEZ

Geoff Johns was the writer of *The Flash* from 2000 to 2005, and his five-year run was quickly considered one of the best of the character's history. Given the sheer number of issues authored, a close reading of all these stories is not possible. The emphasis will be to sample the most vital story arcs (especially in the earlier part of the run) to generalize Johns' overall approach to exploring the character of the Flash as a mythic hero. Johns attempts to situate *The Flash* between the melodramatic mythic hero typical of the superhero genre and the more serious, gritty portrayal of the superhero by Alan Moore (Di Liddo; Klock; Moore and Gibbons).

As any long-term fan of the superhero genre knows, there is an inherently repetitive nature to the generic tropes that are used. The crux of the superhero problem is nicely summarized by Jean-Paul Gabilliet noting how "in an overwhelming majority of superhero narratives; valuables, inventions, or chemicals are stolen, people are abducted, murders are committed, and the onus is on super-justice dealers to restore the order reigning before the event" (Gabilliet 203). To Gabilliet there is an inherent tendency for the superhero narrative to rely upon simplistic dualities of good versus evil and order versus disorder. Johns does not entirely escape this dilemma. Indeed, many of the stories sampled here do fit Gabilliet's description.

However, Gabilliet's argument fits a melodramatic mythic superhero narrative. The melodramatic hero often experiences traumatic events. The hero faces a super-villain forcing the hero to make a hard decision. The superhero experienced severe mental or physical pain and sometimes even death (Jurgens, Ordway, Simonson, and Stern). But the decision is structured in such a way that the essential categories of good and evil are never questioned.

The Flash is not like other heroes—such as Spider-Man or Batman—

151

who by circumstance are marked by tragedy. Wally West has no secret identity for the majority of the five-year run; he retains his red and yellow costume, he strives to act ethically at all times, he rarely curses or drinks, and even his jokes are sensitive, taking the feelings of his enemies into account. Similarly, Keystone City is unlike Gotham City, which is depicted in dark shadows and with a crumbling infrastructure. Moreover, Keystone City is more diverse in terms of race and class than Gotham or Metropolis where those with money and those without live in extreme isolation from one another. The Keystone City in Johns' run has an integrated and strongly working-class character (no doubt reflecting Johns' own roots as a native of Detroit).

This is not to argue that Johns' run on *The* Flash is just light fluff. To humanize Wally West, Johns is willing to allow *The Flash* to enter subjects more familiar to readers of independent comics not beholden to the mainstream superhero genre (Saban). To be sure, the darkness introduced into the Flash is, in the end, rather limited. Johns is willing to play with the deconstruction of certain aspects of the superhero myth but does not engage in any full-throated deconstruction as Moore did with his *Watchmen* limited series (Di Liddio).

Overall, Johns' run in the 2000s was aimed at highlighting the essential core of the Flash as a helpful hero in the wider DC universe and the guardian of Keystone City. Johns' run is best characterized as turning *The Flash* into a semi-serious serial but one retaining the core features of the superhero myth Gabilliet describes. Perhaps the most striking finding is how much Johns tries to not just define *The Flash* for a new generation of readers but reconstruct the internal history of the Flash and especially his relationship to the so-called Rogues (Zoom, Captain Cold, Mirror Master, Trickster), the regular enemies he has fought over decades.

In essence, Johns takes seriously the power of the nihilistic tendencies in the gritty portrayal of the superhero myth. Yet he simultaneously wants to (selectively) make use of the early era of comics from the 1920s to 1930s without losing the sophistication that has come with abandoning the formerly naïve approach to the superhero. The irony is that while *The Flash* tries to overcome the legacy of *Watchmen* by restating and reconstructing heroism familiar to readers of comics in the 1950s and 1960s, it might end up turning the comic into a more postmodern text than Johns had intended.

Deconstructing and Reconstructing Wally West as the Working-Class Hero

During Geoff Johns' run, the Flash is Wally West, the nephew of Barry Allen. Johns carries on the shift in framing the Flash's powers as derived from a mysterious speed-force—introduced by Mark Waid in the 1990s (Hammon-tree 220). Whereas before Barry and Wally were struck by lightning in freak accidents giving them super speed, Waid's retooling makes Barry, Wally, and other similar speedsters as heirs to the speed force which they can tap into.

Wally West's super-speed is so impressive, that imagining situations with a credible threat can prove difficult. Even in the case of Superman, a hero has to make a choice and divide his or her attention. But the Flash can, in theory, fight multiple battles even over large distances. Johns primarily deals with this in two ways: taking away or nullifying Wally's powers and/or enhancing the abilities of the super-villains he regularly fights, the so-called Rogues.

Johns begins his run by throwing Wally into a strange, alternate world. In this world, the Flash has been arrested and is in the custody of the police taken in by a sadistic police officer Fred Chyre. The entire story is reminiscent of Batman and Gotham with a noir atmosphere.

The allusion to *Alice in Wonderland* as text and structure is obvious and explicit. Like other portal-fantasy stories, the Flash has been plunged into a fantasy world that is a nearly identical to the real one but with roles exaggerated. But, the references go beyond *Alice in Wonderland*, becoming a meta-commentary about the long history of the Flash in DC Comics.

In a daze from being beaten by the police, the Flash reminisces about the past Flashes. Jay Garrick is remembered as embodying the "Native American ... spirit, Thunderbird" (Johns 1 "Wonderland Part One: Lightning Strikes"). Barry Allen was a "hero's hero" (Johns 1 "Wonderland Part One: Lightning Strikes"). Wally situates himself proudly, however, as a sidekick (Kid Flash) who represents the "truth" (Johns 1 "Wonderland Part One: Lightning Strikes") and takes his uncle Barry's place as the Flash.

Captain Cold (Leonard Snart) also figures out he is in an alternate dimension and frees Wally. They team up and discover the Mirror Master has put them into this wonderland-dimension. However, the wonderland-dimension is unstable and will eventually collapse and therefore all three must leave. But, in a nod to *It's a Wonderful Life*, Johns first explores a wonderland-reality where the Flash never existed, to establish why the character is so important in the core DC Universe where the Flash has been an integral, but perhaps under-appreciated, part for decades.

Without the Flash, the Justice League fighting Starro in this wonderland-dimension is unable to prevent it from killing Aquaman (Johns 1 "Wonderland Part Two: Lightning Rod"). The absence of the Flash also leads to deaths among the Teen Titans with Speedy and Aqualad dying. Wondergirl is put into a coma. This turns Robin into a revenge-minded killer of villains. The world, in short approaches the reality of *Watchmen* with heroes becoming more extreme in their method and tactics.

Before Flash, Captain Cold, and Mirror Master can return home, however, Mirror Master and Cold are kidnapped by Thinker, a new villain unique to this dimension. Defeated by Thinker's proxies, the Flash is forced to improvise and revise his dismissal of the rogues as "just crooks with gimmicks" (Johns 1 "Wonderland Part Four: Joining the Tea Party"). At the Hal Jordan Museum, the Flash picks up weapons from Green Lantern's villains to help Mirror Master and Cold have a fighting chance against the Thinker.

After defeating the Thinker, the trio return to their home dimension, but discover that Keystone City—the entire city—has been taken into yet another, different dimension. However, upon arrival, it appears Keystone City is gone. Mirror Master and Captain Cold accompany Flash into this dimension, and discover that a man named Grimm has taken the city to punish the Flash. Previously, the Flash had helped Grimm overthrow his tyrannical father and Flash told Grimm to "be your own man" (Johns 1 "Wonderland Part Five: Brother Grimm"). Following this advice leads to Grimm's kingdom falling apart.

Grimm sees the Flash as being hypocritical in merely taking on Allen's mantle as the Flash, contradicting his advice to "be your own man." While the Flash is able to defeat Grimm and return Keystone City to its proper dimension, this thematic emphasis on being your own man again acts as a thematic mediation on what it means for Wally West to be the (third) Flash.

"The Final Race"?

In Keystone City, a prison called Iron Heights is where the captured villains are incarcerated (before inevitably escaping). In another Johns story, a longtime Flash villain, Gorilla Grodd, uses his telepathic skills to have a contingent of gorillas break into Iron Heights and liberate the prisoners. Wally is injured but saved when a villain, Fallout, intervenes. Fallout blasts Grodd forcing him to flee, saying "He [Wally] helped me when no one else would" (Johns 3: "Run Riot Part Two: On the Run"). Grodd, after reading the Flash's mind, has one of his gorilla proxies go after a friend of the Flash's named Zolomon. Grodd succeeds in disabling Zolomon who is now on a path to become the supervillain Zoom, Wally's complete opposite. Enraged, Wally tracks Grodd to Africa. "I don't wear this uniform to frighten anyone," Flash tells Nnamdi, the new ruler of Gorilla City, "and I don't fight for vengeance" (Johns 3: "Dead or Alive"). This self-definition by the Flash is obvious and is deliberate to serve as a counterpoint when the Flash faces a grave tragedy in a future story.

Yet the dialogue is self-contradictory within this very story because the Flash *did* come to Gorilla City seeking vengeance. He has to tell Nnamid, due to Gorilla phobia of human violence, that generally the Flash as a hero is not *defined by* a quest for vengeance. The Flash defeats Grodd and returns to Keystone. But Zolomon has lost the use of his legs and begs the Flash to return in time to restore his mobility.

The Flash refuses on the grounds that tampering with time would be too dangerous. Zolomon's turn to villainy could have been inspired by sheer hatred of the Flash for not helping him. However, Johns frames Zolomon's transformation differently. In his original incarnation, Hunter Zolomon (Zoom) was a fan of the Flash who became steadily insane and killed Flash's wife setting up a deadly cycle of confrontation with the Flash.

Johns changes this slightly but critically. Zoom is no longer a fan but a teacher and one who has no wish to harm the Flash—at least, not initially. As Zoom puzzlingly reasons, the Flash is not reaching his true potential as a hero. The Flash did not help him not due to caution about the "time-stream." For Zolomon, the Flash does not understand true tragedy. He refuses to understand true heroism means, paradoxically, a willingness to do "evil" (Johns 3: "Zoom"). Regaining mobility and now with super speed, Zolomon becomes Zoom to help Wally. At least, in his mind, that is his motivation.

To Zoom, "in order for him [the Flash] to be stronger, he must face the ultimate tragedy" (Johns 3: "Zoom"). Zoom kidnaps Linda and travels through time with her. Rather than killing her, Zolomon instead merely severely injures Linda. But Linda was pregnant with twins. Zoom's attack kills Wally's unborn children. Pressed to the limit, Zoom then decides he will kill Linda after all.

Figuring out Zoom's manipulation of time, Wally is able to stop him and Linda is safe, but this crisis does change him. He contemplates quitting being the Flash altogether when Barry Allen appears to reassure him. As Barry explains to Wally "[i]t's about taking the gifts we've been given and helping as many people as we can" (Johns 3:). The appearance of Allen might appear to break continuity but in keeping with his Infinite-sacrifice the Flash dies while appearing in and out of different time periods. Hence Barry's appearance is pre-destined to occur and possible within the Wolfman narrative.

But Johns does attempt to slightly re-construct recent DC universe history. Hal Jordan, the longtime Green Lantern, went crazy and destroyed the Green Lantern corps. He becomes, initially, a villain, Parallax, and, then, the Spectre, spirit of Vengeance. As the Spectre, he grants Wally West's wish to wipe out knowledge of his secret identity. To West, the enacting of the memory swipe shows "You're well on your way, Hal" (Johns 3). Thus the seeming fall of Jordan, can be read as a detour to his eventual redemption and reconstruction as a hero with West believing "we'll all have our second chance" (Johns 3).

156 The Ages of The Flash

Conclusion: The Super Hero as Narcissist and Altruist

Flash can no longer be a purely "people's" hero because there is indeed systemic corruption and individual failures. Flash's early optimism that everyone can be trusted turns out to be wrong. His friend, Zoom, becomes his worst enemy. Nevertheless, in "Rush Hour," the Flash remains adamant that he not change in any *essential* way: "I'm not going to be like Batman" (Johns, *The Flash* #207, April 2004: 4). As Bainbridge has argued, the DC heroes are mythic in a peculiar sense different from Marvel heroes noting how:

> The cities of the superheroes are themselves archetypes rather than real places. Superman's city is Metropolis, Batman's is Gotham, Flash has Central City, Green Lantern Coast City, Wonder Woman Paradise Island. In this sense the DC superheroes are one step removed from the real world, and this is underlined diegetically as well in the heroes' need for a hideout or otherwise secret base—Superman in his Fortress of Solitude, Batman in his Batcave, the Justice League in their satellite or watchtower [Bainbridge 74].

In other words, the heroes of the DC universe are, typically, God-like and removed from humans in ways that a Spider-Man perennially swinging in New York or the Avengers housed in Manhattan are not. As has, hopefully, been demonstrated Johns has tried to move the Flash closer to the everyday reality of normal human beings.

If the superhero narrative is often marked by lack of innovation as Bainbridge laments, it is not due to the serial format. The serial format may aggravate this problem but this analysis of Johns' run suggests comic book writers choose to keep sharp, structural limits on the characters they represent because they like those limits. As Reynolds notes: "Endless story possibilities can be designed around the theme of the superhero wrestling with his conscience over which order should be followed—moral or political, temporal or divine" (15). Ultimately, that is Johns' true subject in writing the Flash in the early 2000s.

In conclusion, despite Johns' best efforts to make Wally West a concrete icon, the theme of the Flash is, in the end, the Flash and not Wally West. The Flash myth stretches from Jay to Barry to Wally and is the true subject of these stories whatever the ostensive narrative. However, such a focus on the interior of the life of the hero threatens to turn the narrative into an empty postmodern performance. No doubt Johns intended West to be a heroic figure who demands to be taken seriously. But Johns—by keeping deconstructive elements (which assuredly are present) to a minimum and try to persuade the reader that the essential myth of the superhero (with qualifications) remains viable and laudable—ends up continually reminding the reader how fictive the myth of the superhero remains all throughout his run. Or put another way: by making the Flash so blandly apolitical, Johns has raised the dilemma of just what the political function of the superhero is. Which is, of course, the subject of Moore's *Watchmen*, the most iconic deconstruction of the superhero.

Works Cited

Bainbridge, Jason. "'Worlds Within Worlds': The Role of Superheroes in the Marvel and DC Universes." *The Contemporary Comic Book Superhero,* edited by Angela Ndalianis, New York: Routledge, 2009, pp. 64–85. Print.

Di Liddo, Annalisa. *Alan Moore: Comics as Performance, Fiction as Scalpel.* Jackson: UP of Mississippi, 2009. Print.

Gabilliet, Jean-Paul. "Cultural and Mythical Aspects of a Superhero: The Silver Surfer 1968–1970." *Journal of Popular Culture,* vol. 28, no. 2, 1994, pp. 203–213. Print.

Hammontree, D.R. "The Flash." In *Encyclopedia of Comic Books and Graphic Novels,* edited by M. Keith Booker, Santa Barbara, CA: Greenwood, 2010, pp. 218–220. Print.

James, Nick. "Opting for Ontological Terrorism: Freedom and Control in Grant Morrison's *The Invisibles.*" *Law, Culture and the Humanities,* vol. 3, no. 3, 2007, pp. 435–54. Print.

Johns, Geoff. *The Flash: Book One.* New York: DC Comics, 2015. Print.

_____. *The Flash: Book Two.* New York: DC Comics, 2016. Print.

_____. *The Flash: Book Three.* New York: DC Comics, Print.

Johns, Geoff (w), and Howard Porter (a). "Rush Hour." *The Flash* #207 (April 2004). New York: DC Comics. Print.

Jurgens, Dan. *Zero Hour: Crisis in Time!* September. New York: DC Comics, 1994. Print.

Jurgens, Dan, Jerry Ordway, Louise Simonson, and Roger Stern. *The Death of Superman.* New York: DC Comics, 2016. Print.

Kaveney, Roz. *Super Heroes.* New York: 2008.

Klock, Geoff. *How to Read Superhero Comics and Why.* New York: Continuum, 2002. Print.

Kukkonen, Karin. *Studying Comics and Graphic Novels.* New York: John Wiley and Sons, 2013. Print.

Miller, Frank. *Batman: Dark Knight Returns.* New York: DC Comics, 1986. Print.

Moore, Alan, and Brian Bolland. *Batman: The Killing Joke.* New York: DC Comics, 1988. Print.

Moore, Alan, and Dave Gibbons. *Watchmen.* New York: DC Comics, 1986–87. Print.

Pustz, Matthew. *Comic Book Culture: Fanboys and True Believers.* Jackson: UP of Mississippi, 1999. Print.

Reynolds, Richard. *Super Heroes: A Modern Mythology.* Jackson: UP of Mississippi, 1992. Print.

Sabin, Roger. *Adult Comics: An Introduction.* London: Routledge, 1993. Print.

Witek, Joseph. *Comic Books as History.* Jackson: UP of Mississippi, 1989. Print.

Wolfman, Marv, and George Pérez. *Crisis on Infinite Earths.* New York: DC Comics, 1985–86. Print.

Wright, Bradford W. *Comic Book Nation: The Transformation of Youth Culture in America.* Baltimore: John Hopkins UP, 2001. Print.

Profiling the Rogues

Seeking Criminal Intent
in The Flash *of Geoff Johns*

Matthew J. Smith *and* Tod W. Burke

In a series of spotlight issues of *The Flash* published between 2002 and 2011, writer Geoff Johns sought to deepen the motivations for members of the Rogues Gallery by developing their back-stories in greater detail than any writer before. Although most of these characters had clashed repeatedly with the Fastest Man Alive since the early 1960s, writers rarely developed their backstories or motivations beyond a single, explanatory page. Johns' take added a layer of complexity to the overall milieu of the series that helped to enrich longtime reader's understanding of the reasons why these villains would repeatedly challenge law enforcement as most strikingly embodied in the Scarlet Speedster.

Historically, a rogues gallery is a collection of photographs of wanted suspects. In comic book culture the term has been applied to a collection of foes who repeatedly return to vex the hero. The Flash's first encounter with Captain Cold, the first of the supervillains who would become a part of his rogues gallery, occurs in his second appearance in the pages of *Showcase* #8 (1957), appearing in a story written by John Broome and drawn by Carmine Infantino and Frank Giacoia. In the ensuing years, numerous colorfully named foes join with Cold in facing off against the Flash; in 1965, several of them team-up in the pages of *Flash* #155 in another story from Broome and Infantino in collaboration with Murphy Anderson and Joe Giella. The original Rogues Gallery consists of Captain Cold, Mirror Master, Pied Piper, The Top, Captain Boomerang, and Heat Wave, all thieves who made up for the lack of genuine superpowers with novelty gimmicks to challenge the Scarlet Speedster. In the ensuing years these villains, and numerous others who would rotate in and out of their roster, regularly team-up to attempt ever-bolder crimes, only to be thwarted by the Fastest Man Alive.

Given the dictates of comics' Silver Age and Bronze Age storytelling, these villains lacked much in the way of detailed origins or internal motivations; the Flash required a monthly challenge and over the decades of the series' run, these familiar criminals returned time and again to provide it. Occasionally, a rogue's background might be fleshed out a bit more, such as when it was revealed in 1977 that Len "Captain Cold" Snart actually had a sister, Lisa, who turned from a career as a professional skater to become the villainous Golden Glider (Bates, Novick, and Colletta). But it was writer Geoff Johns who offered substantially more detail about the Rogues in a series of spotlight issues during his two tenures on the series, 2000–2005 and 2009–2011.

This essay performs a close reading on these stories, seeking to synthesize two fields of expertise in its analysis. First is the expertise of a Comics Studies scholar deeply invested in both the multi-generation saga of the Flash and keenly interested in the larger body of work produced by Johns. Second is the expertise of a Criminal Justice scholar, who possesses a command of contemporary theory into criminal behavior. The authors hope to provide insight into how criminological theory helps to explain (or possibly contradict) John's efforts to develop the personalities and motivations for characters such as Captain Cold, Pied Piper, Zoom, Mirror Master, Heat Wave, Captain Boomerang, and the Reverse-Flash.

Thus, we analyze John's texts through a lens of criminology, that is, the scientific study of criminal behavior. There are two opposing—although sometimes overlapping—criminological schools of thought:

> Classical criminology is based on the concept of *free will,* viewing the decision to commit crime as a choice made freely by the offender. The positivist school of criminology (positivism) is based on the concept of *determinism,* which holds that criminal behaviors are influenced by outside forces (e.g., biological, psychological, and sociological factors) [Owens et al. 130–131].

While our analysis is performed on fictional characters, we believe that the application of criminological theory helps to better understand how these modern texts achieve a greater degree of verisimilitude, or the illusion of reality, and thus deepen the readers' understanding of the villains as potentially sympathetic figures.

We admit from the start that within these two schools there are multiple criminological theoretical possibilities that could be applied to each of the narratives Johns has produced. We curated a select few to show the utility of theory in helping to interpret these stories and aid the reader in understanding how Johns' more developed characterization rings true with our knowledge of criminal behavior in our reality. In the sections that follow, we begin with an introduction of Johns. We then turn to summaries of the Rogues spotlight issues and offer criminological theories to explain the villains' motivations. We conclude this chapter with reflections on the utility of applying theoretical constructs from other academic disciplines to Comics Studies.

Johns began his career writing comic books in late 1999 and was soon authoring his own series, *Stars and S.T.R.I.P.E.* and co-writing *JSA (Justice Society of America)* before adding the *Flash* assignment to his portfolio in 2000. Johns had studied media arts and screenwriting at Michigan State University before working with filmmaker Richard Donner on such productions as *Conspiracy Theory* (1997) and *Lethal Weapon 4* (1998) before transitioning into comics. At DC Comics, Johns developed a reputation for his rich grasp of the corporate history and revitalized a number of other high-profile series, most notably *Green Lantern.* On numerous occasions, he was trusted with writing company-wide crossover events like *Infinite Crisis* (2005–2006) and *Blackest Night* (2009–2010). In 2010, he was named DC's Chief Creative Officer and began to take on greater responsibilities for directing the course of the company's overall publishing mission and its adaptations into other media, including Hollywood blockbusters. He was one of the chief architects behind 2011's "New 52" relaunch that proved to be a market-winning reboot of the entire line of DC Comics.

In his tenure as a writer, Johns proved to be particularly competent at developing characters' motivations. Nowhere was this more evident than when he chose to cast spotlights on the Rogues in Flash. In seven issues during his tenure, he offered detailed back stories on Captain Cold, Pied Piper, Zoom, Mirror Master, Heat Wave, Boomerang, and the Reverse-Flash.

Rogue File #1: Captain Cold

In the first of these stories, "Absolute Zero," Captain Cold recalls his abusive upbringing and early criminal career in a series of flashbacks set against a modern day mission to avenge the life of his murdered sister at the hands of one of her henchmen. As the story unfolds, Captain Cold storms the penthouse of a Keystone City crime boss who is employing as hired muscle, Chillblaine, an opportunist who killed Cold's sister, Lisa, a.k.a. the Golden Glider. While walking a gauntlet of thugs to get to his sister's killer, Cold's monologue shifts to a series of flashbacks where he recounts having been raised by an alcoholic, physically and emotionally abusive father. His father, a former police officer, was placed on disability after being shot. From his father's mistreatment of his family, Cold learns not to show emotions, lest he be beaten for any tears shed in pain or sadness. Later, Cold leaves home, falls in with a band of would-be robbers, and is dramatically captured by the Flash in his first criminal act. In prison, he dedicates himself to the study of kinetic energy in the hopes of learning a way to slow down the Flash. Upon release from prison, he steals blueprints for a weapon that negates kinetic energy, costumes himself in a stylized parka, and sets out to challenge the Scarlet Speedster. That confrontation, and the many that follow, all end with the Flash triumphant. Back in the present, Cold manages to seek his revenge on Chillblaine and returns to a seedy apartment where he breaks down in tears, admitting to himself, "As much as I hate it—my heart's not always cold" (Johns, Kolins, and Panosian 22).

Captain Cold's motivations as relayed in this story evidences a particular theory of criminology called **labeling theory**. Labeling theory assumes that once a societal label has been placed on a person, that person will self-identify with that label. This then becomes a self-fulfilling prophecy in that the person behaves according to the label. In other words, "if a person is labeled as delinquent, deviant, or criminal, the theory suggests that the person will accept that label and therefore engage in delinquent, deviant, or criminal activity" (Owen et al. 143). This would seem to be the case for Captain Cold, who after his initial botched robbery attempt—and incarceration by the Flash— embraces his potential as a criminal and repeatedly engages in criminal behavior thereafter.

Edwin Lemert (1951) noted that deviant labeling is a two-part process: primary and secondary. Primary deviance is the initial deviant act, but does little to define the person (as the act may or may not come to the attention of those persons who would generate the label, such as law enforcement officers). Secondary deviance occurs when the deviant or unlawful act comes to the attention of others (family, friends, criminal justice professionals) who then reinforce the negative label. This begins the downward spiral into further deviant or unlawful acts and the acceptance of the negative label (Owen et al. 144). Again, Cold does not report engaging in criminal behavior until his act of primary deviance, the initial attempted robbery; only when he is captured and imprisoned does he embrace the label of outlaw and begin to methodically plan a career as a professional criminal.

As explained in the exposition throughout "Absolute Cold," one of the hallmarks of the Captain's career is his leadership of the Rogues. "Labeled persons may find themselves turning to others similarly stigmatized for support and companionship. Isolated from conventional society, they may identify themselves as members of an outcast group and become locked into a deviant career" (Siegel 232–233). Not only does Cold find himself in this phenomenon, but his sister is drawn into it as well. Labeling theory could help explain the motives for multiple members of the Rogues, including the focus of our next case study, the Pied Piper.

Rogue File #2: The Pied Piper

The Pied Piper of Hamelin was, of course, a medieval mythic figure whose supernatural powers were documented by the likes of the Brothers Grimm. Taking inspiration from this folklore tale, John Broome and Carmine Infantino introduced Hartley Rathaway, alias the Pied Piper of Central City, early in the career of Barry Allen. The self-proclaimed "Master of Sound" had discovered frequencies that could manipulate others' behaviors and used this ability to commit robberies until stopped by the Flash. Unlike many of the Flash's other rogues, though, Piper enjoyed a period of character development in the 1990s, when he reformed, became a supporting character in Wally West's *Flash* series, and came out as one of the first opening gay characters in DC Comics (Messner-Loebs, LaRocque, and Marzan 3).

Despite his status as a member of the Flash's supporting cast, few details about Piper's original criminal intent were disclosed until Geoff Johns delved into his motivations in the second of his "Rogue Files" series. Against the framing narrative of Piper professing his innocence for a murder charge to another reformed Rogue turned FBI agent, Piper recalls his origin as the scion of wealthy, if somewhat neglectful, socialite parents. In his reminiscences, he reflects: "At first my parents thought I was *slow*. It took them over two years to *realize* I was almost completely *deaf.* Though they would *never* accept *that.* How could these *perfect* people have an *imperfect* child? (Johns, Justiniano, and Wong 10). Piper's parents spend a small fortune to find corrective apparatuses for Piper's deafness. He discovers a passion for music, but is unable to relate to his parents: "Like I said, it's not that they were necessarily *bad* people. They just … they came from *old* money. I never felt like I could *relate.* All our relatives, my parents' friends" (11). Sometimes Piper would pretend that he could not hear his parents, just to "freak them out," and later conflicts between parents and child stem from his failing out of college and his coming out of the closet (11). He steals money from them and dedicates his life to building innovative musical instruments. In doing so, he discovers frequencies that allow him to manipulate the behaviors of others. "For the *first* time in my *life,* I had some kind of *power,*" he explains. Piper discovers he has control when costumed as a Rogue: "All I wanted to do was make some *noise.* Get *attention*" (12). Of course, he got the attention of the Flash.

One explanation for Piper's original criminal intent may be found in **social control/bond theory**. According to this criminological explanation, "Criminal deviance occurs when an individual's bonds to society (i.e., social bonds) are weak or broken. Social bonds are provided by individuals, groups, and organizations that connect a person to the community" (Owen et al. 142). Clearly Piper experiences weak or broken links in his interactions with his family. Distanced from them by both his initial handicap and then later by dispositional differences, Piper cannot quite find a connection within his immediate or extended family. In one telling scene, Piper is depicted as standing at a distance from a group of cousins, who are saying among themselves that he is a freak. "They all looked *down* on me. Like I didn't belong," he narrates. "*And* I didn't" (Johns, Justiniano, and Wong 11). His turn to crime is thus a reaction to the lack of clear bonds that typically tether people to conventional norms.

Criminologist Travis Hirschi explains that social bonds arise when a person accepts the social norms and develops a social awareness and conscience wherein the individual develops an attachment to and caring for others (i.e., bonding). Piper is depicted as failing to make these meaningful connections early on in life. Indeed, "if these beliefs are absent or weakened, individuals are more likely to participate in antisocial or illegal acts" (Siegel 229). As if to confirm the importance of these bonds, when Piper does decide to reform, he reaches out to amend his relationship with his parents: "I got a *wake-up* call," he reports. "I went to my parents *first*. I apologized ... and they apologized, too. Old age made us all *wiser*. We reconciled as *best* we could" (Johns, Justiniano, and Wong 13). He pursues a more law-abiding path thereafter, evidenced by both his reunion with his parents and his establishing a working relationship with the Flash.

Rogues File #3: Zoom

Unlike the other Rogues that Johns profiled during his tenure as Flash writer, Zoom is his own a creation, debuting as Keystone City Police Profiler Hunter Zolomon in 2001 (Johns, Kolins, and Marzan). For two years, Zolomon is a part of the Flash's supporting cast, aiding Wally West in confronting and capturing many of the Rogues before an attack by Gorilla Grodd restricts him to a wheel chair. When the Flash refuses to use a time traveling device called the Cosmic Treadmill to go back and prevent Zolomon's injury, Zolomon activates the machine himself and is caught in an explosion. This accident gives him time warping capabilities that appear to make him move at super speed (Johns, Kolins, and Hazelwood, "Zoom" 21).

In *Flash* #197, Johns reveals the tortured path that leads up to Zolomon's adoption of the identity of Zoom. Just prior to leaving for college, Zolomon is shocked to discover that his father is a serial killer and his final victim is Zolomon's mother. He dedicates his collegiate studies to understanding the criminal mind and eventually enters the F.B.I. training headquarters, located in Quantico, Virginia. There he meets a mentor, an expert on supervillains, and coincidentally the father of his fiancée. On a field mission, Zolomon makes the call to move on a low-level costumed criminal, the Clown, but misjudges the danger posed by the deranged villain; Zolomon's misstep leaves his mentor dead, Zolomon lame, and his marriage in divorce. But upon discovering his newfound superpowers, Zolomon resolves to teach the Flash to be a better hero by making him experience tragedy and there upon sets out to do so by endangering those closest to the hero. "Who fits the *profile*" of a Rogue, he repeatedly asks himself. Upon adopting his new identity, he concludes, "*I* fit the profile" (Johns, Kolins, and Hazelwood, "Zoom" 22).

But just what profile does Zoom fit? From a criminological perspective, **learning theory** may help to explain his path. Learning theory is based on the assumption that criminal and deviant behavior is learned. Albert Bandura (1973), a social learning theorist, argues "that people are not actually born with the ability to act violently, but they learn to be aggressive through life experiences" (qtd. in Siegel 156). These experiences may come from family members, environmental experiences, and/or mass media. In the case of Zoom, it appears that the source of his deviant inspiration stems not only from his own personal brush with a deviant father, but from years of study into the behavior of supervillains. That repeated and sustained focus on deviants informs his decision to choose a lifestyle that turns him into one of the very monsters he had sought to understand and outwit. Who better to know how to be a Rogue than someone who has studied them so deeply?

Albert Bandura, Dorothea Ross, and Sheila Ross (1961) believe that social learning is based on a system of rewards and punishments, known as operant conditioning. According to this system, behavior may be influenced by one of a number of techniques, including providing negative punishment after a desired behavior (i.e., removing something that a person enjoys) (Owen et al. 138). In Zoom's case, it seems that the loss of his mentor, his wife, and the later the use of his legs—all costs incurred while in the line of duty as a criminal profiler—provides the stimulus to lead him away from crime-fighter to criminal.

Zoom then attempts his own version of operant conditioning. He attacks the Flash's allies and then his wife, causing her to miscarry their unborn twins. In a confrontation he explains to the Flash:

> I need to make you into a hero that will take any risk needed. You must learn. To see what it's like to live with *loss*. So that you will do *anything* in your *power* to help people. People like me. I'm making you a *better* hero, Flash [Johns, Kolins, and Hazelwood, "Blitz" 20].

Zoom, of course, fails to impart this lesson on the Flash and finds himself locked in a cycle of repeatedly confronting the Flash, exactly like the Rogues he so carefully studied as a cop.

Rogue File #4: Mirror Master

The original Mirror Master, Sam Scudder, was another of the Flash's earliest and most recurring foes, having first appeared in the debut issue of Barry Allen's Flash ongoing series in 1959 (Broome, Infantino, and Giella, "Mirrors"). Like many of Flash's early foes, he is depicted as a criminal who happens upon some fantastic gimmick. In Scudder's case, this is some unusual—and heretofore unknown—properties of mirrors, which he repeatedly uses to face the Flash both alone and in the company of the other Rogues. Following Scudder's death in the "Crisis on Infinite Earths" event, a mercenary named Evan McColloch is introduced as his successor (Morrison, Truog, and Hazelwood). Details of his disturbing origin are refined through Johns' efforts in collaboration with artists Steve Cummings and Wayne Faucher.

In this first person account, Mirror Master reveals that he is abandoned in an orphanage as a child with nothing more than a photograph of his parents. Although the matron who runs the orphanage is kind and gentle, the orphanage is plagued by Georgie, an older child who bullies and sexually molests the younger children. When Georgie pulls young Evan out to abuse him one night, Evan fights back, striking the older boy with a rock and then drowning him in a nearby stream. The murder seems justified, if only in Evan's own mind: "Every Scotsman knows—ye never do a good deed just ta brag about. Do ye? Ye just do it cuz it's right" (Johns, Cummings, and Faucher 7). Upon maturing, Evan goes to Glascow, thinking he "might be a writer or work in construction or some nonsense" (8). Apparently unsuccessful in these legitimate career options, he is subsequently depicted in rough company, first engaged in robbery, then reportedly involved in protection rackets, and finally turning to assassination as a profession. On one assignment, he makes the horrifying discovery that he has unknowingly assassinated his own father. Prepared to turn from his murderous ways, Evan is recruited by the U.S. government to be a mercenary with a cover story. He is given the equipment of the original Mirror Master and sent off on missions that, eventually, bring him into conflict with the Flash and frequently into the company of the other Rogues, where he becomes a staple of the gang.

Mirror Master appears to be a product of a **delinquent subculture**. A subculture originates when "a group shares a set of norms that are different from those of the larger society" (Owen et al. 441). Richard Cloward and Lloyd Ohlin argued that within disorganized communities (i.e., communities where there is a lack of attachment with the community due to crime, poverty, and breakdown in the family), delinquents often lack role models and opportunities for success. These individuals may resort to drugs, violence, gangs, or other illegitimate activities in a mean to escape from societal expectation (i.e., "retreatists") (Owen et al. 142).

This certainly seems to be the case for Mirror Master, who is abandoned by his family, bullied in his youth, and freely engages in criminal behavior as a means to find his place in society. In fact, when the government comes along with the costume and equipment of the original Mirror Master, McColloch is actually rewarded for his poor choices. As Walter Miller explains, "delinquency resulted from efforts to achieve a different set of goals from those promoted by social norms—goals that he labeled 'lower class culture'" (Owen et al. 142). Evan's impoverished upbringing leads him to make a choice to associate with a delinquent culture. Miller might explain this as one of the focal concerns that promote criminal behavior in lower-class youth: Fate is the belief that people's lives are in the hand of strong outside forces that guide their destinies (e.g., a delinquent commits a crime with the belief that whatever happens, will happen). This seems to reflect the Mirror Master's disposition. As he prepares to snort a dose of cocaine, he seems resolved to his own fate. "The real world. S'just not for me.... Made me inta somethin' I didn' choose ta be. I ain't ever goin' back. I ain't ever leavin' wonderland" (Johns, Cummings, and Faucher 20–21).

Rogue Profile #5: Heat Wave

Created as a counter-point to Captain Cold, Heat Wave debuted in a story from John Broome, Carmine Infantino and Joe Giella in 1963. Some details of his origin are expanded by Cary Bates, Irv Novick, and Frank McLaughlin in 1978, but it is Geoff Johns and Peter Snejbjerg's 2005 story that most fully details the tragic story of Mick Rory, a.k.a., Heat Wave. Therein, Heat Wave admits: "I'm not like those *other* Rogues. I *know* I have problems. I've known since I was a *kid*. I'm *sick*" (1). He explains how he becomes fascinated with fire as a child and ultimately sets his family home afire just to see the flames. Standing outside the burning structure, he is so captivated by the spectacle that he is unable to do anything to save his trapped family from dying inside. When pranksters lock him in a meat locker on a school field trip, he retaliates by burning down their homes. As an adult he becomes a successful fire-eater until his obsession gets the better of him and he burns down the circus at which he performs. Inspired by the criminal career of Captain Cold, he adopts the identity of Heat Wave. "I was *ready* to commit crimes. To *burn* buildings. All in the name of *robbery*" he reflects. "*The fire* ... it wasn't an illness anymore. It was a *gimmick*" (11).

Heat Wave's motivation seems rooted in an inherent problem he professes, an inherency that could be explained criminologically by **biological theory**. The basic premise behind biological criminology is that human behavior is inherent. Early criminal biological theorist Franz Gall believed that future criminal behavior could be predicted based upon biological traits such as the shape of the human skull, weight, height, and other anthropological features, known as *phrenology* (Owen et al. 131). Modern biological theorists move far beyond the historical perspective (even adamantly discounting extreme biological theories such as phrenology). "Many modern biological theories focus on genetics, in the context of inherited traits that are conducive to crime" (Owen et al. 134). These biological traits have been associated with aggression and other tendencies that, if acted upon inappropriately, may lead to criminal activity. Such appears to be the case with Heat Wave, who admitted is acting upon urges that are inherent, rather than learned. As he reports, he had already acted on his pyromania long before he turned it to a "gimmick" to be exploited as a Rogue. "It's just the urge … the *urge* never leaves you," he admits, even when attempting to reform and leave the Rogues behind (14–15). Heat Wave does not become a criminal by choice—or even by chance—but is essentially wired toward anti-social behavior that he cannot seem to curb nor control.

Rogue File #6: Captain Boomerang

When Captain Boomerang debuted in late 1960, memories of the fading hula hoop craze (which had taken off in 1958) were still fresh in the public conscience. In his debut story written by John Broome and illustrated by Carmine Infantino and Murphy Anderson, Digger Harkness is cast as "Captain Boomerang," the spokesman for the W.W. Wiggins Games Company's promotional campaign to make boomerangs the next big fad. However, Boomerang moonlights as a jewelry thief and gets caught up to no good by the Flash. More than fifty years later, Geoff Johns and Scott Kolins delve into the Boomerang's background even deeper to provide an explanation for his antisocial choices.

In this account, Boomerang reveals himself to be the illegitimate son of the toy manufacturer, Wiggins, and an Australian woman named Betty Harkness. Unaware of his true lineage, Boomerang is raised in a remote section of Australia by his mother and his abusive stepfather. One day, Wiggins sends him a gift, a toy boomerang that the boy masters over time. When a bit older—and apparently left with no better prospects—he uses his prowess with the boomerang to rob a local pawnshop. Given his reputation with the weapon, everyone, including his parents, knows who committed the crime. "*Get out!* You *lazy* goodfornothin' *criminal!*" shouts his stepfather as he assaults the boy (Johns and Kolins, "What" 9). His mother directs Boomerang to America and Wiggins, who rechristens and outfits the lad. But the fad fails to catch on and few boomerangs sell. Boomerang then reflects: "He thought ol' *Captain Boomerang* would excite the kids. But the kids had a scarlet speed-ster to look up to" (10). A passing child grasping a Flash action figure confirms those thoughts, "Flash would beat Captain Boomerang up, wouldn't he, Mom?" (10). Once Wiggins' paychecks start to bounce, Boomerang turns jewelry thief and runs afoul of the Flash. Thereafter, he finds himself recruited into the Rogues: "I never felt more at home than I did with *The Rogues*" (12).

One possible explanation for Boomerang's criminal behavior would be through **strain theory.** Strain theory says that when a disconnect occurs between goals and means of achieving them, some individuals become frus-trated and angry, leading to deviant and/or criminal behavior (Conklin 204–205). Boomerang exhibits this frustration when he chooses to confront limited economic options in his small town by committing larceny; he suc-cumbs again to the strain when his career as a spokesman unravels and once again he is robbing merchants.

The origins of strain theory may be traced back to Emile Durkeim's con-cept of *anomie*. Anomie is "a social condition in which norms (rules of con-duct) are absent or unclear" (Siegel 192). This seems to be the case for Boomerang, where isolation and abuse separate him from the norms of soci-ety. "Anomie inevitably produces strain as individuals try to identify appro-priate norms" (Maguire and Radosh 244). Thus, unable to adapt to find a means for his unusual ability to employ him normally, Boomerang turns to crime. Indeed, as he finds himself accepted by the Rogues in this new lifestyle, he engages in a kind of anomie that Robert Merton calls "rebellion." This involves "substituting an alternative set of goals and means for conventional ones," that is, creating alternate opportunities and lifestyles within the existing system (Siegel 193). This seems to be well-supported by the Rogues as an evolving team of supervillains.

Rogue File #7: Reverse-Flash

Although not considered a member of the Rogues himself, due to his anti-social tendencies, Eobard Thawne, a.k.a. the Reverse-Flash, was the sub-ject of Johns' final villain profile in 2011's *Flash* #8. Like the Rogues, Reverse-Flash had begun his career during comic's Silver Age in the 1960s, launching his decades-long struggle against the Flash in a story devised by John Broome, Carmine Infantino, and Joe Giella ("Menace"). In his first appearance, readers learn that Thawne originates in the 25th century, where his obsession with the historical adventures of the Flash lead him to imitating his super-speed. The two speedsters clash repeatedly in the ensuing decades and their conflicts eventually lead to Thawne's murder of Flash's wife, Iris Allen (not to worry; she was later resurrected), and Thawne's death at the hands of the Flash (with every reason to worry; he too was resurrected). In Johns' 2011 collaboration with Scott Kolins, the reader learns more about Thawne's childhood and early adulthood in his native future ("Rebirth").

In Thawne's future, time is the most precious commodity and the culture is obsessed with efficiency. Thawne is a driven student who resents the arrival of a younger brother into his family. He finds spending time with his sibling, Robern, a distraction from his studies. When caught yelling at a young Robern by his no-nonsense father, Thawne is scolded, "You waste my time. You are a *disappointment*" (5). Later when Thawne's studies lead him to conducting forbidden research into the "Speed Force" that empowers the Flash, his brother, now a police officer, catches him and appeals to him to turn himself in. But then a mysterious figure reaches out from the shadows and chokes Robern. It is Thawne's future-self, traveling through time to eliminate any impediment on his path towards becoming the Reverse-Flash. Subsequent panels in the comic reverse several previous scenes in the narrative, suggesting that time is running backwards. When it stops, the narrative picks up again just prior to Robern's birth, as Thawne proclaims he is an only child.

The story moves forward in time again, and now Thawne's rival for the professorate at the Flash Museum refuses to share important discoveries about the Speed Force. His rival rejects him, saying, "You are not needed here. In fact, you are not *wanted* here" (9). Again, the Reverse-Flash shows up to remove the rival, and history is reset once again with Thawne now the world's leading expert on the Flash. This pattern repeats itself time and again. Next, Thawne's parents interfere in his work and are retroactively killed before they can stop his progress. He meets an attractive reporter and then her boyfriend turns up missing; when she spurs his advances, Reverse-Flash leaves her catatonic. Finally, a mysterious time capsule appears before Thawne containing the Flash's uniform; he finds traces of the Speed Force within it and gifts himself with super-speed. He becomes a hero—The Flash of the 25th century—before reversing course towards villainy.

A number of criminological theories that we have previously discussed could be brought to bear on this final profile. For example, labeling theory could contribute to his pathway. As noted in the story, his father's harsh judgment and the confrontation with his brother suggest that Thawne was conditioned to accept a role as a criminal from the labels placed upon him by his family.

Alternately, social control/bond theory could provide an alternate explanation. Thawne exhibits very poor bonding skills, and when people interfere or disappoint him, his future-self arrives to remove, kill, or maim them. With little regard for those close to him, it seems almost inevitable that he would turn on his greatest hero, the Flash, as well.

Elements of Thawne's story might also suggest some explanatory elements derived from learning theory (e.g., his fast-paced, competitive culture), delinquent subculture (e.g., his lack of positive role models), and biological theory (e.g., his seemingly innate response to lash out at anyone—brother, lover, hero—in his way). There are additional theories in criminology that also might be applied. The point is, of course, that modern criminological studies has a great deal of potential insight to offer into the world of the Rogues. Additionally, these stories are rich enough that valid, alternative explanations could be offered for many of the motives laid out in them.

Conclusion

Geoff Johns, in tandem with his collaborators, used the opportunity he had in the early part of the 21st century to craft a number of Rogue Files that fleshed out the background details on many of Flash's most recurring nemeses. In doing so, he added a layer of complexity to their motivations that few authors before him had bothered to explore. While devoting whole issues of a comic book series to villains might seem cynical to some (perhaps even sinister), the depths of the villains' motives and lack of virtue stands in stark contrast to the elevated and selfless motives of the hero. Johns' triumph with the Rogue Files is that we see them for the flawed figures they are and can better appreciate why they are such stark contrast to the series eponymous hero.

Our efforts here have attempted to show how real world theoretical constructs can help readers to further appreciate the reasons why Johns' characterizations were so successful. His efforts to develop the backstories and personalities of these foes seems to work because the characters' motivations ring true with criminological behavior described in the real world. Such theory is brimming with potential applications in other comics storytelling, including other superhero narratives penned by other creators.

Works Cited

Agnew, Robert. "Foundations for a General Strain Theory of Crime and Delinquency." *Criminology,* vol. 30, no. 1, 1992, pp. 47–87.
Bandura, Albert. *Aggression: A Social Learning Analysis.* Prentice Hall, 1973.
Bandura, Albert, Dorothea Ross, and Sheila A. Ross. "Transmission of Aggression Through Imitation of Aggressive Models." *Journal of Abnormal and Social Psychology,* vol. 63, no. 3, 1961, pp. 575–582.
Bates, Cary (w), Irv Novick (p), and Vince Colletta (i). "One Freeze-Dried Flash—Coming Right Up." *Flash* Vol. 1 #250 (June 1977). New York: DC Comics.
Bates, Cary (w), Irv Novick (p), and Frank McLaughlin (i). "Heat Wave Plays It Cool." *Flash* Vol. 1 #266 (October 1978). New York: DC Comics.
Broome, John (w), Carmine Infantino (p), and Frank Giacoia (i). "The Coldest Man on Earth!" *Showcase* Vol. 1 #8 (May–June 1957). New York: National Comics.

Broome, John (w), Carmine Infantino (p), and Murphy Anderson (i). "Here Comes Captain Boomerang!" *Flash* Vol. 1 #117 (December 1960). New York: National Comics.

Broome, John (w), Carmine Infantino (p), Murphy Anderson (i), and Joe Giella (i). "The Gauntlet of Super-Villains!" *Flash* Vol. 1 #155 (September 1965). New York: National Comics.

Broome, John (w), Carmine Infantino (p), and Joe Giella (i). "The Heat Is On … for Captain Cold." *Flash* Vol. 1 #140 (November 1963) New York: National Comics.

_____. "The Master of Mirrors!" *Flash* Vol. 1 #105 (February-March 1959). New York: National Comics.

_____. "Menace of the Reverse-Flash." *Flash* Vol. 1 #139 (September 1963). New York: National Comics.

_____. "The Pied Piper of Peril!" *Flash* Vol. 1 #106 (April-May 1959). New York: National Comics.

Conklin, John E. *Criminology*. 6th ed., Allyn and Bacon, 1998.

Durkheim, Emile. *Rules of the Sociological Method*. Translated by Sarah A. Solovay and John H. Mueller, MacMillan, 1893.

Hirschi, Travis. *Causes of Delinquency*. University of California Press, 1969.

Johns, Geoff (w), Steve Cummings (p), and Wayne Faucher (i). "Mirror, Rorrim on the Wall." *Flash* Vol. 2 #212 (September 2004). New York: DC Comics.

Johns, Geoff (w), Justiniano (p), and Walter Wong (i). "Rat Race." *Flash* Vol. 2 #190 (November 2002). New York: DC Comics.

Johns, Geoff (w), and Scott Kolins (a). "Reverse-Flash: Rebirth." *Flash* Vol. 4 #8 (February 2011). New York: DC Comics.

_____. "What Goes Around, Comes Around." *Flash* Vol. 4 #7 (January 2011). New York: DC Comics.

Johns, Geoff (w), Scott Kolins (p), and Doug Hazelwood (i). "Blitz Part 2: Into the *Fast* Lane." *Flash* Vol. 2 #199 (August 2003). New York: DC Comics.

_____. "Rogue Profile: Zoom." *Flash* Vol. 2 #197 (June 2003). New York: DC Comics.

Johns, Geoff (w), Scott Kolins (p), and Jose Marzan, Jr. (i). "Rogues." *Flash Secret Files* #3 (November 2001). New York: DC Comics.

Johns, Geoff (w), Scott Kolins (p), and Dan Panosian (i). "Absolute Zero." *Flash* Vol. 2 #182 (October 2002). New York: DC Comics.

Johns, Geoff (w), and Peter Snejbjerg (a). "Rogue Profile: Heat Wave." *Flash* Vol. 2 #218 (March 2005). New York: DC Comics.

Lemert, Edwin. *Social Pathology: A Systematic Approach to the Theory of Sociopathic Behavior*. McGraw-Hill, 1951.

Maguire, Brendan, and Polly F. Radosh. *Introduction to Criminology*. Wadsworth, 1999.

Merton, Robert K. "Social Structure and Anomie." *American Sociological Review,* vol. 3, no. 5, 1938, pp. 672–682.

Messner-Loebs, William (w), Greg LaRocque (p), and Jose Marzan, Jr. (i). "Fast Friends." *Flash* Vol. 2 #53 (August 1991). New York: DC Comics.

Morrison, Grant (w), Chas Truog (p), and Doug Hazelwood (i). "Mirror Moves." *Animal Man* Vol. 1 #8 (February 1989). New York: DC Comics.

Owen, Stephen S., Henry F. Fradella, Tod W. Burke, and Jerry W. Joplin. *Foundations of Criminal Justice*. 2nd ed. Oxford University Press, 2015.

Siegel, Larry. *Criminology: Theories, Patterns, & Typologies*. 8th ed. Thomson, 2004.

Smith, Matthew J. "Johns, Geoff." *Comics Through Time: A History of Icons, Idols, and Ideas: Volume 4: 1995–Present*. Greenwood, 2014. 1575–77.

_____. "Johns, Geoff." *Encyclopedia of Comic Books and Graphic Novels: Volume 1: A–L*. Greenwood, 2010. 326–27.

Minds in the Gutter

The Persistence of Vision and the New 52

SARA K. ELLIS

These are interesting times for the DC Universe and for comics in general. As newer and evolving media threaten the older bastions of television and film, the once obscure and oft-maligned medium of comic books, and in particular, the superhero genre, has proven itself an unlikely weapon in the battle against dwindling box-office receipts, flagging ratings, and waning attention spans. More interesting, however, is how the two juggernauts of the medium have opted for wildly divergent narrative approaches, with one digging its heels into cohesive worldbuilding and the other betting on instability and fragmentation. In creating a unified, extended universe across multiple platforms from blockbuster films to web series, Marvel has become both cash cow and—for as much as can be allowed—critical darling. Meanwhile, DC has opted for a different strategy, allowing for rifts in continuity through investing in its own well-worn tropes of multiverse fragmentation.

It makes sense then, that among the most recent of DC's live action outings, the character to appear successfully on both large and small screens has not been Batman or Superman, but the Flash, and more importantly, his Silver Age incarnation. Despite criticism over repeated, and increasingly angst-ridden storylines, the Flash TV series continues to be the Arrowverse's most highly-rated superhero offering, while Ezra Miller's turn in the recent blockbuster Justice League has been lauded by many—including the film's scene stealer, Jason Momoa—as a rare bright spot (McGloins, "Jason Momoa Says").

Unlike his J.L.A. counterparts—goddess, ruthless billionaire, cyborg, and alien—the Flash evinces a much-needed warmth and everyman quality. The character is perhaps closest to a Marvel hero, having received his powers through a lab accident, albeit of the non–Cold War variety. Yet, Barry Allen also appeals to a present in which the barrage of information and distraction consistently threatens to overwhelm—a persistent anxiety in modern life that we aren't paying enough attention, and more importantly, to the right things. Compounding this uncertainty is the character's narrative positionality as a trigger for parallel worlds. The Flash's 1956 debut was "the first real reboot in superhero comics" ("The Best Character"), an event whose unanswered questions would necessitate the DC multiverse, and persistent source of conflict for Allen, who more often than other heroes, contends with splintered realities—jumping through time, resetting past and future, and continually living in a present from which he feels a slight sense of alienation. "I ... must be on a different Earth," he says in Geoff Johns' Flashpoint, "or trapped in one of the Mirror Master's Mirror Worlds" (#1). "I'm where I'm supposed to be," his New 52 incarnation says, while walking the streets of Central City, "...in the one place that should feel like home. But it's not the same" (Manapul and Buccellato, The Flash #10). Allen's internal monologues are a relatable stream of uncertainty about the authenticity of reality; he faces the double burden of not only being an everyman, but grappling with the realities of every version of that man in existence.

The Flash's creation and DC's subsequent rebooting of its universes, argues Andrew Friedenthal, have been performed as a kind of enculturation to a present in flux. "The average American is more aware than ever that what appears online—increasingly the primary source of information for many people—can swiftly and easily be edited to reflect an updated version of 'the truth' on a moment-to-moment basis ... we have come to increasingly understand that what we read on our computers, tablets, phones, watches, and so forth only reflects a current version of online 'reality,' one which is the culmination of multiple edits, rewrites, and yes, retcons"(148).

From his beginnings, Allen has also shared a more significant connection to the shifts in media that have destabilized our subjectivity, his depictions on the page often delineating and blurring the lines between comic books and more technologically advanced forms of visual media. His very first appearance in Showcase #4 (Broome) presaged that relationship, showing the Scarlet Speedster bursting from a film strip onto the cover, an image that had some scholars scratching their heads. "Is this comic a showcase for art, as in a museum?" writes Douglas Wolk, "A series of frozen representations of reality or representations of something so unreal that a body moving at high speed leaves parallel lines of ink behind it? A movie that isn't really a movie, made out of individual images that the eye can see in or out of sequence or at the same time?" (qtd. in Pedler, 249). Since his first appearance, the Flash and the moving image have been in a state of perpetual relay, tagging and circling one another as they comment on each other's limits and possibilities; however, it wasn't until "Move Forward" (The Flash #1–8)

Francis Manapul and Brian Buccellato's 2011 relaunch of the character, that this back-and-forth would be so thoroughly explored.

Martin Pedler notes how the Flash draws upon and "diverge[s] wildly" from the visual tricks of cinema, showing panels "a millisecond apart" between which Allen has performed a lengthy task; in others, dialogue is split, word-by-word and panel-by-panel to create a temporal frame of reference for his movements. This "elastic temporality" he argues is, more than other superheroes, a specific device of the character (253).

> When Barry Allen first gains his powers, it does not just manifest as hypervelocity ... objects slow down, hanging motionless in the air. It is the same for Wally West. "Time's not frozen. It just looks that way to me…" the most lyrical description of The Flash, courtesy of writer Alan Moore, evokes these same notions of temporality and mobility: "There is a man who moves so fast that his life is an endless gallery of statues." Yet, the Flash is also a statue on these pages. That is why we are always provided with visual cues to suggest his motion [qtd. in Pedler, 254].

Certainly, watching a film and reading a comic book are very different experiences, with the latter providing more agency to the reader to infer the duration of time while lingering on the page. As Dru Jeffries notes, "In a comic book, each panel is available indefinitely for the reader's contemplation; in a film, by contrast, each frame has exactly one twenty-fourth of a second and each shot has a predetermined duration to make an impression on the viewer"(45). Nevertheless, similarities exist, in particular, the use of the "gutter" which establishes not only a functional and metaphorical connection between the Flash and the mechanics of projection, but as discussed below, a specific historical juncture in film history. As with the shutter in a film projector, which intermittently blocks or separates the images projected on the screen, the interruption of drawings on the page allows the reader to create a sense of movement. Jeffries suggests that the Flash may, in fact, be better served by the static image, as his "extreme speed exceeds the representational limits of cinema's fixed number of frames per second" (122).

Refreshingly, in "The New 52," Manapul and Buccellato make no attempt at a "grittier" reboot of the character or his world. Central City is depicted in muted pastels and neat lines, maintaining an almost translucent quality and a flatness that recalls a high-definition computer screen. Barry Allen is self-described as methodical and obsessive compulsive (The Flash #1 and #7), tying him more closely to today's prevalent themes of distraction and information overload, a point telegraphed in the opening pages, wherein Patty Spivot, his New 52 love interest, complains about an unfinished road project in Central City.

"If they want to improve traffic," she says, "Why don't they finish the downtown freeway?" This is where Allen's Yoda and future nemesis, Doctor

Darwin Elias steps in with some foreshadowing: "Finishing that monstrosity will only make things worse…. Ever hear of the law of congestion? Building more highways doesn't reduce traffic—it does the opposite. It increases the volume of motorists and generates even more traffic" (The Flash #1). This bit of dialogue aligns Allen's principal conflict with that of Central City, a connection the two creators hoped to emphasize. In an interview with Speedforce, Buccellato stated that he wanted Allen to reflect the city and vice-versa: "I think the cities reflect the heroes. Flash is as earnest, hopeful, and optimistic as the home he protects…. In many ways, Central City continues to move forward with Flash, while Gotham is anchored to its past in the same way that Batman is haunted by the death of his parents" (qtd. in "Speedforce and TMStash").

Manapul and Buccellato further this motif not only through the hero's rescues of planes, trains, and automobiles, but a stand-off Elias attempts to orchestrate between the Flash and the collective people of Central City. As is revealed later in the series, Elias has conspired to sap the Speed Force to fuel a clean energy monorail. "I may have invented the technology," he boasts to a rapt crowd, "but it was you—the working-class people of Central City— who've made it possible through your hard work" (The Flash #13). The infrastructure of Central City becomes another damsel in the story, to be seized by the power-hungry Elias, along with other villains, and rescued by the Flash. Elias's praise for the collective body of the workers will echo an earlier storyline, discussed below, in which the body parts of Allen's friend Manuel are regenerated into clones. Elias's plot to essentially replace the hero with a fast-moving rail line bears a closer look for another reason, for the initial phase of his plot begins by tinkering with Allen's perception of time, eventually rendering him incapable of distinguishing between probability and outcome.

Troubled by the death of his old friend, Manuel, Allen goes to Elias's laboratory for testing, where the scientist pins his problem not on a lack of physical speed, but the inability of his mind to catch up with his body (The Flash #1). "Look at your brain scan," Elias says. "While your body takes full advantage of your powers, your mind uses only fraction of the speed force energy." "I'm not thinking fast enough," Allen replies, echoing the complaint of every Adderall hooked teen (The Flash #1). A properly ambiguous mad scientist, Elias starts out with the best of intentions, recommending that Allen attempt "augmented cognition" an emerging, real world field that rather than researching the effects and potential dangers of information overload, hopes to use computers to overcome the limitations of the human brain. This is a brilliant update for the character, and one that immediately recalls Grant Morrison's observation that the Flash is "the superhero for now" (qtd. in Sacks, "The Flash Outruns").[1] In a 2011 interview, Manapul admits to attempting a similar approach, hoping to stoke readers' curiosity by dropping scientific concepts and vocabulary into each story to create a more "Googlable" experience. "If you're an inquisitive kid and you Google it," he said in a 2011 interview, "it absolutely expands the reading experience ... their minds are going to start wandering in terms of 'Oh, what about this, what about that?' It allows participation for them to fill in some of the gaps, and fill in their interpretation of what they think happened" (qtd. in "Francis Manapul and Brian Buccellato").

The introduction of "augcog" is also a minor weakness in the narrative, for we never see the process by which Allen is able to tap into his newfound abilities. Instead, the speedster's leap in mental velocity occurs within a mere two page of Elias's suggestion: On one page, Allen is talking with Patty Spivot and the next, he is easily processing a myriad of events at the same time. In their eagerness to move forward with Allen's rapid-fire cognition, Manapul and Buccellato skip out on one of the more interesting science fictional aspects of the story. Whatever is lacking here, however, is also a point at which the two creators push the Flash's visual narrative forward while presenting him with a fresh and dangerous limitation, and one that plays on the hero's distinct relationship with the moving image.

As discussed above, the gutter has been critical to depicting his speed, while its functional and metaphorical similarity to the shutter in a film projector underscores the character's connection to film. Yet, in comic books, it is the reader who does the work of extrapolating both motion and time from the separate panels rather than being passively hoodwinked at 24-frames-per-second. Here, in this two-page spread, Manapul forgoes the traditional uses and transgressions of the comic book gutter, instead depicting Allen as one of Moore's "statues." Nevertheless, he is not in motion as he is in other instances: Like the cinema viewer, Allen is merely taking in the action/s of those around him, including his super-powered alter-ego. He stands in the center of the page, eyes wide as events fan out around him like thumbnails on a computer screen: We see the Flash in action, a produce seller clutching at a bullet wound, a driver about to meet an accident, an oblivious headphone-wearing youth walking into traffic, while Iris West stands beside him holding an apple to her lips.

Static images in *The Flash*, as Jeffries notes, serve a double purpose in "convey[ing] the character's unique subjectivity" (123), and he likens the debut Showcase cover to Eadward Muybridge's revolutionary photographic studies of a galloping horse, which would lead to the invention of the motion picture. "The represented filmstrip, which implies duration by depicting the Flash at various instants, owes more to [these] protocinematic studies ... than to cinema as we actually experience it ... a series of discrete images which could be then be studied independently as instants (121)." But this subjectivity has more often than not referred less to impartiality than to what the reader views through the hero's eyes. In most instances, Allen is narratively positioned as the de facto objective viewpoint; he is the only one questioning the altered realities into which he has stumbled, while those around him—Batman, Superman, his resurrected mother—fail to notice the discrepancies (See Flashpoint). This subjectivity is one that is rarely called into question from the reader's perspective, something Manapul and Buccellato hoped to change in the New 52. "You can't just be a guy who's running fast," said Manapul in a 2011 interview. "There are certain aspects of your life, the way you think will change. When you're used to seeing everything at the blink of an eye, and not really getting to take that all in … what would it be like? … Are you going to go crazy? Are you going to take advantage of it?" (qtd. in "Francis Manapul and Brian Buccellato").

Certainly, the comic book reader has the option to infer motion or study each image as a separate object, but minus the presence of a gutter, it becomes more difficult to follow the narrative flow, each image can be taken as a wholly separate event, connected by likeness rather than causality. The reader is thus forced to question what he or she, and therefore Allen sees, and while Allen believes he has gained more agency, particularly over the chronology of events, he is in fact encountering his own variation of the paradox of cinematic vs. diegetic time. This contradiction is illustrated by Jefries through the infamous climax of Richard Donner's 1979 Superman: "…the construction of a particular film might play fast and loose with narrative chronology— perhaps best embodied in the comic book film by Superman's reversal of Earth's rotation" which "reverses diegetic time, but the linear momentum of the film representing this event continues to move forward all the same" (125). For the Flash, the option to play fast and loose with chronology is an illusion. It is Allen who becomes the de facto gutter as he takes in the multitude of probabilities—The Flash isn't bursting from a strip of celluloid as on the Showcase cover, but metaphorically under its thrall.

Jeffries' allusion to Muybridge also provides an interesting frame for Manapul and Buccellatto's narrative, for it is through the photographer that the motifs of high-speed transportation and the Flash's ramped-up cognition converge. In her 2003 essay, later expanded into a book, Rebecca Solnit bridged the ways in which the railroads and the invention of photography, and later cinema, would influence how human beings experienced time, describing these advancements as "instruments for annihilating time and space"(5,6):

> Before the new technologies and ideas, time was a river in which human beings were immersed, moving steadily on the current, never faster than the speeds of nature—of currents, of wind, of muscles. Trains liberated them from the flow of the river, or isolated them from it. Photography appears on this scene as though someone had found

a way to freeze the water of passing time; appearances that were once as fluid as water running through one's fingers became solid objects…. Appearances were permanent, information was instantaneous…" [15].

This description could easily reference the Flash's unique subjectivity, but Manapul and Buccellato have something different in mind. The second page returns the gutter, as Allen rescues the pedestrian, averts the traffic accident, and keeps the apples from tumbling off the display. The gutter here is still not a blank space: but taken up by Allen's words, separating each panel with short, choppy realizations. "It's amazing. I can see everything before it happens. I can weigh every possible outcome. I can make the right choice. And I can do something about it. Before anyone notices (The Flash #1)."

Allen's above exclamation echoes Merleau-Ponty's description of natural perception, the "age-old way of seeing" before the inception of visual prosthetics. "Everything I see is in principle within my reach, at least within reach of my sight, marked on the map of the 'I can'" (qtd. in Johnston 30). This state, argues Paul Virilio, would be permanently disrupted by the telescope and the development of visual technology, resulting in a "regressive perceptual state" or "a kind of syncretism, resembling a pitiful caricature of the semi-immobility of early infancy…" (qtd. in Johnston 30). In a sense, Elias and Allen's experiments with augmented cognition have, in fact, reduced the Flash to this semi-state of stasis. He freezes, unable to trust his own eyes and his own perception: thus, the "I can" becomes the "I can't."

Rather than relying on thought balloons or the thickly lined black rectangle that separates prose from image, his thoughts are expressed in the blank, line free spaces between panels. Scott McCloud observes that the white spaces in the prose panels are a "Bizarro World version of the comic book gutter: the non-space that "plays host to much of the magic and mystery that are the very heart of comics" (qtd. in Pedler). By making Allen the gutter on the first page, with his internal monologue flowing into a borderless space in the next, Manapul is able to invert the typical panel use, privileging Allen's internal experience over his physical movements.

As Pedler states, in the comic book, "each panel acts as a specific 'now,' a discrete image, waiting to be stitched together with the next" (253) and initially, Allen believes he has gained this agency through his sped-up thought processes. But his rapid-fire cognition has in fact worked to blur the line between probability and outcome. Later, when he, Spivot, and the newly resurrected Manuel are attacked by Mob Rule, an army of mercenaries cloned from the latter's DNA, Allen freezes before their pursuers just long enough to be clipped by a bullet (The Flash #3). Although he is able to react quickly enough to miss the brunt of the shell, he realizes that his enhanced cognition has become more of a danger than an advantage. "…I don't have a handle on my mental abilities," he says, "…and because of that I almost died. I got lost in my thoughts. I got lost in probabilities. I couldn't tell the difference between what I'd done and what I was about to do (The Flash #4)."

It is also important to note that Allen must continually verbalize his observations to the reader. This is not just another example of exposition seeded through Eisner's "desperation device," but provides an inkling of our own limitations in comprehending what we see on the page. Allen's confusion becomes our confusion, with both reader and character confronting their own perceptual boundaries, margins that will be further pushed by Manapul in terms of the body.

The superhero body is also often invoked to draw parallels between the cinema and its depiction on the page. While historically the former has relied on everything from jump cuts to blue screens and the continuing development of digitalization to free the superhero from physical limitations, in comic books, writes Pedler, the body becomes an effect in itself, with the striking costumes and color schemes "[making]superhero bodies visually spectacular" (252). Pedler cites the splash page as an example, likening them to pin ups "[that] function similarly to lavish spectacles in Hollywood epics— slowing down the action to a crawl to be shown in fetishistic detail" (252).

As discussed above, Allen's conflict with Elias pits the collective body against the individual—the Flash vs. Mob Rule and later Elias's attempt to pit him against the people of Central City. In "Moving Forward" Manuel's cloning allows Manapul and Buccellato to incorporate this fetishization into the visual narrative. In an interview with Pop Matters, the artist says he drew inspiration from Buccellato's gifts as a "cinematic storyteller," using the layouts to enhance the narrative and visual subtext. "Going back to the Manuel Lagos scene where we find out how his organs were used for the clones, I was able to create a multi-layer storytelling within a double-pager. In which you can read the story going on within in the panels, but then you can look at the panels themselves, and just the shapes of them also tell another story as" (qtd. in Shathley, "Didn't Think"). In this two-page spread, Manapul's panel layout is created from Manuel's body—more horrifically, parts of it. As Manuel relates his story about being cut up and regenerated into clones, his story is visually depicted in the outline of a hand, or several, being dismembered (The Flash #4). Bits of fingers fly off into the black void of the gutter and as we continue down the page, we see Manuel, or his clone, in a split panel, formed from a torso separated from the lower half of "his" body, as he attempts to crawl away from his executioners. Further down the page, fully generated clones come to "save" their maker in another show of hands as a horrified Manuel recoils. This use of the gutter, of the visceral and disgusting body parts as panels, makes use of the temporal motion of both frame, gutter, and superhero body, while also contrasting both external and internal conflicts between the Flash and his reluctant nemesis: Mind vs. Body and Individual vs. Collective.

Later, Manuel lies face down on the ground, mourning Allen whom he believes to be dead. It is not Manuel's body framing each image, but his tears, leaking down the page to structure a flashback of the two men reuniting: Manuel reappearing to Barry in the lab, Barry clasping the other man's shoulders happy to see him alive, while in the final frame, we have Manuel's clones listening in on the "bromance" (The Flash #4). Once again, it is a product of Manuel's body that forms the gutter, and a humanizing contrast to the previous dissociative use of body horror.

This use of the gutter to underscore the intimacy between the two men highlights another aspect of the Flash's importance and the ways in which his creation has paralleled cinema's socio-historical trajectory. Allen's birthing of the Silver Age helped restore superhero genre to popularity during the post-war years, but perhaps more importantly, created a narrative coping mechanism through which the genre could stand up to the Comics Code Authority. Two decades previous, the largely unregulated film industry began to endure a prolonged period of censorship. The Hays Code, established in 1930, but rigidly implemented in 1934, restricted everything from interracial romance to married couples in the same bed (The Celluloid Closet). Yet while it censored these expressions, along with explicit references to homosexuality and other forms of "indecent" behavior, the result was creative backlash by writers and filmmakers, who created an entirely new set of signs and codes that stood in for what could not otherwise be bluntly expressed.

It is arguable that the Silver Age, with its Utopian idealism, do-it-all technology, and new age multiversity, was a similar eruption against Comic Code restraints on narrative and characterization—one echoing the ways in which Hollywood creatives skirted the lines of censorship and left room for multiple interpretations from the audience. The Silver Age reveled in "pure Camp," as Sontag defines it, "a seriousness that fails … which has the proper mixture of the exaggerated, the fantastic, the passionate, and the naïve"—a description that fits an age that gave birth to Krypto and Comet the Super horse (59). If the realities of human nature could no longer be represented, then reality itself would fracture under the narrative pressure, erupting into an excess of competing identities and timelines.[2]

Manapul and Buccellato's New 52 is mostly devoid of a tongue-in-cheek sensibility, but it maintains the dogged optimism of its Silver Age predecessor and instills a gentleness and emotional vulnerability to the character. This is not to argue that the narrative contains a gay subtext, but that in exploring the emotional intimacy between its male characters, the creators also respect the Flash's role in setting forth the possibility for other selves and identities. Manapul and Buccellato's reboot is one that emphasizes the Speedster's importance in DC's pantheon while exploring his often-uneasy relationship to technologies that have altered the ways in which we perceive our surroundings.

In showing the Flash's own subjectivity as just that, Manapul and Buccellato have offered something new, not only to the Flash, but to the ways in which we read and inhabit comic book characters. The gutter is more than a metaphor or a way to depict movement on the page, but something to be transcended in order to understand and regain agency in our all of our discrete narratives.

NOTES

1. In a 2008 interview, Morrison likened the Flash's abilities to the accelerated experience of modern life. "People are doing more every day, moving faster and I think the Flash can be their hero. I do think he's a superhero for now" (qtd. in Sacks, "The Flash Outruns").
2. It is perhaps no coincidence that the recent television crossover "Crisis on Earth-X" used its multiverse to spotlight queer themes and characters, from the Nazi persecution of gays and lesbians, to its introduction of the Ray and the dalliance between Supergirl's Alex Danvers and the White Canary. Barry Allen's nuptials may have bookended these storylines, but the abundance of parallel Earths allowed more than enough room for their inclusion.

WORKS CITED

The Celluloid Closet, Epstein, Rob, and Eric Friedman. Lily Tomlin and Tony Curtis. 1995. Sony Pictures Classics. DVD.

"Crisis on Earth-X," *Supergirl, Arrow, The Flash, Legends of Tomorrow.* The CW. November 27–28. 2017. Television.

Diagram for Delinquents, Emmons, Robert, Matt Fraction, and Paul Levitz. Sequart Research and Literacy Organization. 2014. Digital Streaming.

Dolloff, Matt. "How Justice League's Flash Speed Shots Were Created." *Screenrant.* November 11, 2017. Web. 1, December 2017. https://screenrant.com.how-justice-leagues-flash-speed-shots-were-created/

Duncan, Michael. "This Supercut of Kissing in Films by Hitchcock Definitely Breaks Hays Code." The A.V. Club. September 14, 2015. Web. 1, November 2017. https://news.avclub.com/this-supercut-of-kissing-in-films-by-hitchcock-definite-1798284232.

Fox, Gardner, "The Flash of Two Worlds." *The Flash* No. 123. New York: DC Comics, 1961.

Friedenthal, Andrew J. *Retcon Game:Retroactive Continuity and the Hyperlinking of America.* Jackson: University of Mississippi Press, 2016. p. 148. Print.

Jeffries, Dru. *Comic Book Film Style: Cinema at 24 Panels Per Second.* Austin: University of Texas Press. 2017. pp. 45, 121–122. E-book.

Manapul, Frances, and Brian Buccellato. "Move Forward." *The Flash* 1–8, Vol. 1. DC Comics. 2011–2012. Print.

_____. "Rogues Revolution." *The Flash* 9–12, Vol. 2. DC Comics. 2013. E-book.

McGloins, Matt. "Jason Momoa Says the Flash Is Best." *Cosmic Book News.* January 12, 2017. Web. 22, December 2017. https://www.cosmicbooknews.com/content/jason-momoa-says-flash-best-justice-league

Pedler, Martyn. "The Fastest Man Alive: Stasis and Speed in Contemporary Superhero Comics," *Animation: An Interdisciplinary Journal.* Vol 4(3): pp. 249, 251, 253–254. 2009. Print.

Rivera, Joshua. "The Most Important Character in the DC Universe Isn't Batman or Superman—It's The Flash." *Business Insider.* May 22, 2015. Web. 12, August 2017. http://www.businessinsider.com/the-fhasl-is-the-best-dc-superhero-2015-5.

Sacks, Ethan. "The Flash Outruns the Reaper." *N.Y. Daily News.* April 29, 2008. Web. 12, August 2017. http://www.nydailynews.com/entertainment/music-arts/flash-outruns-reaper-23-years-saving-universe-dying-article-1.284094

Shatley, Q. "Didn't Think It Was Really Possible: The Manapul and Bucellato Exclusive" Pop Matters. February 21, 2012. Web. 1, September 2017. https://www.popmatters.com/

155003-didnt-think-it-was-really-possible-the-manapul-buccellato-exclusive-24958
81596.html
Solnit, Rebecca. *River of Shadows: Eadweard Muybridge and the Technological Wild West.*
Penguin: New York. 2004. Print. "The Annihilation of Time and Space." *New England Review.* Winter, 2003.Vol. 24, No. 1 pp. 15. Print.
Sontag, Susan. "Notes on Camp." *Camp: Queer Aesthetics and the Performing Subject.* Ed.
Fabio Cleto. Edinburgh: Edinburgh University Press, 1999. Pp. 57, 59. Print.
"Speed Force and TMStash Interview Manapul & Buccellato on Their Move from Flash to Detective!" n.d. Web. 1, August 2017. https://speedforce.org/2013/11/flash-detective-interview/.

About the Contributors

Daniel J. **Bergman** is an associate professor and Program Chair of Science Education at Wichita State University in Wichita, Kansas. His research interests include teachers' interactive classroom behaviors and the role of popular culture in science and teacher education. He has published more than 50 articles in science and teacher education, and writes at www.teachlikeasuperhero.blog.

Tod W. **Burke** is a retired professor of criminal justice and a former police officer. He has authored or coauthored approximately 160 publications, including journal articles, book chapters, encyclopedia entries, and other publications. He earned his Ph.D. and M. Phil. in criminal justice from the John Jay School of Criminal Justice. He is also the coauthor of *Foundations of Criminal Justice* (third edition pending).

John **Darowski** is a doctoral candidate in comparative humanities at the University of Louisville. His research is on the superhero Gothic, tracing the influence of the Gothic on the evolution of the superhero and how both genres work together to reflect the cultural context. He has previous essays published in the Ages of Superheroes series.

Joseph J. **Darowski** teaches English at Brigham Young University. He is a member of the editorial review board of *The Journal of Popular Culture* and has previously edited essay collections on the ages of Superman, Wonder Woman, the X-Men, the Avengers, Iron Man, the Incredible Hulk and the Justice League.

Sara K. **Ellis** is a 2011 Lambda Emerging Writers Fellow and Milford Science Fiction Workshop Alum. She is an assistant professor at Meiji University in Tokyo. Her short fiction has appeared in *Ideomancer*, *Andromeda Spaceways Inflight Magazine*, *Crossed Genres*, and *AE—The Canadian Science Fiction Review*. She has also contributed essays to Sequart's *Teenagers from the Future* and *Shot in the Face*.

Charles W. **Henebry** received his doctorate in English literature from New York University in 2003. Originally a student of emblems—Elizabethan comic books, roughly speaking—he has for the past nine years focused his scholarship on the four-color world of superheroes, from the genesis of Superman's costume change to the impact of the 1960s antiwar movement on Iron Man. He is the author of seven articles in Greenwood Publishing Group's 2014 *Comics Through Time* encyclopedia and long-form essays in *The Ages of Iron Man* and *The Ages of the Justice League*.

Christian **Jimenez** is an independent scholar who has published several essays on race, gender, and in the mass media including "Cynical Tolerance: Gender, Race, and Fraternal Fears in *Sons of Anarchy*" and "Strategies of Containment: Sexual Liberation and Repression in the Sci-fi Genre." He is working on several full-length fictional and nonfictional works on Stanley Kubrick and diversity in science fiction. He has taught courses on China and globalization at Rutgers and Rider University.

Peter W.Y. **Lee** completed his doctorate at Drew University in 2017. He is an independent scholar focusing on American history and culture, with an emphasis on youth culture during the Cold War. He has contributed to many volumes in the Ages of the Superheroes series and has edited *A Galaxy Here and Now, Exploring Picard's Galaxy* and *Peanuts and American Culture*.

Cathy **Leogrande** is a professor in the Teacher Education Department of the Purcell School of Professional Studies at Le Moyne College. Her teaching and research is focused in areas of new literacies, using digital text, media, and non-print material as well as comics and graphic novels, manga, and other popular culture to provide K–12 teachers the skills to teach content to students in inclusive classrooms.

Fernando Gabriel **Pagnoni Berns** (Ph.D. student) works as a professor at the Universidad de Buenos Aires (UBA)—Facultad de Filosofía y Letras (Argentina). He teaches seminars on international horror film. He is director of the research group on horror cinema "Grite" and has published essays in *Divine Horror, To See the Saw Movies* and *Critical Insights*, among others.

Tom **Shapira** is a Ph.D. candidate in the Shirley and Leslie Porter School of Cultural Studies in Tel Aviv University. He is the author of *Curing the Postmodern Blues: Reading Grant Morrison and Chris Weston's The Filth in the 21st Century* (Sequart, 2013) and a contributor to various websites including Multiversity, Alilon and Sequart.

Matthew J. **Smith** is a professor and director of the School of Communication at Radford University in Virginia. He holds a doctorate in communication and a master's in English from Ohio University. He is the coeditor, along with Randy Duncan, of the Routledge Advances in Comics Studies Series. In collaboration with Duncan and Paul Levitz, he is coauthor of *The Power of Comics*. His previous collaborations include *Icons of the American Comic Book, It Happens at Comic-Con*, and the Eisner-nominated *Critical Approaches to Comics*.

Louie Dean **Valencia-Garcia** is a lecturer in history and literature at Harvard University. He studies modern history, urban space, the history of technology, youth cultural production and queer and subaltern cultures in contemporary history.

Liam T. **Webb** is an independent academic researcher, creative writer, and teacher. This is his third published academic piece on popular culture and comic books; a fourth, on horror, will be published later this year. He enjoys literary research as a hobby while working and writing creative fiction on the side. He has been an adjunct professor of English, a city bus driver, an editor, a blacksmith, a logistics manager, and a pharmacy tech.

Index